TALES
FROM THE
JOINT

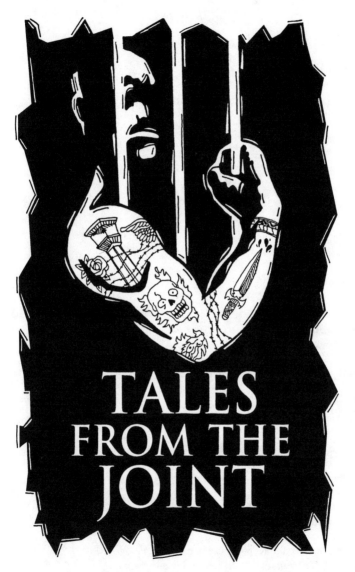

TALES
FROM THE
JOINT

K. HAWKEYE GROSS

PALADIN PRESS · BOULDER, COLORADO

Also by K. Hawkeye Gross:

Drug Smuggling: The Forbidden Book

For Joe Peel

With special thanks to Russ, Stephen, Judy, and Sally

Tales from the Joint
by K. Hawkeye Gross

Copyright © 1995 by K. Hawkeye Gross

ISBN 0-87364-817-X
Printed in the United States of America

Published by Paladin Press, a division of
Paladin Enterprises, Inc., P.O. Box 1307,
Boulder, Colorado 80306, USA.
(303) 443-7250

Direct inquiries and/or orders to the above address.

CONTENTS

PREFACE

THE UNITED STATES OF AMERICA incarcerates a higher percentage of its population than any other nation on earth. A nation that offers more personal freedoms and safeguards from unjust law enforcement now has behind county, state, or federal bars, or on some form of parole or probation, one out of every 250 of its citizens, and in 1994 for the first time ever, there were 1 million Americans locked up in county, state, or federal correctional facilities. The statisticians report that 23 percent of black men between the ages of 20 and 29 are involved at any given time with the criminal justice system, as are 6 percent of white males in the same age group. Furthermore, the numbers continue to mount, to the tune of 200,000 to 300,000 citizens entering prison for the first time every year.

The "war on drugs" has to be recognized as the mighty vehicle of incarceration that has driven the United States to its unenviable position as world leader in the percentage of its population locked up behind bars. And anywhere from 40 to 60 percent of people under the supervision of prison authorities in the United States are there because of a crime involving illegal drugs. As long as marijuana, cocaine, and other drugs that the population enjoys for recreational use are deemed to be illegal and prosecuted aggressively, then prisons are going to remain a growth industry in the United States.

Most of the new recruits who enter prison are scared to death. The media image that portrays prison life as a subculture of violent, psychotic, throat-slitting, gang-raping deviates is indelibly stamped into the brain of every first-timer leaving the free world for the foreboding, dark side of life behind bars.

America is often referred to as the "great melting pot." Well, if that is so, then the nation's prisons are the center mass of a hydrogen bomb. The possibility of the center mass imploding upon itself is precisely the image that movies, television, books, and newspapers love to get across to their viewers and readers. Readers and viewers want the drama and tension of a racial, sexual, economic, and authoritarian nature. What better spot is there to find this kind of drama and tension than in a prison?

Being locked up is the male equivalent of having PMS. It's an emotional roller coaster, and you can never predict, on a day-to-day basis, where the scary parts of the ride are going to be. One day it might be a confrontation with a guard, some other time it might be a bad-news letter from home, or on another day it might be a hostile inmate not liking the way you looked at him.

The Vietnam War gave us flashbacks, postcombat stress syndrome, and encounter groups of every kind to help veterans work through their experiences. However, you never hear any of the terms I just mentioned associated with people who have served time in prison, and the reason is because prison life is generally very different from the image presented by the media.

Prison life isn't all that horrible—most people can survive, and many even turn their prison sentences into a positive experience.

Don't be shocked by the above statement. Drug smugglers don't all carry Uzi machine guns and wear gold chains around their necks, and prisoners aren't all tattooed, muscle-bound psychopaths who walk around the prison yard looking to stick their shank in someone's gut.

For most people entering state and federal prisons, their initial stay will be less than three years. These numbers have increased by 30 percent over the early 1980s because of longer sentences and the elimination of parole at the federal level. The journey of doing time is not unlike that of running a marathon race. You can train all you want, but at some point, you're going to be alone—you run the 26 miles by yourself, and you have to shoulder the burden of ticking off each day of your sentence by yourself.

People who haven't actually served time behind bars can do a fine job writing about the sensationalism and conflict of prison life. However, these people can never hope to capture the subtle emotional swings or comedic farce of day-to-day prison life.

I was sentenced to five years in the Florida prison system. I ended up doing 11 months behind bars, four months at a halfway house, and then two years on parole. *Tales from the Joint* tells of my trek through the Florida prison system. It is a factual account of the people I met and the incidents that happened. I don't recommend the prison experience—no matter how short—to anyone. Being locked up goes against all laws of nature as well as tendencies of the human spirit. However, almost all people who do enter prison are released and successfully integrate themselves back into society. Never underestimate your ability to adapt to even the most adverse situations; 1 million Americans in the prisons of the United States are doing it every day.

Author's note: Television, movies, and the news media have created a stereotypical image of what men locked up behind bars look and act like. Friends who know of my prison experience constantly grope for the politically correct way to ask me the delicate question they all want to know the answer to—did I get fucked up the ass by a muscle-bound black man with a 13-inch dick, and then become a love-slave to his sexual desires?

I've always considered that a fair question, and I'll answer it right now and save you from having to worry about my having become a cowed "fuck boy" once I went behind prison bars.

No—I never took it in the ass; I emerged with my sphincter muscle undamaged.

However, media images aside, the reality is that the question should be rephrased. I should be asked if I got fucked up the ass by a muscle-bound (or scrawny) black man, white man, redneck, Chicano, Asian American, neo-Nazi, Crip, Blood, Aryan Brother, or savings & loan swindler, because no race or group has the exclusive franchise on butt-fucking in prison—it can sneak up behind you from the person or persons from whom you least expect it.

A LOT OF MONEY OR A LOT OF TIME

T HERE WAS NO DOUBT THAT I WAS GUILTY. My lawyer, Russell Cromwell, and I decided to go to trial in the hope that somehow the state of Florida would screw up the prosecution and we would be able to win the case on a technicality. Russell believed that the state had at least a 10 percent chance of butchering any case that it prosecuted, even if it was something as cut and dried as a pilot landing his twin engine Aero Commander 680F at the Stuart, Florida, airport with all the cabin area windows covered in tinfoil to prevent passersby from seeing what's inside the aircraft.

I was going along with my mentor in the marijuana-smuggling business, Mike Buff, and we were carrying out a plan that he had executed successfully three months before in a much more ostentatious smuggling aircraft, a Howard 250. Not only was the Howard 250 the highest-profile marijuana-smuggling aircraft there was, but the one Mike was flying had no door on it; he had removed the door to load the 3,000 pounds of marijuana in Colombia and couldn't get it back on. However, even with no door—which allowed the gas boy to see right in and

1

observe the tarp-covered cargo, as well as giving the pungent, unmistakable odor of Colombia's most successful export crop a direct conduit to the heavy, humid night air—Mike still had no problems buying gas and then flying away to a final unloading destination in Ohio.

Mike convincingly made the case that if he could pull off a refueling in a Howard 250 with its cargo door missing, then fueling up a six-seater twin like the Aero Commander 680F would be a sure thing.

We had covered the windows with tinfoil because we didn't have time to have curtains installed. Mike and I both knew that tinfoil looked suspicious, but it was either that or cancel the whole trip because our Colombian suppliers couldn't hold our 2,000-pound cargo any longer. We either came to get it or we waited another six months till the new crop was harvested. Mike didn't want to wait an extra six months.

The airplane was mission-ready—except for window curtains. I proposed that we spend two days flying around Georgia and Florida, making gas stops every hour and seeing what the reaction was to our tinfoil-covered windows. Amazingly, no gas boy, mechanic, or anyone with whom we came into contact mentioned them. Mike convinced me that we had to make this trip and that we'd have no trouble refueling in Stuart. That didn't make me feel any more confident about how unusual I thought our airplane looked, but I deferred to Mike's previous experience on marijuana-smuggling flights.

When it came time to launch for Colombia, I hopped in, strapping into the Aero Commander as Mike's copilot for the 24 hours of nonstop flying we were looking at to go from Fort Lauderdale, Florida, to Santa Marta, Colombia, then back to Ohio with a refueling stop in Stuart, Florida.

For the first 10 minutes of our refueling stop, it looked as if Mike's deductions were correct. The gas boy came out with the fuel truck and gingerly climbed up on the wings and started pumping in the 200 gallons I had requested. But then a sad thing happened: the fuel truck ran out of gas after having pumped only 50 gallons into the tanks. This caused the gas boy to have to climb off the wing, retract the hose, and then drive the gas truck over to the underground storage tank to refill. This added 30 minutes to the refueling process, which meant we were still on the ground when Deputy Sheriff Newhouse landed after completing his twilight pleasure flight along the intracoastal waterway looking for waterborne drug smugglers.

Deputy Newhouse pulled his Cessna 172 up next to our Aero Commander and was immediately suspicious. He asked to look in our aircraft; we refused, explaining that we were heading to Cape Kennedy to pick up some radioactive space experiments for NASA, hence the covered windows to prevent any radiation leakage.

Newhouse heard out our story while scrutinizing how Mike and I were dressed. Somehow he just couldn't accept that NASA would entrust two guys—obviously around 30, who sported long hair, mustaches, jeans, and T-shirts—to transport its multimillion-dollar space experiments. The deputy sheriff announced to us that we weren't leaving until we opened up the locked passenger cabin door so that he could make sure we weren't carrying contraband.

Opening up the passenger compartment door wasn't an acceptable option for Mike and me. After all, we had our rights as American citizens against unwarranted searches, and surely this was just such an unwarranted search. However, Deputy Newhouse saw it differently. He was looking at an airplane full of dope, and he wasn't accepting the argument from the two dopes who flew the plane that they weren't going to let him see inside because the law books said they didn't have to open the door unless a search warrant was present.

Deputy Newhouse had the gas boy pull the gas truck in front of our aircraft to prevent us from leaving, and then the maneuvering began. First, we demanded that he remove the fuel truck so we could depart since we were not under arrest. Newhouse countered by getting on his police radio and requesting backup assistance. I upped the ante by entering the aircraft through the pilot's front door and starting the engines while Mike paid the gas bill. Newhouse smiled as three police cars arrived on the scene, one containing the sheriff of Martin County, Jeff Hall. It was obvious that I wouldn't be able to taxi forward for departure, and Mike told me to shut down the engines. Sheriff Hall told Mike that we weren't leaving until he saw inside the passenger compartment and that, if we had nothing to hide, we should be willing to open the door. Mike refused. We waited.

About 45 minutes later, a U.S. Customs officer arrived and announced that he had the legal right to search, without a warrant, any vehicle within 50 miles of a U.S. border. Sheriff Hall handed the Customs man an ax and offered Mike one last chance to open the door with the key or else watch the door turn into metal shavings, which the Martin County Sheriff's Department would not pay to have repaired no matter what was found in the aircraft. Seeing that he had nothing to gain by refusing to open the door any longer, Mike made it clear to Hall that he would open the door with the key as long as the sheriff agreed that Mike was not giving him any consent to enter the aircraft, but rather was opening the door to prevent damage to the aircraft. Sheriff Hall agreed to this stipulation, and Mike inserted the key in the lock and opened the door.

Two police officers moved into position next to Mike

and me as we watched Sheriff Hall pull out his flashlight and stick his head into the passenger compartment. The smell of fresh marijuana filled the still night air as Sheriff Hall whistled softly.

"Men, I think these Yankee pilots just bought us a new helicopter for the department" were his first words upon discovering that the passenger compartment of the Aero Commander contained nothing but burlap bags stacked to the ceiling, each bag containing approximately 40 pounds of marijuana.

Florida law at the time only differentiated between more than five grams (about one-sixth of an ounce) or less than five grams for a charge of felony possession of marijuana. Mike and I had a cargo of about 1,200 pounds, or 576,000 grams, so Sheriff Hall didn't have to whip out the calculator to decide to place us under arrest for felony possession of more than five grams of marijuana.

The sheriff complimented us on how well we had conducted ourselves during the bust, asked us if we had any weapons in the aircraft, read us our constitutional rights, and remarked that he hoped our aircraft was paid for free and clear because he was seizing it for the Martin County Sheriff's Department.

Mike and I were handcuffed, loaded into a patrol car, and driven away from the spot where two hours earlier we had celebrated the joy of being back on American soil and the anticipation of a large payday. We were en route to the dark world of the Martin County jail.

Mike and I had both been U.S. Air Force pilots for six years and attended numerous air force survival schools. At the survival school in Spokane, Washington, we had played POW-in-Hanoi for three days, being locked up in cells where you could neither stand up nor lie down. Our private cell at the Martin County jail was much better than the air force accommodations, and we settled in, knowing that our smuggling co-conspirators would eventually figure out that we hadn't shown up to unload in Ohio and would send legal aid.

Once the attorneys, L. Chaney McCullom and Russell Cromwell, arrived, the legal games began. Mike and I had kept our mouths shut and that pleased Chaney greatly, since he was sure our constitutional rights had been violated by Deputy Sheriff Newhouse in detaining us from leaving the airport.

The attorneys jousted with the prosecutors for Martin County on deciding what charges to file, setting a bond, reducing charges, lowering the bond, securing the bond, and finally determining the conditions for our being released on bail. We walked out of the county jail with assurances from our attorneys that we would probably never be going back, at least not for the crime we had just committed.

The attorneys filed motions, hearings were held on the motions, the judge ruled on the motions, appeals were filed on the motions, and, as each day took me further from the day of the arrest, I began to actually believe what the attorneys were saying: that we were going to win the case. Therefore, if we were going to win the case, then I'd be not guilty. Not guilty was the same thing as saying that I hadn't committed the crime, which meant that I was an innocent person whose years of service in the armed forces of the United States had resulted in my being singled out for unjust prosecution.

My warped logic was brought back to reality when Russell advised me that all the glorious motions and paperwork he and Chaney had filed had not resulted in the case being thrown out of court, and that Mike and I were going to have to stand trial for the single charge of possession of marijuana, more than five grams.

The prosecutors offered us no plea bargain, nor would they offer to "cap" the possible five-year sentence at a year or two in exchange for changing our plea from not guilty to guilty. With absolutely no inducement to plead guilty and avoid a trial, except that the judge might take kindly to the fact we had saved Florida the cost of a jury trial, we jumped in to test Russell's "10 percent botch-up rule" and play the judicial system's high-stakes game of legalized gambling.

The trial began and the state of Florida marched forward with a can't-lose case as though it was the U.S. Olympic basketball Dream Team playing against Iraq, a day after Saddam had announced that Iraq would win "this mother of all games" because it was God's will. It didn't look good.

However, on the third day of the trial, which up to this point had been nothing but a parade of state witnesses establishing the chain of where the marijuana had gone once it was unloaded from the aircraft to where it was ultimately burned in an incinerator, a glimmer of light appeared.

Russell brought up the point that it would be nice if the state could establish that this bunch of twigs was in fact marijuana and not 1,200 pounds of lawn clippings. The state responded by saying that it was waiting on its expert DEA chemist, who would be arriving that afternoon.

That afternoon came, and no expert DEA witness arrived. The next day the state concluded its case, and still no expert witness. The judge was upset and gave the state one more day to get its witness on the stand. "If you haven't produced this witness by tomorrow, I will dismiss this case due to the state's inability to prove that the alleged contraband is, in fact, marijuana," the no-nonsense judge proclaimed.

Was this it? Our 1-in-10 longshot had happened? We spent that evening listening to assurances from Chaney, who never lacked for confidence, on how he knew the state would screw this prosecution up.

Chaney's fantasy bubble burst precisely at nine the next morning when the state put its expert witness on the stand to confirm that what was in our aircraft was, in fact, marijuana.

Closing arguments were made, the judge instructed the jury, and 25 minutes later the jury returned to deliver the verdict. Mike and I were guilty.

"We'll win the appeal," Chaney parroted every lawyer's first words after he has lost a trial.

By now I wasn't listening to Chaney's statements of how a miscarriage of justice had been served, but rather to the pragmatic observations of Russell who surmised that our chances of winning an appeal were substantially less than the 5 to 7 percent of appealed cases that are reversed in any given year.

"Get ready for jail time" was Russell's sagacious summary of the future of our case.

I was ready to go to jail, but the criminal justice system didn't want to rush things. Mike and I stayed out on bond while presentencing investigations were done. The actual sentencing didn't occur till six weeks after the jury had pronounced us guilty.

We were looking at a maximum sentence of five years. Chaney confidently guessed that he'd have the judge in tears with his plea for leniency for these two brave air force pilots who had served their country in Vietnam, when it was not fashionable to do so, and who then couldn't find airline employment because of the deep recession the country was experiencing. "One year tops and you can give me a bonus if it's less than 60 days" was Chaney's final guess on what the judge's sentence would be.

Mike and I, along with our lawyers, sat at the defense table and listened to the state prosecutors ask for substantial jail time as a deterrent to others who might be thinking of getting involved in drug smuggling.

Chaney was elated as he leaned over to whisper to us just before addressing the judge with his plea for leniency: "This is very good, the state didn't call you drug-scum or dangerous felons. Get ready for probations."

Chaney talked for 30 minutes, but no tears appeared in the judge's eyes. When he finished he sat down and once again whispered to us, "It's going to be probation; I can feel it."

The judge shuffled some papers, blew his nose, adjusted his glasses, took a sip of water, and spoke. "This is a very clear-cut case to me," he said as he looked Mike and me straight in the eyes. "If you men would have succeeded in your drug run, you would have made a lot of money. But you didn't succeed, you got caught, and for that I'm going to give you a lot of time. Maximum sentence for each of you, five years in the Florida state prison system."

Chaney immediately sprang up from our table and requested that our bond be extended. Before deciding the amount of the bond, the judge asked the state lawyers their thoughts on the matter—the state wanted it raised, Chaney argued against the raise, the judge set a new bond figure, we made bond, and we walked out of the courthouse once again, still free men.

Our appeal of the search and seizure and the illegal detention question dragged on for more than two years. During that time Mike hired a new lawyer to handle the appeal, a famous South Florida drug lawyer named Melvin Kliner.

Mike was paying Kliner $40,000 to write what would amount to a six-page brief—over 10 times what he had paid Chaney and Russell combined to handle our case at trial. But Kliner offered "a wink." Kliner never specifically said that the fix was in, but he strongly hinted that his connections were so great at the appellate level of judges that the appellate court would vote to suppress the evidence because it was illegally seized and that would be the end of our case.

Twenty-five months after the original verdict, the appellate court upheld the lower court's decision; we had lost once again. Kliner's explanation was that he had been betrayed by one of the judges on the appellate court.

Kliner asked the original judge in Stuart to extend the appeal bond again so that we would be out of jail while our appeal to the Florida Supreme Court was in progress. The judge refused this extension. It was time to check in to the Florida state prison system.

I had made a significant amount of money in the drug-smuggling business while I was out on appeal bond, and I was grateful to the judge for giving me that opportunity by his granting of an appeal bond. Now I was going to get to experience what doing a lot of prison time would be like. I didn't think I'd be as thankful to the judge for this opportunity.

LAST CHANCE TO BE A FUGITIVE

A FTER OUR APPEAL WAS DENIED, the clerk of the court advised our appeal lawyer, Melvin Kliner, that Mike and I were to surrender ourselves at the Martin County jail on December 18 to begin serving our five-year sentence for felony possession of marijuana.

Three weeks before our surrender date, Mike called me and announced that he wouldn't be accepting Florida's request to be domiciled in its prison facilities for the next five years; he was leaving the country and would become a fugitive from justice.

No one I knew had ever been to prison. None of the lawyers I dealt with knew anything about how the prison system worked, nor did they know any previous clients from whom I could get some on-the-job information. The only useful piece of information I was able to glean came from Melvin Kliner, who stated he was fairly certain that I wouldn't be serving the whole five years of the sentence; it would be more like two to three years, and then I would get paroled. If this was true, then before even having to serve one day, my sentence had effectively been cut in half. However, after having listened to

11

three years of lawyers' assurances about impending victories concerning motions, verdicts, and appeals, I wasn't placing a whole lot of credibility in anything I heard come out of a lawyer's mouth.

I was a 33-year-old, college-educated, white boy, who had flown jets for the United States Air Force. I had gotten married for the first time one month before I was due to check into the joint because not only did I love Karen, but I didn't want either of us to be alone while I was locked up. I was 6 foot 4, weighed 200 pounds, and had been a bouncer during college. My guess on what life in prison would be like came from the movies, and I was hoping that it would be closer to *Cool Hand Luke* than *Midnight Express*. In the last conversation I had with Mike before I turned myself in, I related this observation to him, and he quickly countered with, "Yeah, but don't forget, neither of those movies had any black sexual predator convicts in them who are serving life sentences for child raping and other sexual perversions." Mike laughed after he spoke, "You sure you don't want to join me in the Bahamas?"

That wasn't the answer for me. I had gone into the military when everyone was telling me I should try to get out of it, and now leaving the country to become a fugitive to escape a couple of years behind bars didn't sound any more appealing than going to Canada had to escape a two-year military stint.

Actually, I was more worried when I had gone to Vietnam than I was about going to prison. My job in Vietnam had been a forward air controller (FAC); I was the bait that flew low and slow over a target and then directed the fighters and bombers on where to drop their ordnance. Low and slow over a target didn't seem conducive to returning to the United States alive, but it worked out fine. I flew 330 combat missions, got shot at 80 percent of the time, and, after getting five missions under my belt, became more concerned about avoiding the Pan Am 747s in the landing pattern at Ton Son Nhut Air Base than with the small arms and 50-caliber machine gun bullets that the Vietcong and North Vietnamese Army were shooting at me.

Dying in Vietnam had been a real possibility; I didn't think that was something I had to worry about in prison. I had my reporting date; it was time to go and get it over with.

CHECKING IN

I DROVE THE 90 MILES FROM FORT LAUDERDALE to Stuart with Karen and my brother John. Karen had moved in with her sister and brother-in-law, who lived in Fort Lauderdale, so she would be able to visit me once we found out how visitation worked, and John was in South Florida working on a marijuana-smuggling mission that our group was preparing to execute over the Christmas holidays.

I was supplying the Piper Aztec aircraft that had a modified fuel system so it could fly the 1,300 miles from Colombia nonstop to South Florida, as well as the four-wheel-drive pickup that would meet the aircraft. Gene Blass would be flying the Aztec, and John would be driving the pickup. The plan was to land on a seldom used stretch of road 10 miles west of Vero Beach at 3 A.M. One other vehicle would be involved to illuminate the touchdown point and then block the road to any other traffic. The plan was to unload the aircraft's cargo onto the truck right on the road, with the whole process taking no longer than four minutes. If the plan worked, my equipment-rental-fee agreement with Gene amounted to $50,000, which would be collected by 15

John in the form of 200 pounds of the marijuana cargo.
John would sell the marijuana and then turn the money
over to Karen. What's more, if this mission worked once,
there was no reason it couldn't work again and again. I
couldn't participate directly, but there still was the chance I
could be making some big money by just sitting in my
prison cell.

Melvin Kliner suggested that I wear a coat and tie when I
reported to the Martin County jail to begin my jail sentence.
His thinking was that I would make an excellent first impression on the jail personnel who would be in charge of me until
I was transferred to the Florida state prison system. I declined
Kliner's advice and chose for my checking-in wardrobe a
worn but attractive gray flight suit that the air force had
issued to me before I had begun undergraduate pilot training
in Del Rio, Texas. For shoes, I selected a pair of Etonic running trainers, and my only accessory was an $8 wristwatch.
On the shoulder pocket of the flight suit, where I had carried
my grease pencils so I could keep track of the air strikes I was
working, I now carried two toothbrushes; in the five large
pockets—where I had carried survival equipment, maps,
checklists, and M16 machine gun ammo clips—I now was
armed to the teeth with paperback books.

During our last visit two days before I was to report,
Kliner had told me to report to the jail by two in the afternoon. At 1:30 P.M., I parked the pickup four blocks from the
jail so no law enforcement officials would see me getting out
of a vehicle that was programmed to be used in a smuggling
mission, said ta-ta and good luck to my brother, and then
began the walk to the jail with my wife.

Karen and I held hands, and I did most of the talking
as we navigated our way to my loss of my freedom and
the interruption of our life together. Karen had her family in South Florida for support, and I had no doubts

that we'd survive, as a couple, my upcoming period of incarceration.

We had a long hug and kiss outside the door of the jail, and then it was time to get it over with.

Karen and I walked up to the counter, behind which sat an overweight, middle-aged jailer, smoking a cheap cigar and intently reading the local newspaper. I thought the whole jail would swing into action as soon as they saw me, whom Sheriff Hall had described to the local newspapers as a drug-running Yankee who threatened the very fabric of life in Martin County, but all the jailer did was stare at me blankly for a second and then rebury his head in his newspaper.

I waited at the counter, and when it became obvious that the jailer couldn't care less that I was there, I said, "Excuse me, sir, I believe you are expecting me to check into your jail today."

Luckily, I didn't infringe upon the jailer's sacred donut-eating time, but I had come close by interrupting paper-reading time. The jailer wrinkled the paper back together, set it down next to the coffee pot, and grimaced as he stood up to indicate the discomfort his lower back was feeling with the position shift.

"What's your name?"

"Gross, Kenneth Hawkeye, sir," I responded in military mode as if addressing a superior officer.

"Well, Gross, Kenneth Hawkeye—I've got nothing on this sheet about you. Who told you to show up here? That's one strange name you have. What's your crime?"

Karen whispered in my ear that she thought the jailer was confused with how I gave him my name. "Sir," I answered, "my attorney from Miami, Melvin Kliner, told me to report today by 2 P.M. I've got a five-year sentence for possession of marijuana handed down about two and a half years ago, and I think you're confused on my name—it's first name Kenneth, middle name Hawkeye, and last name of Gross."

The jailer stretched his back in a backward arch while rubbing it with his left hand. "I got a list of three guys who are supposed to show up today, and none of them have anything close to the name you're telling me. Are you sure you want the Martin County jail?"

"I'm just doing what my attorney said. My bondsman is Jack O'Connel, and if Sheriff Hall is in the building I think he'd remember me."

"OK, I know Jack; write your name real clear, and I'll go find the sheriff and see if we can figure this thing out."

I wrote my name on the piece of paper the jailer handed me, and Karen and I stood waiting at the counter, each having no idea how there could be confusion about a prisoner showing up to begin serving his sentence.

In three minutes the jailer returned, closely followed by the sheriff of Martin County, Jeff Hall. Sheriff Hall could have been in a Marlboro commercial. For a man in his late 50s, Jeff Hall was aging well. I hadn't seen him since the trial, and his deeply tanned face had developed a few more weather lines, but he still was an imposing figure of the law in his Western-cut sportcoat topped off by a brown cowboy hat.

The sheriff swung the horizontal counter top back on its hinges and walked through, extending his hand. I shook his hand and introduced Karen.

"How come you're showing up today?" asked the sheriff of Martin County. "And how about your buddy Buff? Where's he?"

I repeated the facts on how Melvin Kliner, famous drug lawyer from Miami, had told me to report, and I also told the sheriff that I hadn't talked to Mike Buff in months and had no idea where he was.

"I don't know how you get your information," the sheriff

responded, "but you and Buff were supposed to report here on November 2; that's almost six weeks ago. I've had a warrant out for your arrest for failing to appear since 10 November. You're going to catch another charge."

"I never heard those dates," I said in a shocked voice. "My wife and I sat in Kliner's office two days ago and listened as he made the phone call, making sure everything was set for me to turn myself in to begin my sentence."

"Should we call Kliner?" Karen interjected.

"I don't care what he has to say," Hall announced. "The judge's order says November 2; that's the date you were supposed to be here."

I had no idea of what was going on. I gave Karen one final hug and kiss and told her to call Kliner as soon as she got back to Fort Lauderdale and tell him to get this confusion straightened out. Karen walked out the door, waved from the other side, and was gone.

"Your wife's mighty pretty," Sheriff Hall commented after Karen had left the building. "How long you've been married?"

"Four weeks."

"Well, maybe I can offer you a way to get back to her a lot sooner than you thought. The boys in Broward County are feeling like idiots that your partner Buff was able to bond out on his charges down there; I'm sure you know what I'm talking about. We'll talk about it later."

The sheriff was right; I did know what Mike's plans were as far as his pending legal matters. He was disregarding his order to report to serve his sentence, and he was also disregarding the new charge he had picked up in Fort Lauderdale for selling 1,500 pounds of marijuana to an undercover police officer.

When Mike was arrested for the sale to an undercover officer he was brought before a magistrate, who set a bond of

$60,000 for the charge. Neither Mike nor his attorney, once again Melvin Kliner, had expected that any bond would be set because Mike was already out on appeal bond for our case in Martin County. However, the electronic impulses didn't transmit properly, and the magistrate never knew about the appeal bond until Mike had posted his Broward County bond and was 24 hours removed from his jail cell. This new charge made it clear to Mike that he wasn't going to participate in his proposed rehabilitation to be monitored by the Florida prison system—he was going underground and becoming a fugitive.

This kind of screwup happens all the time, but the worst part was that a Fort Lauderdale newspaper reporter did a story on the incompetence in the Broward County court and jail system, which made several county employees look lazy and inept in the way they went about protecting the public from dangerous criminals. Sheriff Hall, no doubt, wanted to show his big-city neighbors to the south that his department was capable of avoiding such mistakes.

I was taken back to the administrative area of the jail where I was fingerprinted and photographed. Then I was put in a two-man containment cell in the administrative area that allowed me to watch the jail personnel as they went about their jobs.

As soon as the barred cell door slammed shut I felt disoriented. I knew where I was and I knew Karen had just left, but I also knew that screaming out to open the cell and let me get out of there was not the solution to my situation. I had felt this kind of confusion only once before, and that was during jet pilot training in the air force. I was on a check ride with an evaluation pilot in the T-37 twin-engine jet. We were about 20 minutes into the ride when the oil pressure light for the left engine flashed red. I assumed that it was the check pilot testing my skills on an emergency procedure and pointed out the emergency and started going through the checklist. The last item on the checklist was shut the engine down, which the check pilot told me to go ahead and do.

After the left engine was turned off, the next expected step was for the check pilot to tell me that I could go ahead and restart the engine and that we'd continue with the ride. Instead, he told me to check my parachute lanyard because if we lost oil pressure on the right engine, we were going to have to bail out of the aircraft. I checked my equipment and then looked out the canopy to the West Texas scrub land 25,000 feet below. I did not want to eject, I did not want to be in this situation, and I wasn't leaving my piece of still-flying metal. Those thoughts went through my mind as I watched the instructor run the throttle of the good engine back and forth to confirm that the right engine was running correctly.

I sat there stoically for a period of 30 seconds with nothing to do but stare at the brown earth five miles below and try to battle the primal instinct I had that I wasn't going to bail out. However, the debate in my brain ended when the instructor informed me that we were heading back to the base for a single-engine landing. The emergency was over, both with the aircraft and my inner self, and the engine loss was nothing more than something to whoop it up about with my classmates for the rest of the day on the flight line.

But back in Florida, the cell door was shut, and I didn't want to be in that situation; I wanted to leave and join Karen outside the Martin County jail and get the hell out of there. The debate in my brain began again as I felt my body temperature rise and sweat start to form along my hairline. I grabbed the bars of the cell door, and, at that point I beat back the panic impulses when the practical, rational, clear thought that I was in jail seized control; it was no dream, no fantasy, but the reality of my life at that time. There was absolutely no one in that jail who cared one bit about me or my state of mind; I was on my own with no parachute or support systems.

I sat down on the steel bunk in the cell and looked at the surroundings. No one was looking at me; no jailer was running to get Sheriff Hall to advise him that his smuggler prisoner was sweating along his collar line and might need some assurances that the staff of the Martin County jail was there to make his stay as pleasant as possible and that if he had any problems, just to let the sheriff know. The air force survival school training kicked in; it was time to internalize all emotions: I was a POW of the marijuana wars; I was alone; my jailers would exploit any weakness I displayed—no whining, no sniveling, and no panic—I was there to follow the rules and survive the ordeal.

There were two other two-man holding cells next to the one I occupied in the administrative area of the jail. Prisoners were brought down from the upstairs cell blocks for phone calls, attorney's visits, or counseling sessions, and then put in these cells until a jailer was available to escort them back to their cell block. This coming and going of prisoners—combined with the movements of jailers, police officers, and jail trustees—ensured that there were always conversation and activity in the central area.

After an hour of watching the routine from my holding-cell vantage point, a jailer came by and asked if I wanted a jail-issue orange jumpsuit or if I would rather just wear what I had on. I told him I'd keep my flight suit, and he let me know that he'd be moving me up to cell block C right after the 4:30 evening feeding was completed.

As the jailer was walking away, a commotion erupted from one of the enclosed rooms on the other side of the open area from where my cell was. The door flew open and an obese black woman in her 20s was being dragged out of the room by a male and female jailer. The black female prisoner was wearing a loose-fitting, gray, jail-issue dress and shower thongs. She was grabbing onto the door frame, and the jailers were having a hard time getting her to let go.

"I won't take that schizo medicine," she bellowed like a cow stuck in a fence. "You got no right to make me take that stuff!"

After a minute of this noise and standoff at the door's threshold, Sheriff Hall appeared to see what was causing the uproar. He grabbed the nightstick from the female officer and gave a good crisp whack to the prisoner's knuckles, which were clasped around the door frame. The lady screamed and said she wanted to call her lawyer to report police brutality. Hall didn't reply to this comment and teed off on her knuckles again. This time she released her grip and was pushed forward into the open administrative area.

Protesting every shove with a scream of pain quickly followed by a threat and obscenity, the fat prisoner was funneled to the corridor that ran in front of the holding cells, which would eventually lead to her cell block.

When she was in front of the holding cells, she pulled her dress up over her waist while bending over and backing her exposed ass right up to the bars of the first holding cell.

"Somebody fuck me," she yelled. "Stick it in that pussy. Come on, you niggers; I ain't got all day."

The jailers thought this was pretty funny and let her slowly move her exposed ass down the bars. I couldn't see what the men in the other two holding cells were doing, but I could hear their comments.

"Sister," said a male voice in a deep black accent, "you better clean the shit out of that booty before anyone is going to be able to fuck it, and you got so much fat on that pussy no one is going to be able to find it."

The jailers were laughing at the comments being made
by the holding-cell prisoners, and let her continue her wad-
dle along the bars of the holding cells. When she got in
front of my cell she dropped her head lower so she could
look up through her spread legs and see who was in the
holding cell.

"Come on, white boy, fuck me. Stick something in this
pussy. Show those black motherfuckers how it's done."

She was gyrating her ass against the bars like the
primitive dance that bees do when they enter the hive.
She kept up her stream of trash-talking till she had
reached the end of my cell and then Sheriff Hall gave
her a good smack with the nightstick on her exposed
butt, and she moved on down the hall to the women's
cell block.

When Sheriff Hall returned from the women's cell
block and passed our holding cells, one of the black jail
inmates asked him if he had fucked that pussy.

Sheriff Hall had an easygoing, folksy way about him,
and he stopped while holding up the wooden nightstick.
"Here, Jermaine, smell this because it's as close as you're
going to get to a piece of ass in the next three years."

"Piece of ass, I don't think so, sheriff," added another
holding-cell inmate. "Pussy, maybe; but ass, he'll find someone's ass to stick that black snake into."

"Fuck you," yelled Jermaine in a laughing voice.
"You're the only one in this jailhouse who would fuck a
fat, flabby, black pussy like that. Hell, even the white boy
wouldn't touch it. Hey, white boy, how come you didn't
slap that pussy?"

Sheriff Hall had stirred up the monkey cage. It wasn't
dialogue that you would find on a "Bob Hope Special," but
some of the one-liners that the black holding-cell inmates
threw out about the obviously mentally ill woman they

had just seen brought some heavy laughs from Sheriff Hall and my holding-cell mates. Just because you were in jail didn't mean you couldn't laugh, preferably with someone, but if any opportunity to laugh at someone arose—that was OK too.

LEROY THE JITTERBUG

CELL BLOCK C AT THE MARTIN COUNTY JAIL was composed of six 4-man cells, with each cell having a sliding, steel-barred door that opened into a narrow passageway. The other side of the passageway was a barred partition that formed one of the walls of what was called the "dayroom." In the dayroom were four metal picnic-type tables, a sink, an open toilet, and a shower stall. The four-man cells were 10 by 12 feet, with an upper and lower bunk welded to the opposite wall. Situated in the back of each cell was a sink, an open toilet, and a mirror of polished steel welded to the wall just above the sink.

At 5:30 in the morning, a jailer would roll back all the doors so that it was easy to move from the cells to the dayroom to take a shower or do morning exercises. At 6:30, the jailer would reappear and close all the doors before the breakfast trays were passed through the food service square into the dayroom. If you wanted breakfast, you had to be in the dayroom, or you had the option to just stay in your cell and try to sleep through the noise pollution of steel-framed doors pounding against their steel lock- 27 ing mechanisms, the constant "whoosh" of high-pressure toilets flushing, the clunking on and off of faucets, and the staccato pelting of streams of water hitting the rubber shower curtain, plus the verbal conversation of those who woke early and wanted to eat breakfast.

This was a formidable amount of noise, but even so only half of the prisoners would be in the dayroom when the food trays arrived, with the rest preferring to try and cover their heads with their flimsy pillows or various articles of clothing to keep the noise of the beginnings of another day in prison out of their heads.

Every few hours a jailer would appear to roll the doors to allow movement between the cells and the dayroom, but never would they be left open for more than a few minutes. The most freedom available in cell block C occurred during that early morning period when one could move from his cell to the dayroom and back as many times as he pleased before the breakfast trays arrived. It was just a taste given to us by the jailers, and only available to those who would wake up and get out of their bunks. If you didn't want to wake up, then you had to confine your movements from cell to dayroom, or dayroom to cell, only when the jailer saw fit to roll the doors.

No TV, telephones, private radios or cassette players, newspapers, or magazines were allowed. The only contact with the outside world in cell block C was the speaker inserted into the ceiling of the dayroom. For a few hours in the afternoon and evening the local radio station would be patched through that speaker. With no clock on the wall, no wristwatches allowed, and no windows to tell whether it was day or night, the gauging of time was never much better than a guess as to how much time had passed since the 6:30, 11:00, or 4:30 feedings.

The social life in cell block C centered around the steel

picnic tables in the dayroom. These four tables dominated the 60- by 15-foot dayroom where all meals were eaten, as well as being the location of the card games that were constant from 7 A.M. to 9 P.M., when all prisoners had to leave the dayroom and return to their cells.

The only card game played was a hybrid between hearts and bridge called spades. Once in a while a game would form that involved the betting of cigarettes or candy bars, but most of the games were just a cumulative process wherein each hand and bidding procedure provided the opportunity for the players to exercise their vocal cords by spilling out challenges and put-downs to the other players.

Paperback books were allowed, as well as writing materials, but since at least a third of the prisoners residing at any one time in C couldn't read or write, that assured that there were always two card games going on during the hours that the dayroom was open.

The Martin County jail served a wider range of functions than that of providing a place for drunks and vagrants to spend the night. Anyone arrested in Martin County moved into one of the three cell blocks until he could make bail or came to trial. Secondly, if someone was sentenced to less than a year, he served that sentence in the county jail and not one of the Florida state prisons. Also, you could have been sentenced to more than a year in the state prison and still serve months in the county jail as you waited for bed space to open up in the vastly overcrowded state system.

Thus, the makeup of prisoners in a cell block at the Martin County jail could contain a widely varied group in terms of age, type of crimes, and sentences being served.

When I began residence, cell block C comprised the full gambit of crimes, ages, and racial backgrounds. There was a 50-year-old white man who was being held on a $200,000 bond for murdering his wife. There was a 70-year-old white guy who was awaiting trial for sexually molesting a minor. Then there were four young guys between 18 and 23 years old awaiting trial or serving sentences of less than one year for possession of personal-use amounts of marijuana or cocaine. We had two black men in for burglary, another black guy in for drunk driving, a white guy in for not paying his child support, a 30-year-old white guy in for car theft, and a 19-year-old Hispanic in for breaking into tourists' cars at the beach and stealing wallets and purses. Finally, added to this motley crew was Leroy, a 17-year-old juvenile delinquent who already had a two-page arrest record for car theft, dealing marijuana, shoplifting, truancy, assault, robbery, burglary, and forgery.

Leroy was a good-looking white boy who was never going to see five feet nine. His parents ran a popular restaurant in town, and when it became evident that they couldn't control Leroy, they worked out a deal with Sheriff Hall and the local prosecutor for Leroy to serve a year in the county jail so he could get a good dose of what life would be like for the next 20 years if he didn't drastically change his ways.

This attempt at behavior modification was obviously failing. Leroy was thriving in the Martin County jail. He had taken his one bed sheet and dyed it black by using the ink from a ballpoint pen. He then strung his black bed sheet around his bunk to seal off the light from the bare light bulb that was on 24 hours a day in each cell. Leroy also would pad each ear with a sock and then hold them in place with a bandage he told the jailer he needed for his knee. This sleeping arrangement allowed Leroy to stay asleep until just before the 11 A.M. meal.

After making his appearance for food, Leroy followed this up with "arts and crafts." For Leroy "arts" was either doing, or having done to him, a crude jailhouse tattoo.

These were done by inserting ink from ballpoint pens into the skin with either sewing needles or safety pins. The more areas of your body that were covered with these amateur, silly tattoos, the more "street" status you had in Leroy's criminal mind. Leroy told me that he figured it would take him about five years to get both arms, his chest, and his back inked in. He was right on schedule. He had been in the county jail nine months, and he had both shoulders covered and was moving down his left arm.

"Crafts" for Leroy involved the making of "shanks." In a county jail setting, where prisoners are so tightly controlled and monitored, possessing a homemade knife was unnecessary. However, Leroy was in apprenticeship for the state prison system or maybe even a federal joint like Leavenworth or Atlanta, and he and a few of the other teenagers in the cell block would work on the various techniques of removing the bristles from a toothbrush, melting the plastic, and then inserting a razor blade where the bristles had been. Raw materials in the cell block were very limited; however, Leroy and his buddies were relentless in trying to turn paperback books, plastic eating utensils, and zippers into weapons that could penetrate the skin.

Leroy didn't see himself as a teenage offender doing a year in a county jail for being a punk with low self-esteem. Leroy saw himself as a convict—not an inmate or a prisoner, but a convict. He'd strut around the dayroom with the sleeves of his T-shirt rolled up on each arm around a pack of Marlboros, showing off his meager upper arms that had foolish-looking drawings of a girl on his left biceps and extensive scabbing on his right upper arm from a work in progress. He'd have the handle of his toothbrush showing out of a front pocket to let any would-be aggressors know that he was "armed," and he'd constantly talk about how he had it all figured out about how to make thousands of dollars a week by stealing cars from rich people in Palm Beach. Leroy's dream life involved days full of smoking, drugging, drinking, fucking, robbing, stealing, and fighting. All this fun would be interspersed with years he knew he'd have to spend in the joint, but so what? To Leroy, prison time was just part of the job description of being an outlaw, and, besides, it would be an educational time to learn about other aspects of the criminal life-style from old-timers, as well as to provide the time to get more tattoos etched into his skin.

When Leroy and his pals were in shank production or tattooing sessions, they didn't make much noise. However, after the 4:30 feeding, Leroy and his buddies became like a bunch of kittens who wanted to play. The problem was that in a bare room made out of cement and steel bars and where all chairs, tables, and benches were welded to the floor, there just wasn't anything to play with, except the plumbing.

The Martin County jail would not put youthful offenders in cells with older prisoners, and this meant Leroy and three like-minded young idiots shared a cell. Therefore, after the dayroom was cleared and everyone was in his cell, it meant that no one with any sense could have access to the party boys in cell number four. If there were no comic books to read, no cigarettes to smoke, no sexual conquests to analyze, or no criminal endeavors to discuss—in short, no intellectual activity for these underdeveloped minds— then Leroy, as leader, liked to do what he called the "jail-house rock."

Leroy thought it was great fun to cram his shower towel into the toilet and keep flushing the high-pressure system until, not only had he backed up and flooded his cell, but also every other one in the cell block.

Everyone would yell at Leroy to quit the bullshit, but he didn't care; he was locked down in his cell, and no one could get to him. Once the disgusting jailhouse toilet water started to leak through the floor to the offices on the ground floor, this would immediately bring up a jailer (or Sheriff Hall if he was in the jail), and he'd take Leroy out of the cell block and beat the shit out of him before giving him a mop and bucket to clean the mess up.

The punishment for Leroy didn't stop with a jailer's beating. The next morning, when the doors would roll at 5:30 A.M., three older prisoners, who didn't appreciate having to sleep 18 inches above the stench from the residue of a backed-up toilet, would grab Leroy from his bunk, drag him into the shower, beat him up a bit, and then stick his face in the toilet bowl.

This took the playfulness out of Leroy for about a week; then his boredom factor would rise, and he'd start out by constantly flushing his toilet and making his "jailhouse rock" cracks. A few nights of this and then he'd do it again. He knew what was coming, but he didn't care; to him those few moments of flushing, gurgling, and then the erupting of the plume of toilet water from each of the seven commodes in cell block C was great fun and showed everyone in the jailhouse that you could never break his spirit.

The prison slang for guys like Leroy and company was "jitterbugs." For Leroy, the moment was all that mattered. There was no future; there were no consequences; there was no need for considerations. The purpose of life was to react to whatever whims and stimuli entered his world. This failure to even consider one's actions is what made jitterbugs a wild card of the prison population.

In the Martin County jail, Leroy didn't have the freedom of movement to "gang up" with other inmates and participate in the culture that flourished in prisons for young offenders. These institutions were known as "gladiator schools" because so many individuals and gangs were trying to out-macho their fellow convicts—without regard to what the punishment could be—that there was a constant war going on within the prison walls. Most of these kids saw no future for themselves beyond a life of criminal activity, and whether that activity took place inside prison or out on the streets made no difference. The weak were to be preyed upon, respect was to be fought for, and if someone had to be "shanked" then just do it. It didn't make any difference if a kid only had a month to go on his sentence—you pick up another couple of years for a stabbing, so what?

Older prisoners who had been in the system hated to be in contact with the youthful offenders. There was no reasoning with them, and you could never really predict what their reactions might be. If you snitch on a fellow inmate, then that's worthy of a shanking; however, to get cut up when you asked a jitterbug to turn down his radio because you were trying to sleep made no sense.

A sociologist might lament Leroy's lack of self-esteem brought on by a dysfunctional family unit and analyze his poor performance in school due to peer pressure to fail. However, to the prisoners over the age of 22 who were sharing cell block C with Leroy, he was just an ignorant jitterbug who thought he knew all the answers, and to Sheriff Hall and the jailers of the Martin County jail he was a teenage punk wiseass who showed no interest in the jailhouse rules. However, Leroy's mother must have loved him because when she would show up for a weekend visit, they'd stare at each other through the Plexiglas visiting window and both would have tears running down their cheeks as Leroy swore on his prison-issue Bible that he was studying hard for his GED high school equivalency test and was thinking of attending junior college as soon as he got out. It was all very touching, especially if you were privileged to witness Leroy's conversation with his cellmates right after his mother left.

"Hey, Leroy," Ralph would start in, "how come your eyes are all red?"

"Hey, you stupid motherfucker," Leroy would reply, "the stupid bitch put $50 in my account. I'd say that's worth a few tears."

Leroy had the attitude of a convict, he had a good start on having enough "jailhouse" tattoos on his body for like-minded young punks to think he was a "badass" for having done time, and he carried his peewee shank around the way a NFL player might show off his Super Bowl ring. However, there was one other area of jailhouse life that Leroy wanted to experience, a part of prison mystique that has fascinated voyeurs of prison culture for centuries: Leroy wanted to be a dominant predator male—he wanted to do some butt-fucking.

Few Hollywood movies have been made about life behind bars that don't contain at least one scene centering around a prison rape. The public is fascinated by the concept of predator males and females forcing sexual acts on weaker, docile inmates so as to establish dominance over them. The drama involved in these scenes is so predictable that it is now a movie-making cliche to have the scene where a gentle, unfairly accused, white boy is cornered by four body-building, iron-pumping, scowling black men, and then spread-eagled across a chair so that each attacker can take his turn fucking the ass of the screaming white boy. This is such a strong media image, whether it be written or visual, that people who have never been to prison believe that almost everyone who enters the convict world is going to come out a broken spirit who has had his masculinity subjected to repeated gang rapes by the gangs of sexual predators who are all sneers and violent pelvic thrusts.

As a result of this unavoidable media image, the public not only perceives life behind bars as a battleground of bull elks vying for the breeding rights to the female members of the herd, it also sees the predator males portrayed as the meanest, baddest, most feared convicts in the joint. The nightmare of anyone who has never been to prison, and of some that have, is for a black man who looks like Mr. T or Mike Tyson to come up to you and say, "Blood on my knife, or shit on my dick, white boy, what's it going to be?"

When Leroy would get into an argument with one of his cellmates the words that usually were the mainstays of his conversational pattern, such as "motherfucker," "fuck," "asshole," and "piece of shit," would quickly be augmented with "sissy," "bitch," "punk," and, the most demeaning of them all, "fuck boy."

Leroy could outverbalize his cell block buddies in the game of put-down and humiliation, and he could kick their ass if it got down to actual blows. However, these guys were Leroy's friends, and butt-fucking a guy you liked would be a homosexual act, not an act of domination and humiliation.

Three weeks after I arrived in cell block C, a new member was deposited in our 300-square-foot world of concrete, porcelain, and steel. Jason was a vagrant in his mid-20s and had the dirty, disheveled appearance of someone who was homeless and living on the street, which is exactly what he had been doing. He had been begging during the day and sleeping in the park at night. Stuart, Florida, is not used to seeing society's losers appearing in public, especially a Caucasian who certainly looked like he could be doing work to support himself. As the complaints from the downtown shop owners mounted, Jason was advised to take his backpack and get out of Martin County. When he didn't respond, Sheriff Hall arrested him for aggressive panhandling.

When Jason arrived in cell block C, he immediately

went to a corner of the dayroom, just like a dog who has been beaten too much and quakes at any human movement for fear that it is a boot about to kick him again. Jason didn't say a word to anyone; he didn't play spades; he didn't read; he just sat.

Leroy said a few words to Jason the first day he arrived, but he got no response, just a blank stare from Jason, whose liquid eyes begged Leroy to leave him alone. Leroy threw off a few comments to his buddies about what a pathetic piece of shit Jason was and lost interest. That is, he lost interest until two days later when Jason was sitting on the toilet bowl in the dayroom (there was no toilet seat) taking a crap.

(Few jailhouses have enclosed stalls for the toilets, nor are there toilet seats. The lack of toilet stalls is so a prisoner cannot have a sanctuary where he can be out of sight of jailers, and no plastic toilet seats to sit on not only makes it easier to clean the toilets, but also removes a piece of strong plastic from the list of potential materials that a prisoner could use to improvise a weapon. Jail procedure for taking a crap requires the inmate to balance on the thin rim of the toilet bowl, and then when it is time to wipe his ass, to tilt up to one side and insert his hand underneath to use the toilet paper to tidy up the booty hole. Then, before getting off the rim, the user flushes and remains seated until the gurgling sound that indicates a successful flush has occurred. However, if the water starts to rise in the toilet bowl, indicating a possible overflow situation, then it is permissible to abandon the sitting position before getting soaked.)

Leroy was playing spades and had a direct view of Jason sitting on the toilet. Jason finished his business and flushed the toilet, but something had caught Leroy's eye, a very important part of the process had been skipped.

"He didn't wipe his ass," Leroy exclaimed as he stood up from the metal picnic table. "What kind of filthy pig are you?"

Jason got a look on his face like he was a deer on a road and a car's high beams were catching him square in the eyes.

"Don't you know what toilet paper is for?" Leroy continued. "I'll bet the bitch don't wear underwear either."

Leroy walked over to the petrified Jason and grabbed the back of his jeans just inside the rear belt loop and pulled up.

"No fucking underwear! What a piece of shit."

The confrontation couldn't go any further because Tim the jailer arrived to roll the doors and clear the dayroom. Once everyone was back in their cells, the doors were rolled, and for the next two hours Leroy and cellmates kept up a barrage of conversation speculating on what kind of person would be so low as to not wipe his ass after taking a shit. Jason didn't respond to the comments; he just lay on his bunk in quiet panic that he couldn't just disappear into his corner and be left alone.

Leroy was agitated. Jason had violated the sacred jailhouse etiquette on defecation. He wouldn't play cards—all he did was sit in a corner and look scared. Moreover, Jason wasn't a convict; he was a pathetic vagrant who not only didn't have the balls to be a criminal, but didn't even have the self-pride to get a job and support himself.

When the cell doors rolled at 5:30 the next morning, only three of us got up and left the cells. Jason went to his corner of the dayroom and sat down, I started doing my exercise sequence, and Leroy appeared from his exotic-looking bunk enclosure with a notebook.

Leroy started right in on Jason. "Get into the shower and clean your ass up, you piece of shit," Leroy commanded.

For the first time in the three days Jason had been in cell block C, he spoke. "Look, Leroy, I don't want any trouble— just leave me alone, please."

Leroy was standing over Jason, who was still sitting on the cement floor. "You don't want trouble, then get into that shower. You're going to give everyone in here a disease from the maggots that are growing in your ass."

"Please, just leave me alone," Jason pleaded as he stood up to face Leroy.

Leroy slapped Jason in the face and pushed him back against the cell bars of the dayroom wall. "Don't give me this 'please' shit; get your ragged ass into that shower, or I'll throw you in there."

Jason put up his hands to protect his face from Leroy's slaps. "Move bitch," Leroy continued as his speech pattern changed gears into the dialogue of the sexually dominant. "You're nothing but a punk. Come on, sissy, you want to hit me? Come on, bitch, hit me."

Jason weakly kept his hands up, but made no effort to deflect Leroy's slaps, which were catching him square on both sides of his head. "You like getting bitch-slapped, don't you, bitch?" asked a smiling Leroy.

Jason just took the hits. While this was going on, I took a seat at one of the metal picnic tables to watch the confrontation play out. In the joint everyone quickly learns to mind his own business. If something doesn't directly involve you or someone with whom you are allied, then you don't get involved. I wasn't going to fight Jason's battles for him. He had to at least try to protect himself.

After 20 more slaps from Leroy, Jason said he'd go to the shower if Leroy would leave him alone. Leroy quit hitting him and motioned for him to move over to the shower. Jason quickly took off his shoes, socks, pants, and shirt and entered the slippery cement shower stall. He pulled the piece of plastic along the runner to extend it and give him some privacy, and then he turned on the water.

If any of the other prisoners still in their bunks were awake, it was unnoticeable because there was no stirring or movement. These guys had managed to sleep through five minutes of Leroy's loud taunts and physical assault on Jason.

Once Leroy had Jason positioned in the shower, he went to the notebook he had carried into the dayroom and pulled out some folded sheets he had concealed between the pages. Leroy stared at me as he moved back to the shower stall. He knew I was watching him, but he didn't care. Leroy's most glorious moment of convict life was about to occur, and he saw no reason why I would want to prevent it from happening.

When Leroy got to the shower curtain, he pulled it back and shut off the water. Then he took a piece of adhesive tape, which was one of the items he had removed from his notebook, and quickly attached it to Jason's mouth so he couldn't yell for the jailer.

"You're either going to get my shank or my dick up your ass, fuck boy . . . bend over," Leroy commanded.

Jason tried to push back out of the stall, but Leroy had him blocked and rammed him forward so his head cracked against the cement, in tandem with reaching out and giving Jason a blow to the stomach so he'd double over. Now, Leroy had Jason pinned into the corner of the shower stall. He unfastened his Levis and pulled them down, and grabbed the bar of soap with one hand while keeping Jason bent over with the other. Leroy shoved the wet bar of soap into Jason's crack and lathered up his asshole. However, Leroy didn't have an erection, so he started to masturbate with quick, hard strokes to get his dick hard. But it wasn't working, so Leroy played his ace in the hole. He reached behind him and grabbed a folded piece of paper that was on the floor. Leroy got the paper unfolded, and in it was the centerfold pinup from *Playboy*. He plastered the playmate picture on the back of the bent-over Jason and resumed rigorous masturbation.

"Motherfucker!" yelled an exasperated Leroy. "All right bitch, I'm going to let you turn around so you can suck my dick."

There had been enough commotion that Leroy's cellmate, Ralph, had awakened and lifted his darkened bunk veil to see what was going on in the dayroom. What Ralph had a clear view of was Jason bent over in the shower with a picture of a *Playboy* bunny plastered on his back while Leroy pulled his own sex organ trying to get it hard.

"Hey, Leroy can't get his dick hard," blurted out Ralph to anyone who was awake enough to listen. "Come on, Leroy, you can do it; jack that dick."

Leroy turned around to see a grinning Ralph staring at him through the bars of the cell. "Too bad," Ralph commented. "You know what this means: if you can't fuck, then you're going to get fucked."

"Leroy, leave him alone," I said. "Let him out of there."

I left my perch on the picnic table and stood up in case Leroy decided to come at me with his toothbrush. But his spirit had collapsed. I was half a foot taller and outweighed him by 50 pounds, and, sharpened toothbrush or not, Leroy knew I could easily kick his ass in a fight. An ass-kicking from me, coupled with the humiliation of his attempted rape of Jason, was too much for Leroy for one morning, so he grabbed his playmate off Jason's back, pulled up his pants, and walked back to his bunk.

"The bitch didn't have any fight in him," Leroy said as he pulled his darkened veils down to keep the light out of his bunk area. "How can you fuck the pussy if he won't fight? I don't want to fuck homosexuals. I'm no faggot."

Those were Leroy's last words on his failed sexual prowess. Within an hour, a little birdie had gotten word to Sheriff Hall on what had happened in cell block C. Jason was pulled from the cell block, and Sheriff Hall gave him

$50 and put him on a bus to Miami—Jason was disrupting his jailhouse, and for the good of the other prisoners he had to go.

Leroy stayed quiet and subdued for the next two days as he worked through the tangents that his failed sexual assault meant to his stature in the jailhouse. But, by the third day, he was on the mend, and within a week he had flushed a towel down the toilet and flooded all the cells in the cell block. Leroy was a jitterbug at play, and jitterbugs never stay immobile for long.

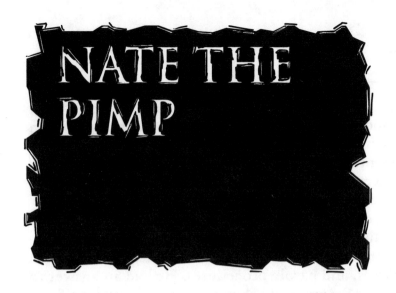

NATE THE PIMP

W HEN I ARRIVED IN CELL BLOCK C of the
Martin County jail, I was put in a cell
with a 45-year-old black man. For the
first week of my stay, it was just the two of us in the
four-man cell. As I emptied my flight suit of the
books I was carrying, I told the man my name and
offered him the loan of any of the paperbacks I had
brought. The man replied that his name was Nate
and all he read was the Bible.

For the next four days Nate didn't say a word to
me. His day revolved around an hour grooming session in front of the mirror in the morning to meticu-
lously pluck and trim his beard, followed by some
exercising in the dayroom. Nate spoke to no one.
All the rest of his waking day, if he wasn't eating,
toileting, grooming, or exercising, he lay on his
bunk and read his Bible.

I was new to prison life and was trying to glean
as much information as I could about how the process would work once I was moved from the county
jail to the state system. Unfortunately, the only person in the cell block who claimed to have been
through the Florida system was Leroy.

Leroy spun a tale of how he had been to a gladiator school on the west coast of Florida but had gotten in trouble for fighting and had been shipped out of the juvenile facility by the head of the prison to an adult correctional facility near Gainesville. I didn't know any better and was happy to be getting advanced information on what to expect. I asked Leroy questions about the living arrangements, visiting privileges, job assignments, recreation facilities, availability of educational classes, and parole procedures. He had an answer to every question, and I thought he was doing me a favor and bought him a couple of packs of cigarettes to show my appreciation.

One night in the second week of my incarceration, Leroy was doing his "jailhouse rock" and had blown up the toilet in Nate's and my cell. We had an inch of toilet water on the floor, and Leroy was yelling that he was ramming another towel down his toilet to try and get another eruption. Nate calmly lay on his bunk as our toilet gurgled and read his Bible.

When the second plume of water rose out of the toilet and came splashing down on the already-drenched floor, Nate had had enough. He slammed his Bible shut and yelled down to Leroy that the ass-whipping he was going to get the next morning when the cell doors were rolled was going to be extra special. Leroy yelled back for Nate to get fucked and that if Nate tried anything he'd stick his shank in him. Nate laughed out loud and shook his head at Leroy's audacious comments.

"That boy is the biggest fool I've ever seen," Nate said as he spoke to me directly for the first time. "I've been hearing all that shit he's told you about the state system. He don't know anything; the only jail cell he's ever seen is right here in Martin County."

"How do you know?" I replied in a questioning voice, not wanting to challenge Nate's statement.

"Because I've been there twice and am heading back for a third trip. The jitterbug is just talking to exercise his jaws. Tomorrow, I'm going to shit in the toilet before I cram his head in it; this bullshit has got to stop."

The next morning Leroy took his ass-whipping without putting up a fight, but that quickly changed when Nate dragged Leroy back to our cell to dunk his head in our toilet where Nate had deposited a fresh six-inch turd during his morning bowel movement.

I watched from my bunk as Nate easily overpowered Leroy's attempt to get away and held his head in the water for a good three seconds before letting him up for air. When the act was done, Nate threw Leroy out of our cell and told him the next time he overflowed our toilet he was going to put some of the overflowed water in his cup and make Leroy drink it.

Leroy scrambled back to his cell to wipe his face and tried to roust his homeboys to launch a counterattack on Nate. Leroy wasn't subtle about calling his cohorts to arms.

"The nigger turd touched me; I'm going to kill the motherfucker," Leroy ranted in a decibel level that awoke everyone who was trying to sleep through breakfast.

However, Leroy's mates weren't interested in taking revenge on Nate, and Nate wasn't bothered at the spate of "niggers" flying out of Leroy's mouth.

I thought Leroy's use of the most demeaning word in the English language would cause Nate to immediately return to Leroy's open cell and bring him back for another breathing lesson in our toilet bowl. However, Leroy, who was always running his mouth, probably hadn't noticed that the blacks in the Martin County jail weren't address-ing each other as "man," "blood," or "soul brother" anymore; they were using *nigger*. I had hated the word and refused to use it ever since the time when I was in the seventh grade and Danny Cortesi had called my basketball teammate, and the only black kid in my school, Willie Jackson, a "stupid nigger" when he missed the free throws that caused our team to lose. Willie Jackson was by far the best athlete and most popular kid in our school, but when Cortesi blurted out the ultimate put-down, Willie didn't respond with a like insult; he just started crying. He walked over to his parents, who were watching the game, and they too started to cry. Just from that scene, I knew that *nigger* was a word I didn't want in my vocabulary. Even when I heard other people use it, the word triggered a response of wanting to avoid a person who could so casually use a word that had the power to make people cry and feel inferior.

However, in conversations between blacks in the Martin County jail, *nigger* was used as a filler word, much like "you know." If you hear a taboo word used enough, it starts to lose its danger. Up in cell block C, *nigger* was no longer a dangerous word that defined the dominance that one race had held over another for the 400 years that African slavery has been in the historical record. *Nigger* was just another word, like asshole or motherfucker, and had lost its racial meaning. In fact, the term had become a form of acceptance; if a black prisoner thought a white prisoner was a pretty good guy, then it was OK for the white inmate to use it as a friendly greeting.

Leroy and Nate certainly weren't pals, but Nate was impressed with the attitude Leroy had been able to keep after 10 months of county jail time. Leroy was still flushing towels down the toilet, still getting the shit beat out of him, and still coming back for more.

"Leroy," Nate yelled, "I ain't flushed my toilet yet. You

want to bring your buddies over to my house and show them what you washed your face in this morning?"

Nate was amused, but when Leroy didn't respond he settled back down on his bunk, opened his Bible, and began the day's reading.

Since Nate had declared Leroy's knowledge of the Florida prison system to be fictitious, I asked him if he could fill me in on what was going to happen once I left Martin County. Nate spelled out the way he remembered things happening when he was last in the state system seven years earlier.

"From the county, you go to Lake Butler Reception and Medical Center, where you get classified; then they move you over to the Butler Transfer Unit, where you sit for a month; and then you get shipped to your destination prison."

That was about it as far as Nate's knowledge was concerned. He didn't pretend to know much about the destination prisons, except that they all were different, but he was able to answer my basic questions on phone facilities, visiting privileges, recreation, and education.

After this transfer of information, Nate started to speak to me during his beard-grooming sessions. I had grown up on the North Shore of Chicago, where you were more likely to win the lottery than see a black person strolling around town. My first extended stay away from this lily-white environment was when I went to college at the University of Colorado in Boulder, which had fewer than 200 black students out of a total enrollment of around 20,000, with most of the black students being athletes. After graduation, I had entered the U.S. Air Force as an officer/pilot, again an almost all-white career field. There had been a few black air force maintenance people in my unit, but they were enlisted and I was an officer, which meant there was very little interaction besides the standard "how's it going" greetings. In all, for the first 30 years of my life I had never been in a situation where I had a black friend, and my whole perception of life for a black man in the United States of America had come from the media via books, newspapers, and TV shows.

Nate's "house" was right next to mine, separated only by three feet of open space. Nate had surveyed the playing field where he was supposed to compete in the American version of the game of life, and he had deduced that it was heavily stacked against him. To attain the material things he wanted and to feel useful, Nate had known that he was going to have to modify the rules as set forth by the 70-year-old multimillionaire white people who ran and controlled the wealth of the United States of America.

Nate told me how his parents had worked in the vegetable fields west of Palm Beach and how, during picking time, they'd pull him out of school to help. He had quit school when he turned 16 because his family needed him to pitch in a wage, but after two years of full-time field-hand work he had quit and tried to enlist in the U.S. Army. Even in the era when the army desperately needed men for Vietnam infantry service, Nate had been turned down because he couldn't pass the intelligence test.

What followed was a series of minimum-wage jobs where no skills were required and no opportunity for advancement existed.

By his mid-20s, Nate was back in the vegetable fields and living in an abandoned shack with no water, heat, or plumbing. By this time, the big growing operations were having trouble getting enough local labor to work the fields, and they had resorted to bringing up seasonal workers from Mexico, Haiti, Jamaica, and the Bahamas. Most of these workers had stayed in the fields from sunrise to sunset, lived in worse conditions than Nate had, and sent almost all of their paychecks back to their home countries. These imported workers hadn't required much, just a TV to observe the American dream that they certainly weren't a part of and the accouterments to liven up their one night off, Saturday night—mainly liquor, marijuana, and girls.

Nate had stepped in to provide the imported field hands what they needed. He had started by being the "fence" for stolen TVs that he would sell direct to the migrants for a third of what the cheapest ones in a used-appliance store would cost, and then he had expanded to provide Saturday night parties to the bachelor camps at the big growing operations.

Nate had provided the rum cheaper than the migrants could buy it for from the company store, the marijuana, and the girls. Each man got a fifth of rum, a half-ounce of marijuana, and one screw with a girl for $20; if someone wanted to screw a second time, it cost him another $5.

Within a month, Nate had elevated himself from what he called a "nigger dirt farmer" to a position where he didn't have to work in the fields, but rather could concentrate on getting TVs from his homeboys in Palm Beach and providing the Saturday night entertainment for the foreign migrants.

"All of a sudden I had money," Nate confided to me. "I went from always owing the company store for just food and cigarettes to having dollar bills in my wallet. You take a nigger dirt farmer, who has never had nothing, and give him $10,000 a year . . . well, he's going to fuck up because he ain't used to having money like that. I was just like an athlete who gets signed out of high school. You see it happen all the time—they buy the Mercedes, the fancy jewelry, the clothes, and hit the nightclubs every night; then if they get another paycheck, they get into the cocaine and pussy once a week. When it's all over, they're broke, and all they've got to show for it might be some bullshit bracelets worth 10 cents on the dollar for what they paid.

"When I became a $10,000-a-year man, I could handle that," Nate went on to explain. "However, when I became a $50,000-a-year-man, that's when I started to fuck up bad. I bought a stolen Cadillac and got popped, my marijuana supplier gave my name up as his biggest customer, and one of the bitches stabbed a guy then told the cops she worked for me. Since all that shit came down, it's been a pattern: I go to jail for a couple of years and then I'm on the street for three before I go back again. Sometimes it's the county jail, sometimes it's probation, and sometimes it's the state—it's just part of the job."

Nate was telling me his story because this time he was worried. The district attorney had told him the next time he showed up with a felony that he was going to try him as a habitual offender, which meant he would be in the joint for 10 years minimum. Nate could accept his one to two years at a time in the joint, but 10 years was a whole different story. His dilemma was that if he was going to keep providing his criminal services, he would have to move himself up a notch and become management so he would be far enough removed when arrests were made. This elevation on the job ladder would mean he'd have to start dealing with payoffs, lawyers, and turf battles with other niggers—in other words, big business. His other option was to get a legitimate job when he finished doing his current two-year sentence.

During beard-picking time, Nate would continually go over his future with me; petty crime was the only life he knew where he could make good money, and it was the only opportunity that America had ever offered him. On the other hand, he had already paid for this opportunity with five years of down time in the joint, and if the next conviction carried a dime sentence, then he'd be over 60 when he got out. Nate was having a mid-life crisis that he couldn't contain by his constant Bible reading, because on Saturday, which was visiting day, his three "bitches," as he called his prostitutes, would dutifully pay a call and remind him what he would be giving up.

Sheriff Hall had no legal reason not to let the prostitutes visit. They had no criminal record, had properly filled out the paperwork (on which they listed their relationship to Nate as "cousin"), and were never found with anything illegal on their person during the purse search and body patdown that was always performed before any of them were allowed in the corridor leading to the cell block. They were always well dressed and well mannered as each waited for her opportunity to visit with Nate for 20 minutes.

If the ladies had names, I never heard them, because if Nate wasn't referring to them as "bitches," he was calling them "field-hand niggers." Despite Nate's reading his Bible all week, and his ladies' patient and circumspect behavior in the visitor's waiting area, once Nate laid eyes on one of his bitches through the Plexiglas window, his face would contort into a mean-looking scowl, and he'd start in with a series of demeaning put-downs that the women would not challenge.

"All right," Nate would start out, "how many bucks did you all fuck out at Dole camp #2 last night?"

"Nate, honey, we did 32 guys with the party price, and then five guys came back for seconds" would be the answer that everyone in the cell block could hear.

"Not bad, but, look, you got to get some weight off that ass; those Latin guys don't like fat women, you hear? How about the Cadillac, you get the payment in?"

There were no niceties in Nate's conversation, and he would get so mad at them that his face looked like he was having a brain aneurysm. But the ladies would take it, and then they'd be right back there the next week to report to

Nate on how the numbers were at the migrant camps they had serviced.

When the visits were over, Nate would leave the day-room and return to his bunk for a five-hour session of reading his Bible.

About the only time you could count on Leroy having his mouth shut was when Nate had a visit going on. Leroy viewed this as classroom time, with the subject being how to treat a woman so she'd take abuse, give you most of the money she earned, and be devoted and loyal while she was doing it.

At the end of one such visiting session, Leroy couldn't contain himself any longer—he had to know how Nate was able to so dominate his bitches, even from a prison cell.

"Come on, Nate, tell me the secret," Leroy would plead. "Is it a nigger thing? I'm getting out in a couple of months; I'd like to get a couple of white bitches working for me."

Nate couldn't help but smile when Leroy expressed such enthusiasm for the various strains of criminal activity he came across in the jail. "Leroy," Nate calmly answered, "you're a fucked-up jitterbug, and you'll never know anything until you read this book. It's all in the Bible."

Leroy was a sponge: he wanted to know how to smuggle drugs from me, how to run a string of bitches from Nate, and anything else he could find out from various criminals in the cell block. But I had underestimated how serious he was about the few ridiculous suggestions people would throw his way until the next week when Leroy's mother brought him a Bible. All of a sudden Leroy was a regular visitor to Nate's house with proposals that he and Nate study passages together.

Leroy was so anxious to find out the secret of Nate's control over women that he was trying to suck up to Nate under the pretext of Bible study. There was a masterful con job going on here, but who was conning whom? I never heard Nate give Leroy a 10-point program on how to be a successful pimp, but I did see Leroy reading and contemplating his Bible. Leroy even told his mother that not only did he want to go to junior college when he got out, but he might want to become a minister, a prison minister no less, where he could help troubled youths like himself.

Leroy had picked up a new trick from the master to add to his arsenal. He now began to explain his thoughts and actions to his homeboys by quoting scripture. The Lord's work was being done for strange reasons.

GOOD COP-
BAD COP

I STAYED IN THE MARTIN COUNTY JAIL for six weeks
as Sheriff Hall played "good cop-bad cop" with
me. The bad cop was threatening to file a felony
charge of failing to appear because I had followed
my lawyer's instructions and checked into the
Martin County jail on the day he told me to. What I
didn't know was that the date my lawyer had given
me was five weeks after the date specified in a letter
to him from the clerk of the court for Martin
County. However, the good-cop side of Sheriff Hall
let me know that this matter of reporting late could
be easily forgotten and I could be on my way to a
possible reduced sentence if I would just cooperate
and tell him where Mike Buff could be found.

The cell blocks in the Martin County jail had
no phones; therefore, to make a phone call, even to
your attorney, you had to make the request to a jailer
and then wait days for him to find the time from his
busy schedule of magazine reading, donut eating,
and soap opera watching to pull you out of the cell
block, take you downstairs, and wait while you made
the collect call. My problem was that the honorable
Melvin Kliner was never available to accept the   5 5

call. After two attempts, I quit trying and began dealing with him through letters that I would send to my wife so she could make a copy and then forward to him.

After four weeks, I was still sitting in cell block C and was very concerned that Sheriff Hall's threat of a new charge for failure to appear was a real possibility. Kliner had not written or called Karen or me. He was supposedly out of town doing a trial and couldn't be reached. At this point, Karen called the lawyer who had handled the original case, Russell Cromwell, and asked for advice on what she could do to break the logjam and get me rolling out of the county jail and on my way to the Florida prison system.

Russell visited me at the county jail and spent the morning gathering documents and talking to the clerk of the court about why the discrepancy in reporting dates had occurred. It obviously hadn't been my fault. Russell knew from weekly phone conversations, plus being the best man at my wedding, that Kliner had given me the December 19 reporting date back in early November. But Russell had also seen the court document that clearly stated the reporting date to be November 2. The problem link in this chain of events had to be Melvin Kliner.

With Russell's help, I wrote one last letter to Kliner and told him I was retaining an attorney to file malpractice charges against him, seeking $1 million in damages unless he immediately solved the problem of the new charges Sheriff Hall was threatening against me for failure to appear. Karen sent the letter by registered mail so that Kliner couldn't claim he hadn't received the correspondence.

Within three days, Kliner called Karen and told her there was no need to file a lawsuit against him; he had talked to the people in Martin County and the misunderstanding had been solved—I would be getting shipped out of Martin County within two weeks.

Karen and I had heard a lot of bullshit and outright lies from Kliner over the past two years; thus, Karen took the initiative and made a special trip up to Stuart to try and meet with the sentencing judge in my case to make sure that Kliner had done what he claimed to have done.

After Karen had sat in open court for three hours, the judge noticed her and asked why she was there. This was the opening she was hoping for, and she was invited back to his chambers, where she showed the judge the paperwork we had accumulated regarding the reporting date discrepancy, along with a list of the latest phone conversations with Kliner saying the problem had been solved.

Whether the judge was impressed with the organization Karen displayed in his chambers or whether he was dazzled by her beauty, I don't know, but he immediately called in the clerk of the court and Sheriff Hall to get to the bottom of the problem.

Karen waited outside while the three men were meeting, and 10 minutes later she was ushered back in and advised that her husband would be on his way out of the Martin County jail as soon as transportation was available and that no new charges would be filed.

I couldn't be sure, but through bits and pieces of conversation with Sheriff Hall during our good cop-bad cop sessions, I developed a conspiracy theory whereby Kliner, the clerk of the court, and the sheriff were working together to try to force me to cooperate and give up Mike Buff's underground hideout so he could be arrested.

The sheriff wanted the accolades and publicity he would get if he returned the bail-jumping Buff to the Fort Lauderdale police. Melvin Kliner wanted Buff captured because he knew that Buff would pay him a huge fee to defend him against the Fort Lauderdale marijuana charges he had bolted on. The clerk went along with the plan because he would be doing the sheriff a favor, as well as getting a kickback of a certain percentage of the fee that Kliner was paid by Buff. However, the plan centered around my being sufficiently worried and scared about an additional five-year sentence to give them information on where Mike could be found.

It was a good plan, and everyone had something to gain, including me. And the sheriff even sweetened the deal for me by offering to intercede with the sentencing judge and tell him that I had provided significant cooperation and to recommend a sentence reduction, which the sheriff thought would get my sentence down to something in the area of six months—to be served right in the Martin County jail where I would immediately be made a trustee!

However, the sheriff, the clerk, and Kliner hadn't figured on two things: 1) that Karen would be able to meet with the judge and disclose the problem I was having, and 2) that I would never "turn over" on Mike Buff.

A person usually forges his or her closest friends during times of stress and challenge. Such a period might occur during an academic situation, an athletic competition, or a survival situation. For Mike and me, our friendship began during Air Force Undergraduate Pilot Training, or UPT, a situation that involved a bit of all three: academics, athletics, and survival, plus a lot of stress regarding imminent failure and the challenge of flying supersonic jet aircraft.

It was a strange time for the U.S. Air Force. Because of the rapid buildup of the air war in Vietnam, the air force was forced to look for pilot candidates outside the reliable pool of Air Force Academy graduates and ROTC program graduates. Mike and I both found ourselves at UPT in Del Rio, Texas, by way of the air force officer candidate program, which we had both signed up for to avoid being drafted by the army.

This pressing need for pilot trainees had severely curtailed the effectiveness of the air force's security checks, so the air force had not discovered Mike's juvenile arrest record in the Dayton, Ohio, area. The air force also didn't discover Mike's run-ins with authorities at the University of Cincinnati and why he had transferred to Southwest Oklahoma State.

Both of us wanted to blend in with the other 80 clean-cut, motivated, outstanding products of America's universities, which made up UPT class 70-05, but we were square pegs trying to fit into round holes, and we couldn't quite squeeze in.

Within the first month of flight training, Mike had gotten into trouble for brawling in the officer's club, as well as for taking his motorcycle on a joyride on the only bit of green grass that existed in Del Rio, Texas—the sacred Laughlin Air Force Base nine-hole golf course. Luckily for Mike, the base commander liked Mike's background as a football player and arm wrestler and gave him one last chance to get with the program and control his drinking, which is what usually led to his problems.

As for me, within that first month of UPT, I was somehow suspected of being a leftist, a member of Students for a Democratic Society (SDS), and a plant in the air force. The only basis for this accusation was a story I told at the officer's club bar one evening about Bob, a friend of mine at the University of Colorado who had lobbed a few sticks of dynamite onto the roof of the Boulder police station. The blast blew a hole in the roof of the cop shop, but no one was hurt. Even though Bob had considered this as nothing more serious than a college prank aimed at a police department that was continually giving him tickets for noise violations at his parties, the fact was that the incident was seen as an attack on law enforcement in a college town that was experiencing a lot of conflict because of the Vietnam War.

I had nothing to do with Bob's fireworks display, and certainly not the SDS, but the fact that I was called into my section commander's office and grilled meant that my hope of going through the program as just an ordinary pilot trainee wasn't going to happen.

Along with our outside troubles, Mike and I had problems inside the program as well. Neither of us was what the air force would call a "natural stick." We were both hacking the program, but just barely, accomplishing and mastering flight maneuvers right at the last possible moment so we could pass the various check rides and not wash out of the program. Neither Mike nor I had ever flown before, and for us to receive just 30 hours in a Cessna 172 single-engine trainer, then go right into a 300-MPH jet for 90 hours of training, followed by a leap into a T-38 (which could go Mach 1.3) was like an 8-year-old kid going from learning how to ride a two-wheel bike to driving an Indy 500 race car in the course of a year.

The pressure to hack the flying part of the program, pass all the academic courses, and withstand outside scrutiny of whether or not we belonged in the air force in the first place drew us together first as friends and then as roommates.

We spent 52 weeks together on the flight line going through the most intensive program in the military. When we weren't talking flying, we were thinking flying, and when we weren't thinking about flying, then we were worrying about flying. After six months of this, Mike and I agreed that between 7 and 9 each night we'd go out to dinner and all talk about flying would be barred. We both had to have a break because there had to be more to our personalities than the fact we were about to become air force pilots.

We both managed to graduate from the program, and

Mike went on to fly B-52s, while I became a forward air controller (FAC). We each did our year in Vietnam, and after we got back to the United States we stayed in touch. I didn't see much of Mike, but just before we were both about to get out of the air force, he suddenly appeared at my house in Fort Walton Beach, Florida, and asked if he could stay a couple of weeks.

While still on active duty, Mike had taken three weeks of leave and was working with some high school friends of his to put together a marijuana run. Mike was the pilot, and, unfortunately, he had crashed the Beech-18 aircraft on takeoff out of Sabring, Florida, but he had gotten away from the accident site before the police had arrived to investigate the crash. He wanted to lie low at my place and see whether any law enforcement personnel showed up at his apartment on Loring Air Force Base in Maine. When no one showed up in Loring looking for him, Mike went on home.

I lost track of Mike after that and knew nothing of where he was or what he was doing for two years. But, by chance, we ran into each other at a bar in Boulder, Colorado, and found out we were living within two miles of each other. Once again, we became inseparable—only this time the purpose wasn't to learn the skills needed to fly supersonic jets; it was to put together missions to smuggle marijuana from Colombia into the United States.

Mike and I had some disagreements during the four years we participated in boat and aircraft missions, but we always knew we could trust each other to do his best toward the success of the mission. He'd flown on my wing at supersonic speeds, and I'd flown on his as he led us through thunderstorms to an instrument landing at Laughlin AFB—to turn over on Mike Buff to save a year or two or five from my sentence was out of the question. Obviously, Sheriff Hall didn't know what it was like to strap on a T-38 and be part of a two-ship formation where you take turns leading while flying 50 feet above the ground at 600 MPH. In combat, if you can't trust your wingman, then don't engage in the battle.

In the smuggling business, people constantly talk about how they'd do the time if they got caught and never betray anyone in the group. That kind of macho talk is lovely . . . except when the group does get busted, and all of a sudden group members panic and start making deals with law enforcement to try and save their own ass from going to jail. That's just the way it is: the fear of jail, coupled with the long sentences that law enforcement is able to demand from judges, makes it a fact that if law enforcement officials want someone to cooperate in an investigation, then they are more than likely going to be able to get that coopera- tion. The list of people who have told various law enforce- ment agencies to get fucked when they offer inducements to get the cooperation they want is very short.

If I had been facing a 20- or 30-year sentence, I can't say that I wouldn't have considered Sheriff Hall's offer. However, I had received nothing but optimistic news regarding how much time I was going to have to serve since I had been sentenced to five years for my one count of pos- session of more than five grams of marijuana. I had thought originally that five years meant five years in the joint, but then Kliner had told me that I'd get paroled somewhere between the one-third and one-half point of my sentence, and now here was the sheriff offering to take me down to six months. There was no decision involved; there was nothing Sheriff Hall or Melvin Kliner could offer me that would cause me to tell where they could find Mike Buff.

If they found Mike, I knew he'd end up spending at least six to eight years in prison. I wasn't going to snitch on one of my best friends, to drop eight years on him while saving myself a year to 18 months. It wasn't the "code of the smuggler" or "honor among criminals." Mike and I were partners, warriors welded together by our T-38 formation flying 50 feet above the ground, as well as our smuggling adventures in the jungles of Colombia. Mighty fine partners don't try to improve their fate at the expense of the other; besides, I couldn't conceive of helping a scumbag trickster liar like Melvin Kliner get another $50,000 fee.

Good cop-bad cop—I politely declined all of Sheriff Hall's overtures by telling him that I had no idea where Mike was hiding out.

"I thought you were smarter," the sheriff told me during our final meeting. "G. Gordon Liddy did seven years to protect President Nixon, that makes sense, but why would you want to protect Buff? My offer is always open. You get to Raiford and don't like what you see, get back in touch with me and we'll work something out."

"I'll do that, sheriff," I replied, but what I was thinking was that he couldn't understand what it feels like to slap hands in a high-five after getting a DC-3 off the ground in Colombia when it is loaded 35 percent above its gross weight limit with marijuana, or bashing forearms after climbing down from our T-38s after completing a formation flight where our wingtips were never more than three feet apart as we skimmed over the West Texas scrubland at just below supersonic speeds.

Mike and I were battle-tested warriors. I had seen the tracers go whizzing by my aircraft from weapons of war. Now it was time for another side of war: the mental test of incarceration. A warrior can fight his battles in many ways, but never at the expense of those he knowingly goes into battle with. That was a noble thought to do time by!

YOU'VE GOT NOTHING COMING

BEFORE KAREN MET WITH THE JUDGE and got the failure-to-appear confusion worked out, she often would have news of late-breaking legal developments concerning this problem on her weekly visits to the Martin County jail. There was no way to receive this information except for Karen to try and shout it through the Plexiglas of the visitor's window and for me to answer in the same high-decibel voice. This allowed everyone in cell block C to hear what I was saying about my legal problems, including Nate.

As Nate and I got to know each other better, he often would remark about how in the early days of his criminal endeavors, he had never been given a lawyer or public defender to advise him about his legal situation; he'd just go before the judge, get sentenced, and that would be it. However, Florida, like all other states, now had to provide every accused person with an attorney if that person couldn't afford to pay for one. Nate thought that the attorneys who had previously represented him had never saved him any jail time or prevented him from being convicted of a crime he had committed.

65

"All lawyers have ever done," Nate told me, "is add a bunch of bullshit to getting caught. They create this expectation that they are going to do all these great things, and it's all a bunch of lies. I liked it better before; all that's happened now is adding a new step to the process, where a guy in a suit tells you about all the mistakes law enforcement has made and how your constitutional rights have been violated, and how you're going to win the trial—then you still get found guilty. I don't care if you got the public defender or you're paying a guy big money, all they do is talk shit. Shit-talking lawyers—that's all I've ever seen, and it sounds like that's what you are dealing with now. Right?"

"I can't believe for the money my partner is paying this guy that he won't at least return my phone calls," I answered, "and this guy is supposed to be one of the best criminal lawyers in South Florida."

"The more you pay them, the more they'll fuck you," Nate said. "There's only one lawyer motherfucker that's ever done shit for me, and he didn't charge me a dime—a white dude, too—wouldn't take no money from anyone."

"How did he support himself then, if he wouldn't take a fee?"

"He didn't have to," Nate chuckled. "The state was supporting him. Joe Peel . . . Judge Joe Peel, he's probably the most famous convict in Florida; he's gotten thousands of guys out of the joint."

"I've never heard of him. Where's he now?"

"Still in prison," Nate replied. "They'll never let him out. I think he's in for a double murder or something like that. I saw his name in the paper a few months ago for some death row convict that he got released."

Nate told me how he had first gone to prison in the late sixties. He went in for a two-year stretch, which normally would have meant a minimum-security institution.

However, Nate had punched a guard when the guy wouldn't give him his mail, and that had landed him in Raiford, which was Florida's maximum-security prison.

Joe Peel had already been in prison 10 years by the time Nate got to Raiford. Prison authorities had tried everything they could to prevent Joe from doing legal work for inmates, including keeping him in solitary confinement for seven years. But Joe still managed to get legal work smuggled out. After being constantly embarrassed by the assistance Joe would receive from guards and other prison employees who helped him get his legal work—sometimes written on toilet paper—out of his cell, the prison authorities decided to put Joe back in the general prison population and secretly hoped that Joe would be killed by another inmate who was unhappy with the legal help he had received from Joe.

Nate met Joe after Nate had been turned down for parole. As a first-time offender for a nonviolent crime, Nate was expecting to be paroled on his first trip in front of the parole board, but they had turned him down citing his "assault on a guard" as proof that he wasn't yet ready to rejoin society. Nate asked Joe if there was anything he could do about the parole decision. Joe had checked over Nate's paperwork and discovered that the proper disciplinary report had never been filed for Nate's punching the guard. Joe filed an appeal with the parole board, arguing that the guard-slugging incident couldn't be used against Nate in his request for parole since it wasn't documented, and the parole board agreed. Nate was back on the streets of Palm Beach within the month.

"I offered to pay him everything that I had," Nate added. "All I had to give was a carton of cigarettes, but he wouldn't take anything. I'll never forget what he said: that he knew he was going to spend the rest of his life in prison and he had already received the best thing I could give him—seeing me get out of the joint. No white man had ever shown that kind of interest in me before. After I got out and started working again, I sent him a money order for $50. A couple of weeks later, I got a letter from him with the money order enclosed. He told me he didn't need anything and to take the money and start a college fund for my boy; after all that time he had remembered that I had a kid. I've never run into him since that first stretch. I owe that motherfucker something, I know that."

"Maybe you'll see him this time through," I injected.

"You never know," Nate said as he stroked his beard. "They're always transferring him from prison to prison, at least that's what they used to do. He's the best damn lawyer in the state, I know that."

Seven weeks after I arrived at the Martin County jail to begin serving my five-year sentence, I was shipped off to the state prison system. As disgusting as the conditions were in cell block C, I had gotten used to them. Now I felt the same apprehension of what awaited me in the state system as I had when, halfway through my tour in Vietnam, the officer in command of our four-man, four-airplane FAC unit had announced that we were being assigned a new mission. Major Womack told us that we no longer would be flying in the Rung Sat region below Saigon, but that now we would be the lead unit doing top-secret forward air controlling in Cambodia.

Flying missions in Cambodia was more dangerous because no U.S. ground forces could come across the border to rescue us if we were shot down and there were more 50-caliber machine guns to shoot up at us and even rumors of SAM missiles and MiG jets ready to pounce on our lightly armed spotter planes. I was upset about the change of missions because I thought I was going to die over the flatlands of Cambodia. But that was foolish thinking, since I had been through the same mental exercise five months earlier when I arrived "in country" to do battle with the Vietcong and NVA. It wasn't the thought of dying that had worried me; it was the change from a dangerous "known" situation to a dangerous "unknown." Dying is dying, whether it is in a situation you are used to or an unfamiliar one; there is no difference—you still end up dead.

Getting shipped off to the state system was just the same. If getting butt-fucked was what worried me, then whether it happened in the county jail or state prison didn't make a whole lot of difference—it was still getting butt-fucked.

My first stop after leaving Martin County was the Lake Butler Reception and Medical Center located near a complex of Florida prisons about 30 miles north of Gainesville.

Lake Butler was primarily a classification facility. Every prisoner entering the Florida prison system had to go through Lake Butler, where he received a quick medical check, filled out some paperwork, took a few tests, and got to voice a request to a caseworker about which prison he would prefer to serve his time in. The procedure at Lake Butler took five days to complete, and then a convict was loaded into a bus and shipped the 15 miles over to the Butler Transfer Unit (BTU), where the normal wait was from four to eight weeks for classification to be completed and a permanent prison assigned.

Both of these institutions were maximum security. They had triple chain-link fences topped with razor wire and armed guards in gun towers to prevent even the thought of escape. The best part was that we lived in dormitories and had the freedom to move about the yard during daylight hours.

Within a day of arriving at Lake Butler, I started to hear the name of Joe Peel. The first time I heard Joe mentioned was by a couple of guys ahead of me in the line waiting to get lunch. One guy remarked to another that he had put in for a "call-out" to see Judge Joe Peel so he could get some advice about his case.

The next day in the yard, a group of black guys were talking about how Joe Peel had won some court case that prevented the state from taking away a guy's good time.

As I was leaving our cell in Martin County, Nate had given me one last piece of advice: keep my mouth shut and don't ask any questions till I could get a handle on who was full of shit and who wasn't. I was following Nate's suggestion. However, by listening, I got the impression that Joe Peel lived at the Lake Butler institution, and it sounded like he was operating a law firm.

The move over to BTU didn't stop the name of Joe Peel from popping up. The name was like a hit record; you would turn on the radio and if you ran through all the channels you were bound to hear it. As I moved about the yard during the course of the day, I was bound to hear someone talking about how Joe Peel had done this or Joe Peel had done that, and the name began to take on a mythical quality for me; he was Robin Hood, Jean Valjean, Crazy Horse, and Mother Teresa rolled into one, and he was close, just 15 miles away if I could believe the guys who claimed they had just had an audience with the great man in his law office at the Lake Butler Reception and Medical Center.

The caseworker I had been assigned during my short stay at Lake Butler said he was going to recommend that I be assigned to a permanent prison in the Miami area, since I was a nonviolent offender and my wife and her family lived in Fort Lauderdale. Karen was visiting me every weekend once I got to BTU, and that involved a four-hour drive to Orlando on Friday after she got off of work, then a further three-hour drive from Orlando to the prison early Saturday morning so she could be in line at 8 A.M. and be one of the first to get in for a visit.

We visited until the 2:45 P.M. departure time, and then Karen would drive back to Orlando, spend the night, and continue on to Fort Lauderdale on Sunday morning. This routine took her whole weekend away, not to mention that it was very expensive. It was costing more than a $100 just to spend five hours with me. My getting assigned to a prison in the Miami area would cut the driving down to one hour each way and reduce a three-day trip to a half-day commute.

Eight weeks after checking in at the BTU facility, I was shocked and disappointed to be awakened at 4:30 A.M. and told to pack my shit, I was getting transferred to my permanent prison assignment. I was going back to the Lake Butler Reception and Medical Center as a permanent inmate of the facility.

By nine that morning I was back at Lake Butler and in the office of the same caseworker who had told me I would be going to the Miami area. He told me that inmates went where the open beds were, and South Florida was overcrowded. He gave me a piece of paper to apply for a transfer, but added that I'd be out on parole before a transfer ever came through.

"Sorry, we couldn't get you down south," the caseworker said. "Eighty percent of Florida's population is south, and that means 80 percent of the inmates, but we only have two facilities south of Palm Beach. We've got 32,000 inmates in the system, of which 26,000 are from South Florida, and there are only 3,000 beds down there. That's the problem, and that's why you're up here to do your sentence."

There weren't any magic words I could utter to get my assignment changed. The air force had a saying that aircraft and duty assignments were ultimately based on the needs of the air force no matter whom you knew. Likewise, the Florida prison system assignments were based on where the beds were available.

My caseworker was in a chatty mood. I had been outside his office with a bunch of other inmates who were on the bus from BTU to Lake Butler, and when they were called they had gone into the office and had been out two minutes later. But when I got in the office, the caseworker leaned back in his chair and was giving me advice, as well as a pep talk, on how to be a successful prisoner.

"I'm seeing a lot more criminals come through the system like you," chatted my caseworker as he lit up a cigarette. "Guys with college backgrounds, first-time offenders, non-violent, and just about all of them are in for drug crimes. Being a permanent inmate at Lake Butler isn't bad; there are only about 300 of you, and we don't assign anyone under 26 to be a perm."

"How come?" I questioned, following Nate's decree to keep all conversation to a minimum when addressing a free man.

"Because we want older, more stable inmates to try and keep the bullshit to a minimum with all the transient inmates that come through for assignment—no jitter-bugs, so you shouldn't have to worry about some idiot doing something stupid. I'm probably going to be the most sympathetic guy you can talk to, and if you have any problems, put in for a call-out to see me. Some guys come in and think they've a say in what goes on around here; they want to complain and make suggestions and snivel to anyone who will listen about their plight. No one in this institution likes a sniveler. Just remember this: you've got nothing coming from anyone; expect nothing from the Florida Bureau of Prisons and you won't be disappointed."

My caseworker was a white man in his late 20s. On the wall of his office was his framed diploma showing a degree in sociology from Florida State University. I had the feeling as I listened to him that he was concerned about the new breed of drug-smuggling criminal he was seeing pass through his office.

"You're at a disadvantage," my caseworker explained. "Most of the inmates you're going to be in contact with have done a step-by-step progression to end up here. These are people who started robbing, stealing, and burglarizing when they were teenagers. They've been through juvenile programs, foster homes, and detention camps, and then they graduated to adult offenders and probably caught some probation and county jail time. By the time these guys get to prison, they've pretty much decided that prison time isn't something to be afraid of. They have homeboy friends they've met at other institutions, and they know the games and tricks to play that can keep each day from being too boring. But, with the drug hysteria going on in Florida, just about every druggie getting caught is catching a sentence to an institution; no judge is giving out probation or a 'taster' sentence to a county jail because they don't want to be labeled as 'soft' on drugs and have to take the abuse from the politicians and reporters."

My caseworker went on to establish his liberal credentials by telling me that he had smoked pot and thought it was ridiculous to lock up people over a weed that has adapted to climates and soil conditions all over the world.

"I'll see what I can do about getting you a transfer, maybe after your first progress report in six months; but just remember—you've got nothing coming" were my caseworker's concluding remarks.

A guard wearing the tan shirt/brown pants uniform of the institution appeared to lead the new perms of Lake

Butler to the permanent barracks, which I had no idea existed during my first five-day stay at the facility. Before we had exited the administrative building, one of our group asked the guard if he could make a phone call to tell his wife that he had been transferred so she wouldn't go to BTU, as she was planning on visiting him on Saturday.

"No phone calls, convict" was the curt answer from the guard who spit tobacco juice into a Pepsi can with the top removed that he carried around with him.

"Come on, there's no time to mail off a letter so it will get to her in time," challenged the convict.

The guard dropped his can of brown spit and grabbed the inmate by the collar and pushed him up against a wall. "You address me as 'boss,' and don't you ever ask an employee of this institution to do anything for you. You want something, you put it in writing, you hear—you got nothing coming from me. Take off your shirt and clean up that spit."

The guard was speaking the strangest dialect of the English language that I had ever heard. It was a form of Southernese originating deep in a 50-pound beer gut and filtered through a golf-ball-size wad of chewing tobacco.

The interior of Florida north of Gainesville has a lot more in common with rural Georgia and Alabama than with the exciting feel of Miami and Orlando. Lake Butler, BTU, and the maximum-security prison at Raiford were all part of a prison complex centered around the town of Starke. These prisons were the economic engine of the area, and most people living in and around Starke worked at the prisons or had a relative who worked at one of them. These people were rural rednecks and crackers, and if Interstate 75 hadn't been built to bring the Yankee tourists heading to South Florida through their area, the McDonald's, Burger Kings, and Pizza Huts would not have appeared, and the region would have looked pretty much as it did in the 1920s, when the first prison construction had begun on the Raiford prison.

As we walked along the sidewalk leading to the permanent barracks, our escort officer would offer greetings to the other prison employees we passed. Their conversational exchanges would have given the CIA code crackers trouble. If I ever did have something coming from the guards who spoke this strange language, it was going to be tough to understand what it was. Maybe that was the reason the guard said that all requests had to be in writing: they couldn't understand English unless it was spoken in their form of dialect.

Processing and in-briefings took the whole day, and by the time I had been assigned a bunk and given sheets and a blanket, it was close to 8 P.M.

My new home was a dormitory where double bunks were spaced three feet from each other in four rows of 20. There was a TV room as well as a shower room. Access to the whole dorm was controlled by one door, next to which sat a guard protected from the inmates by a steel-mesh cage.

I made up my lower assigned bunk and lay down to survey my new surroundings. Even though it was only April, with outside temperatures in the 50s, it was sweltering in the dorms. Approximately 150 guys living in such close proximity, combined with the steam coming out of the shower room, had the dorm temperature in the high 80s. There was neither air conditioning nor fans to combat the heat, just the louvered open windows that ran the length of both sides of the cinder-block dorm building.

The flow of inmates was from the TV room to the bunks and from the shower room to the bunks. People were talking in groups of two or three or resting on their bunks reading mail or listening on headphones to the one radio channel that was piped into the dorm. The guard was sitting in the TV room watching a baseball game with 10 other inmates, and my first impression was that life as a permanent inmate at Lake Butler was going to be a lot like life in military barracks.

As I was taking in the sights, two black guys in the dorm evening attire of boxer shorts, T-shirts, and shower thongs sat down on the bunk next to mine and began looking at a *Playboy* magazine that one inmate had just received in the mail. As these guys were looking at the magazine, another black guy came over and asked if he could see the magazine next.

"Can't, man," said the owner of the magazine. "I've got to give it to Joe Peel. Check with him."

My attention shifted from the panorama of the dormitory to the black men sitting on the bunk next to me. After 10 minutes the visitor got up and left, and the remaining man laid back to take another look through the pictures in the magazine.

I turned toward the black inmate and said, "Say, I heard you mention Joe Peel. Does he live in this dorm?"

The inmate didn't look my way but responded, "Yeah, his house is on the other wall."

"Which guy is he?"

"He's not here right now; he's probably in the hobby shop," explained my next-door neighbor.

This was an unexpected bonus to being assigned to Lake Butler; I was going to be living in the same dorm as Judge Joe Peel. For the next hour, I watched the entry area from the TV room into the dorm. I knew that Joe was white, and I figured he had to be in his 50s. Whenever a new man entered who fit those two criteria, I'd ask my bunk neighbor if that was Joe Peel.

However, after three such inquiries had elicited a "no," I could tell that I was annoying the man whom I was going to be living next to for the foreseeable future, and I quit asking. But I kept looking, waiting for some telltale sign that would indicate which inmate in my dormitory was the great Joe Peel.

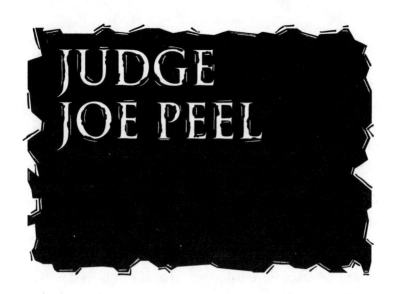

JUDGE JOE PEEL

THE CLUE I WAS WAITING FOR to solve the mystery of which inmate was Joe Peel arrived at a few minutes before 9 P.M. and was about as subtle as Elvis Presley's entry onto the stage in Las Vegas. Joe looked like a heavyweight fighter moving down the aisle to get to the ring as he was flanked by six other men, each one asking questions of the man in the middle.

The man who was the center of all the questions was 5 foot 10 and in his early 50s. He had graying black hair, wore thick glasses, and entered the dorm holding a cup of coffee and cigarette in one hand and a legal brief in the other, which he was trying to read. My sight line of Joe's entry passed right across my neighbor's bunk. When he heard the questions bombarding Joe, he looked up from his *Playboy*, and without even looking my way said, "There he is; that's Joe Peel."

Joe was wearing a white T-shirt and blue gym shorts, and even while handling a cup of coffee, a cigarette, a legal brief, and dozens of questions from all the inmates, he still was able to make quick small talk with anyone who said "hi" to him as he moved down the corridor to his bunk.

7 9

Once Joe got to his bunk, he propped up his pillow and lay down, alternately taking a drink of his coffee and a drag from his cigarette, as a line began to form to have an audience with the great man himself.

Joe Peel was handsome. He had a dazzling smile even though his teeth were stained a light yellow from a life of chain-smoking, and almost two decades in some of the harshest prison conditions that Florida could provide had not dampened the enthusiasm and alertness his blue eyes displayed. My first impression was that if this man donned a three-piece suit and English wing tips he would win, hands-down, the lawyer's beauty contest.

When the line had dissipated, I walked over to Joe's bunk to introduce myself. When there was a break in the legal talk he was having with two guys sitting on stools next to his bed, I moved forward and caught his attention.

"Mr. Peel," I started out, "I've been hearing about you for the last three months, ever since I entered the Martin County jail. I just got here today. I've always been interested in the law and was wondering if there was anything I could do to help your law work?"

"Have you been to law school? And call me Joe," he replied.

"No, but I was accepted to a law school in the Southwest before I went in the air force, and I can type."

"Good," answered Joe, as the word "type" seemed to pique his interest. "We just won Terry's parole appeal, and he'll be getting out in two to four weeks. Maybe you can take his place in the law library. I'll talk to you tomorrow about it."

My next-day meeting with Joe Peel never materialized. There was never a minute of his waking day when he wasn't surrounded by an entourage of at least three people. I'd see him in the bathroom brushing his teeth and people would be talking to him, and I'd see him right before lights out when he would come in from the hobby shop and answer his last questions of the day. There were simply too many people trying to get a word in with him for me to have a chance to discuss my clerking for him. I put in for a call-out to the law library, a process that would take at least three weeks, because it looked like that might be the only chance I could get to make an appointment with Joe.

While I was waiting to meet with Joe, I wasn't exactly idle. As a permanent inmate at Lake Butler, I, like everyone else, was expected to work at some job that contributed to the running of the institution, which drastically cut down on the idle time I had. I was given a job outside the prison walls, which allowed me to be outdoors by myself and gave me the opportunity to formulate my escape plan.

I worked for the free man who ran the water plant, and all I had to do was go around once an hour to check the pump gauges and make a note of each reading in the logbook. The free man, who was my boss, was a retired army enlisted man in his 60s. He never said a word to me; he just sat in his chair and listened to country music on the radio while reading his monthly magazines about hunting and guns.

The first day I was cleared through the gates to walk the 50 yards to the water-pumping station I learned all I needed to know about Lake Butler. The free man pointed me toward the water tower and told me to climb up and get a visual reading to compare with the floating pointer on the side of the tank. Climbing the 10-story ladder to the metal walkway surrounding thè water tank gave me a spectacular view of the facility and surrounding countryside.

The Lake Butler Reception and Medical Center was built on the site of a former army airfield. During World War II, the U.S. Army Corps of Engineers had built scores of these airfields in Florida for use as training bases for military pilots.

After the war, many of the bases were closed, but the runways were left intact and the land was turned over to municipalities for commercial use. Some of the bases had been given to the state for forestry projects or prison sites, hence Lake Butler.

The standard design for these complexes was to have three runways in the shape of a triangle, which meant that no matter which way the wind was blowing, you would never have to land into more than 30 degrees of crosswind. At Lake Butler, only one of the runways was maintained, and that runway ran along the northern perimeter fence and was used when the parole commissioners flew in on a state airplane or when state prison officials visited on official business. However, from the water tower, I could easily see where the other two runways had been laid out. One of them had been dug up and the land reclaimed for the prison construction site, which I could tell from the slight discoloration of the grass where the removed runway path met the still active runway. That still left the third part of the triangle. This part started in the southeast and ran on a heading of 330 degrees to intersect the eastern threshold of the still active east-west runway. The concrete at the northwestern third of this runway was used as building slabs for employee housing as well as for the power plant buildings, but beyond the water-pumping building, 4,000 feet of cracked and crumbling concrete that was almost overgrown with weeds still remained.

The escape would be simple. Gene, one of my smuggling buddies, would buy a junker Cessna 150 with no radios for a couple of thousand dollars. Then he'd get lined up on the abandoned runway to land from the southeast at about 7:30 A.M., a time when I'd already be cleared through the gates and the sun would still be low in the east to make seeing the plane from a guard tower hard. I'd be doing my inspection of the water tank, so even if a guard did happen to look my way he wouldn't think it unusual to see me walking by the runways. But a guard probably wouldn't even look because the focus of his attention was in the prison yard itself—so he'd always have his back to the direction from which the plane would appear. The pilot would make his final approach and land at idle speed to keep noise to a minimum. He'd plan the touchdown point so as to be able to stop and turn around right at the base of the water tower. I'd hop in, and off we'd go. From touchdown to airborne, the whole escape wouldn't take more than 90 seconds.

We'd fly 50 feet off the ground to an airport in the Florida Panhandle area, change to another airplane, and disappear. Even if someone at the prison happened to see the identification numbers of the aircraft that picked me up, it wouldn't matter because, eventually, the airplane would be found abandoned at the drop-off airport where we had changed aircraft, and the plane would have been registered in a fake name and address and paid for in cash. All an investigation might uncover would be a vague description of what the person who bought the plane looked like.

My escape plan was done. If I couldn't do the time, I could just leave—and I wouldn't take the easy escape route by running into the woods and getting picked up on the road two miles away, which I could easily see from my water tower vantage point. No, I'd execute an escape worthy of an United States Air Force combat FAC pilot who had 330 missions in Vietnam to his credit; I'd log one more combat mission against the Florida Bureau of Prisons and gain some style points, which I was sure prisoners everywhere would appreciate.

Thus, during my first visit to the top of the water tower at

Lake Butler, I had gained a certain peace of mind. I was sure that Gene would fly the plane in if I asked him, and I was equally certain that he'd be able to land, pick me up, and be airborne again before any guard knew what was happening.

Once I knew my escape plan could work, I didn't give it any more thought. What I needed then was some way to make my prison time go by as quickly as possible so I wouldn't have to resort to an escape attempt, and that involved getting a prison job that was more stimulating than taking readings from water-pump gauges. I figured that's where Joe Peel came in.

The movements of Joe Peel began to fascinate me. He was always up before the 5:30 A.M. lights-on buzzer, and almost as soon as he sat up, rubbed his eyes, and put on his glasses, an inmate dorm orderly would appear with a cup of coffee. He'd light up his first Marlboro of the day and shuffle off to the bathroom.

Within 15 minutes, he'd be shaved, showered, dressed, and surrounded by people asking him for legal opinions. As soon as the door was unlocked from the dorm to the corridor, Joe would exit to the canteen, where he'd get his second cup of coffee and then seat himself on a bench to try to read the morning paper. But he never could because other inmates would come by and utter the nine most common words said in the permanent dorms: "Joe, can you take a look at my case?"

When the outer dorm doors were open at 7 A.M. for inmates to move freely to their work assignments, I'd see Joe and his three orbiting planets walk the quarter mile to the prison administration building where inmate access was restricted.

However, it was at lunch time when Joe moved from the law library in the administration building to the chow hall that the crowds would become frenzied. The path to

the chow hall intersected with the route that the transient inmates had to take to the chow hall, and even
though the turnover of transient inmates was almost 100
percent every five days, nearly every time Joe made this
walk he would be recognized by a transient who had
encountered him at another prison. Once the word went
out that Joe Peel was walking to the chow hall, he would
be besieged by transient inmates asking him to get them a
call-out before they got transferred to BTU so that they
could get help on their cases.

The same scene would result when Joe left the chow
hall to go back to the law library. Around four I'd catch a
glimpse of him at his bunk, changing from prison whites
into shorts, and then he'd be gone again, not to be seen till
he reappeared in the dorm right before lights out.

For the first week that I was at Lake Butler, as far as I
could tell, Joe Peel was never alone. There was always
someone talking at him or blocking his movement with
questions, but he didn't seem to mind. He always smiled
and looked upbeat, and no one he encountered seemed to
go away disappointed. This wasn't a politician working the
crowd, nor a movie star making you think you'd entered his
world by a wave of the hand. Joe Peel was a god, and what
he offered was hope—hope that if he got involved with
your case, he could get you out of prison.

At the beginning of my second week as a permanent
inmate at Lake Butler, I added a new facet to my prison routine: jogging. The grounds of the institution were beautiful.
There was an abundance of free inmate labor to cut the grass,
tend flower beds, clip hedges, and maintain the softball field
where the prison team practiced and where Lake Butler host-
ed a Fourth of July tournament for Jaycee teams in the local
area. Around the perimeter of the softball field was a narrow
path where permanent inmates were allowed to walk, jog, or

run. After ending my work shift at the water plant, I'd get cleared back through the prison gates, change to shorts, and walk over to the softball field and run for 30 minutes.

The second day I was out running, Joe Peel and his three constant companions showed up and did a brisk walking workout on the path around the ball field. Since I was running, I would lap them every five minutes, and I could hear the legal talk going on and see Terry DeWitt, who was Joe's chief law clerk and always by his side, make his notations on a yellow legal pad.

After I had finished my run, I walked a couple of laps to cool down. This time Joe and his three mates came up behind me, and as he was passing, Joe asked if I would join them for a few trips around the ball field.

Joe remembered me, and he introduced me to Terry DeWitt, Jack Green, and Elmo Ott, all three of whom I recognized from my previous observances of the Joe Peel entourage.

Terry DeWitt, Joe's main assistant in the law library, was a handsome man in his early 30s who talked in a rapid-fire, high-pitched North Florida accent. Elmo Ott was also in his early 30s, wore glasses, and looked like an accountant; he was introduced to me as the designated typist for the law library. Jack Green was in his 50s and had balding black hair and a pockmarked complexion. Jack didn't say much, but Joe introduced him as one of his oldest friends in the prison system; they'd done more than 15 years together.

No one asked me any questions as we marched around the field. I just listened to Terry and Joe discussing cases they were working on, with an occasional comment from Elmo on when he could type the paperwork for a certain document and get it filed.

I quickly became another planet revolving around Joe

Peel's sun. Most of my interaction was in the early morning around the canteen and then in the afternoon at the exercise track. I stuck with Nate's advice to keep my mouth shut unless someone asked me a direct question. I was an outsider who didn't know the cases they were working on, the people they were talking about, or the details of the dramas that were occurring around the prison.

Making friends in prison is a lot different than at college or in the military. Most people entering prison probably have a homeboy or a friend of a friend who is already there and can introduce them around and vouch for their being good, standup guys. I, on the other hand, knew no one in the prison system, and that would make other inmates edgy. The biggest obstacle that a new, unknown inmate has to overcome is the suspicion that he is a "snitch," who has been planted by the Bureau of Prisons to expose other inmates. This happened all the time; an inmate would make a deal with the justice system and be inserted into a prison population to try and get information on an eclectic group of items ranging from drugs being smuggled into the prison to state equipment being stolen to moonshine being brewed by inmates. These state-inserted snitches often would try to get close to particular inmates in order to testify in court that the targeted inmates had told the plants about crimes the targeted inmates had committed.

It didn't really matter whether a snitch had actually been told anything. A good snitch knew what the authorities were hoping to hear and would tell them just that as a way of reducing his own sentence or securing better conditions in prison. And it was his word against the other inmate's.

As an inmate with no homeboys to vouch for my criminal character and honor, I was immediately suspect. Added to my lack of credentials was the fact that I was making subtle errors in the unwritten code of inmate etiquette that existed at Lake Butler.

The first mistake I made was lining up in the black line to get into the chow hall. There were two lines to get into the chow hall—one line for whites and the other for blacks. On the first day I arrived at Lake Butler, I noticed that the lunch line on the black side had only a few people, while the white line had more than 30. Thus, I got in the black line and went on through. I obviously saw that one line had only blacks and the other only whites, but for that whole first week if the black line was significantly shorter, I used it.

Second, during one of my first walks on the softball field with Joe Peel and entourage, I had asked Jack Green (who I was quick to learn had a reputation around the prison as a man of danger—and deservedly so—with a penchant for privacy) what he was in prison for. Jack had responded with a chilling stare. The conversation went on to other areas, and I didn't realize I had just committed a serious faux pas.

I had no idea that I was arousing suspicion in other inmates. When I received a call-out to go to the law library the second week I was in residence, I thought it was just the bureaucratic response to the original request I had made to get an audience with Joe Peel.

The law library was situated in the prison administration building and had one large window that looked out to the visiting area. Access to the law library was controlled by Sergeant Wilkerson, the free man who ran the prison post office. A person possessing a call-out slip would present it to Sergeant Wilkerson, then receive a pat-down search and be let into the building. Once in the building, he would go around the corner and sit on a bench that was along the wall of the visitors area. Only one inmate was allowed in the law library at a time, and it was Terry DeWitt who would escort an inmate out of the law library when his appointment was finished, and then call for the next in line to enter. Other guards and officials in the administration building would constantly come by and look in the window to make sure there was nothing strange going on in the library itself and to keep tabs on the inmates who were sitting on the bench, waiting their turn to get an audience with Joe Peel. If you talked above a loud whisper while waiting on the bench, a guard would remove you, and you would have to start the process all over again by putting in for a new call-out request.

The law library itself wasn't much bigger than an average-sized bedroom. Along the windowed wall looking out on the visiting area were two metal desks, each one having an IBM Selectric typewriter on it. Terry DeWitt sat at the desk closest to the office door, and Elmo was at the desk behind Terry's. Along the rear wall of the room ran a Formica counter, and this is where Joe Peel resided. The counter was cluttered with books and transcripts of court proceedings. Covering every square inch of wall space were bookshelves filled with law books. It appeared that every book had its assigned place on the shelves when not in use, and that these three men were not simply wasting time— they were doing real legal work. Most of all, the law library was air conditioned because it was in the administration building, making it the only air-conditioned room that an inmate could have access to on the Lake Butler premises.

I had the last appointment of the day. When I entered the office, Terry and Elmo stopped what they were doing at their desks to listen to what Joe had to say.

"Terry is heading to work release either this Tuesday or the following Tuesday," Joe began. "Sergeant Wilkerson lets me pick the people I want to work in this office, and I'd like you to take Terry's place."

"I'd definitely like to do it," I replied, feeling like I was getting invited to join a prestigious law firm on Wall Street. "Who handles the job assignment transfer from the pumping station?"

"Don't worry about that," said Joe. "Starting Monday you'll be on the access list for the administration building."

"Great," I injected, and then the fact dawned on me that I would lose my access to outside the prison walls and my ability to execute the great airborne escape plan. "If this job doesn't work out, what will happen? Would I go back to the pumping station?"

"I'm sure you could," Joe countered.

"This is the best job in the joint," injected Terry. "I've got an air-conditioned office, Sergeant Wilkerson is a great guy, and you'll learn a hell of a lot about the law, plus you're getting the top good time job allowance that the state will give—six days a month. If you're not going to parole out, that good time is a big deal."

"Just one thing we need to talk about," Joe said with a serious look on his face. "When you're working in the law library with me, every inmate knows that I don't take money, don't ask for money, and I do the best I can no matter what color a guy is or what kind of crime he's in for. It's always been that way with me and legal work in prison, and that's what I'll expect from you too. If anyone working in here started taking money for the legal work we do, not only would we lose people who don't have anything or any way to pay us, but Colonel Dooly would immediately get word from some snitch, and he'd close us down. Will this be a problem for you?"

"Definitely not."

"I'm going to tell you straight up," Elmo chimed in, "I think you're a snitch. You go snitching about what goes on in here, what other cons tell us, and you can do some major damage. You don't know anyone in the system who can vouch for you?"

I was shocked at being accused of being a snitch. I went into detail with my inquisitors about my crime, the arrest, the trial, the appeal, and what Florida lawyers had handled my case. Elmo had a copy of the book that listed all Florida lawyers and law firms, and he looked up the names as I referred to them.

"I'm not a snitch," I insisted. "I got a five-year sentence, and the only deal I've been offered was to turn in my partner's whereabouts in return for keeping me in the county jail for six months or so, and I wouldn't do that."

"Well, there's no way we can confirm that, is there?" continued Elmo, in an aggressive tack. "If you're not a snitch, how come you were asking Jack about his crime, and what are you doing hanging out with the blacks in the chow hall?"

Before I could answer, Joe took control of the inquiry and ended what was developing into a confrontation between Elmo and me.

"Elmo is a little testy today because someone snitched him out about the card game he was running," Joe said. "If you have any trouble with officials wanting to know information, just tell me. The ACLU is the reason we're able to do this, and they'll sue any individuals, along with the bureau and the state, if they try and interfere with what we do."

Elmo and Terry left to go to softball practice, leaving me alone with Joe for the first time. Joe chain-smoked his way through 30 minutes of explaining what I'd be doing in the law library. It was the first time in almost four months that I had had a conversation of more than three sentences that didn't have at least three "you knows" and four "motherfuckers" in it.

Joe told me that he had his best success in parole appeals and on appeals of cases from guys who had been assigned a public defender, lost their cases, and thought that was the end of the line.

"The state of Florida legislature just passed a whole new system for people to get parole," Joe said. "It used to be that you went before the parole board once a year, and if they were in a good mood, or you walked in with your Bible and your grandmother, you'd get parole. There was no rhyme or reason as to why one guy would get paroled and another wouldn't. However, six months ago the legislature passed a set of guidelines that set specific times for parole, depending on the crime committed and other salient factors like previous prison stretches, if violence was used, age, educational background, and a few others. It's really pretty interesting what they did, and the new system lets everyone have a pretty good idea of when they'll get out if they keep a good prison disciplinary record."

"My attorney didn't tell me anything about this," I answered. "How do you figure out your time to parole?"

"Hardly anyone in the Florida criminal bar knows about this parole guidelines system yet. It's so new that this office is probably the expert on how to go about appealing decisions of the parole board if they don't conform to the legislative intent."

"How's that?"

"Well, take a look at this sheet," Joe replied as he pulled a sheet of paper out of a file he had on his counter. "These are the guidelines for parole for specific crimes in the Florida criminal code. Then over here are the questions to figure out your salient score for chances of parole success. Let's figure out where your parole guidelines will fall. How old are you?"

"Thirty-three," I answered with an intense interest in what Joe was figuring out.

"Any prior felony convictions?"

"No."

"Educational background? College grad, right?"

"Yes."

"Did you use a gun or any violence in your crime?"

"No."

"Any other jail terms you've had to serve?"

"No."

"OK, you're as clean as you can get on this matrix. You've got a salient score of zero. Now, we just have to find the crime category. It looks to me that you'll be in one of these three: possession of marijuana under 100 pounds, possession of marijuana between 100 and 2,000 pounds, or possession over 2,000 pounds. What did they catch you with?"

"Twelve hundred pounds."

"Then we take your salient score of zero on the left side of the chart, and move over till we get to possession of 100 to 2,000 pounds, and here's your framework for parole—11 to 15 months."

I stared at the numbers thinking that already Judge Joe Peel has given me the best piece of legal news I'd ever gotten, and it hadn't cost me a dime.

"Eleven to 15 months," I repeated. "Who decides which one it's going to be?"

"That's where the parole commissioners come in. They have discretion on when to release on parole, within the framework of the recommended-months-to-release chart. And if the parole board thinks the framework dates are too lenient for a specific individual, then they have to submit a brief stating why they want the individual to serve more time, and the demand has to be voted on by the full board of seven parole commissioners in Tallahassee. I've only seen a handful of cases come back from this new system, but already we're starting to see strange stuff. Guys are being placed in the wrong crime

category or given higher salient scores than are warranted
by the questionnaire. They bring in the sheet they get
back from the parole board. We look it over here, and if
it's not right, then we write up a parole appeal."

"And lawyers on the outside aren't doing this?"

"I tell you, this is so new," Joe reiterated, "that I don't
know how many lawyers on the outside have handled this
type of appeal. Your main job working here is going to be
writing up these appeals, and we don't do it on the form
sheet that the parole board sends back with the date. We do
it in legal form, so if we have to take it to district court to
sue the parole commission to change the date, then we've
got our paperwork in order."

"Joe, I've already been in about four months. This
means I might be getting out in seven more months, eleven
on the outside?"

"That's the numbers as I read them," he smiled.

"You sure you want to use me if I'm only going to be
here seven months?"

"Hey, it gets better than that. Most people go to a work-
release assignment three to six months before their paroles
You could be out of here before football season."

Joe was giving me good news, not once, but twice.

"That's how I knew there was no chance you were a
plant, like Elmo thinks," Joe continued. "You're going to be
out of here so fast there would be no incentive."

"Is he going to spread his thinking around?" I asked.

"No, I'll talk to him. I think he's a little upset that
Terry's getting out so fast. He doesn't want to see him go.
And, as for you only being here a few months, that's fine.
You'll be able to help me a lot while you're here."

That evening I wrote two long letters: one to Karen to
tell her about the new time frame we were looking at until
I got out and the other to Russell Cromwell to see if he

knew anything about the parole guideline system that Joe
had showed me. It was obvious to Joe that the sentence
the judge handed down really didn't mean anything.
What mattered in terms of how much time you had to
serve before you were paroled was where you fell on the
matrix. In my case, the one-third to one-half of my sentence served until parole that Melvin Kliner, Esquire, had
told me I would have to do had just shrunk to more like
one-fifth to one-fourth. It amazed me that the self-pro-
claimed major drug attorney of South Florida didn't know
this was happening.

Joe said that the new parole system was the smartest thing
Florida could have done to control prison overcrowding.
"This state has more people on death row, incarcerates a higher percentage of its population than any state except Georgia,
and has a bunch of old-timers that control the politics of
taxes. These people are so antitax that they couldn't care less
that they have the worst schools in all the 50 states, and the
lowest per capita spending on social programs of all states
except Mississippi and Alabama. I saw firsthand when I was
thinking of running for lieutenant governor in the late 1950s
how these people are so conservative that they even blocked
a small state income tax that would have gone directly to
schools. Since then, it's even gotten harder to get financial
matters done up in Tallahassee."

I had little knowledge of the political workings in
Florida. "How's a new parole system that no one seems to
know about going to help prison overcrowding? It seems so
obvious," I remarked when Joe had stopped talking to take a
drag on his ever-present cigarette.

"Think about it a second," Joe proclaimed as he
exhaled. "You have a rich state that contains a very conservative, elderly population base. Old rich people in South
Florida are in direct conflict with a younger, immigrant

population that is mostly Latin and black. The spending on social programs is almost nonexistent, and the crime rates are soaring. The old-timers want long sentences, and the judges are happy to hand them out. However, the old-timers refuse to pay for new prisons, and the legislators in Tallahassee know that if they pass big budget increases they need new taxes, and this will cost them their jobs. Hence, no new taxes, long sentences by draconian judges, and the prisons get overcrowded. Look what the legislature just did; they basically said, 'Go ahead, judges; give out huge sentences all you want—we'll just cut the time to parole. Everyone is going to be very happy about this.'"

"How about the newspapers?" I replied. "Won't they jump on this when some murderer who has a 60-year sentence gets out after only doing eight years like it shows on the matrix?"

"I don't think that's going to happen much," Joe suggested. "First off, for the last five years if you get a first-degree murder conviction in this state, you get a mandatory 25-year sentence without parole. Anyone with a murder conviction before that might catch a small break, but unless he has at least 10 or 12 years in, the commissioners will probably file the brief for a longer time served beyond the recommended parole dates. Also, notice that for the violent crimes like armed robbery, second-degree murder, and kidnapping, the suggested parole framework is way up there; these guys might actually serve more time than they did under the old system. And there's a clause in the new system where a judge can check off that a person he sentences is not eligible for parole until he has served at least one-third of his sentence."

"How do you know all of this in detail, while I've never read anything or heard anything from my lawyers?" I asked, amazed at the knowledge Joe had.

"I helped draft the legislation. I worked with some ACLU attorneys and bureaucrats for the state to come up with a guideline system that would work. They hardly even debated what we proposed, so it didn't get much publicity, and that's why so few attorneys know about the changes."

As soon as Terry left for work release, I moved right into the desk closest to the door. I started out by typing up the briefs that Joe would write on his yellow pads. I was with him constantly; we'd walk to the law library together, break for lunch, come back for an afternoon session, then go to the softball field for exercise. Plus, he got me clearance to be an apprentice leather worker, so I could come and go in the hobby shop where he spent his evenings working on leather projects.

I had heard the basic background story of how Joe ended up in prison from Nate when I was in the county jail. But once I became a perm at Lake Butler and began working in the law library, there was no way I could glean any more details regarding Joe without it looking like I was trying to pry out information that was none of my business. Still, with all the time I was spending around Joe, I naturally heard fragments of his past from everyday conversation. He had worked in Tallahassee with the parole commission, and he had once thought seriously about running for lieutenant governor. However, since I was rarely alone with him when these informational tidbits were spoken, I couldn't stop the conversation so Joe could explain to me the details of what he had said.

The lines to see Joe Peel at the law library never seemed to end. Often we'd have 30 guys lined up at 8 A.M. and it would take us till 3:30 P.M. to see them all. Joe would be at his back counter trying to write something, and I'd call a guy in, start a file, interview him as to what he wanted done, and then pass him back to Joe. It was chaotic. Joe would be trying to work on a brief, talk to a inmate, annotate the new guy's file, drink his coffee, and smoke a cigarette all while answering questions from Elmo and me about things we were typing. Then the file would be put aside, and another new guy would be ushered in.

We saw all the inmates who put in for a call-out, but we were being overwhelmed. Once an inmate's file was stacked, it would be weeks until it was looked at again, followed by more weeks before Joe could commence writing what the case required on his legal pad. Frequently, by the time a piece of legal work was ready to be mailed, the inmate had moved from BTU or Lake Butler to his permanent prison assignment, and we had to use the interprison mail system to get his work to him. Once all this was done, we had often taken too much time and had missed the strict filing deadlines that exist in the court system.

I saw right away that the problem was Joe. All who came to the law library wanted to see Joe about their case. They didn't want to discuss the case with Elmo or me; they wanted to deal directly with Joe. Because Joe often knew inmates from previous years in the prison system and they'd start talking about old times, throwing the schedule into even more disarray, we'd have guys who sat on the bench all day and did not get in for their appointments. Even though Joe sent everyone he saw away with a smile, it was obvious to me that we weren't getting much work done.

After a month of watching us fall further and further behind, I was able to make two changes that solved the case load problem. First, I was typing so many parole appeals that I became an expert on the format Joe used to prepare the appeal, and I started to write the appeals myself, eliminating Joe from the process completely except to proofread my finished drafts. Second, I talked to Sergeant Wilkerson, and he cut down on the number of call-outs he issued per day.

Plus, he set a new schedule for when an inmate could visit the law library on a call-out, from 8 A.M. to the lunch bell. Now, instead of coming back from lunch to find 20 more people waiting on the bench, we'd come back and have the rest of the afternoon to write, type, and deal with the legal work we had to generate.

Joe loved this change. He was far too nice a guy to initiate such a revision himself, but he realized we weren't doing anyone much good if we didn't produce the legal work necessary to meet the filing deadlines. With me writing the parole appeals and typing them up, Joe could handle the other work such as divorces, appeal of convictions, and pleas for new trials. Once Joe had written these briefs, he handed them over to Elmo who would type them up.

We got so efficient that often I would interview a guy in the morning about a parole appeal or a reduction in sentence motion and have it written, typed out, approved by Joe, and ready for the inmate's signature the next day so it could be mailed off.

Almost every day, a guy I had done a parole appeal for would stop by the law office to thank us for getting his time reduced and offer us some money or cigarettes. However, we never took a thing. Joe would just look up from what he was doing and smile, "That's fine, real fine," he'd say. "I'm glad we could help you. Try and do something good with that extra time when you get out, OK?"

Our "law office" led the state in handling successful appeals of assigned parole dates. Constantly, we'd get letters from attorneys around the state asking for advice on how to handle a parole situation for a client. I'd type up the letter with the information, Joe would sign it, and we'd mail it off—no charge.

I could tell in minutes after seeing a guy's statement from the parole board whether the board had made a mistake or not. If the parole board had made a mistake, we'd lay out the argument in a two-page legal brief and demand a correction.

For example, the difference in time to parole regarding a robbery where a gun was used was 50 percent higher than a robbery where no weapon was used. If an inmate came to Joe and me and swore that the parole representative had it wrong—if the rep said he'd used a gun in his robbery conviction when in fact he hadn't—then we would draw up a document and send it to the clerk of the court where the inmate was sentenced requesting the sentencing document.

When the document came back to the inmate and showed that he was sentenced for robbery with no enhancement for using a weapon, then we would have the paperwork ready to prove that the parole commission had made a mistake in calculating the inmate's time to parole. On the other hand, if the sentencing document came back supporting the classification for the crime committed that the parole commission had assigned, an inmate would almost always suddenly remember that, yes, he had had a gun in his pocket that day, even though he *never* intended to use it. We would go ahead and appeal the crime classification anyway, but we would lose the appeal.

Often the correction appeal would come back, and the time to be served before parole was reduced so drastically that the inmate would be released within weeks. The law firm of Joe Peel and Associates knew what it was doing.

I didn't realize just how well we were doing until one day when I was walking from the law library to the chow hall for lunch. Joe was bogged down with a group asking him questions, so I walked on ahead. A black kid in his late teens walked alongside me and thanked me for the successful reduction of sentence motion I had written for him. As I was walking away, I heard a friend of his come up and ask who the tall white guy was. "That guy works in the law library," the black kid explained to his pal. "He's almost as *bad* as Joe Peel; got 18 months knocked off my sentence and didn't charge me a motherfucking dime."

I looked back and saw that Joe had a big smile on his face and was pointing at the black inmate who had told his friend how bad I was. He accelerated to catch up to me, then put his arm around my shoulder. "Did you hear that?" he exclaimed. "You're almost as *bad* as me; that's the word on the street."

By the time I started working with him, Joe had been in prison for 19 years. He had been locked up so long that most inmates and prison workers had no idea of what Joe had been sent to the joint for. "He murdered some judge in Palm Beach," most of the convicts would say if they were explaining the history of Joe Peel. However, that wasn't quite the correct explanation of the sensational crime that ended Joe's promising life as a free man, as I was soon to find out from Joe himself.

Six weeks after starting work as Joe's secretary/clerk, Stephen Jamison, a private Gainesville attorney, was cleared through to the law library to have an attorney-client meeting with Joe. I stood up to leave and wait in the visitor's room until they were finished, but Joe told me to stay; he wanted my advice on what Steve had to say.

Stephen Jamison, who was in his early 30s, had become well known to the Bureau of Prisons because of his work for the ACLU on prison reform. The bureau, in a rare act of cooperation, had transferred Joe from Raiford to a road-camp prison in Tallahassee for the specific purpose of working with Stephen to draw up a plan to bring Florida into compliance with federal prison regulations, as defined by a judge's ruling in a successful ACLU lawsuit. Stephen and Joe had remained close since this initial collaboration five years ago.

When the blueprint of the Stephen Jamison-Joe Peel plan was accepted by the Bureau of Prisons, Joe was shipped back to Lake Butler from the Tallahassee Road Camp. Lake Butler was designated as the flagship prison law library in the state. Florida correction officials knew they were being closely watched, and rather than try to keep ex-judge Joe Peel away from the law library system, they'd demonstrated to the ACLU their intent to comply by putting Joe in charge of the Lake Butler law library, as well as the development of a program to train other inmates as law clerks.

Like so many people that Joe had come into contact with, Steve wanted to be a part of any effort to get Joe a parole from his life sentence. Steve was a handsome man, who wore his hair over his collar, and he exhibited the enthusiasm and confidence that led one to believe that there was no legal challenge he couldn't handle.

Once Joe introduced us, Steve looked around the small office, then closed the door that led to the visitor's room so he wouldn't accidentally be overheard by a prison employee in the vicinity.

"Old man," Steve began, "I'm going to get you out of here." Joe looked my way and rolled his eyes while a smile came to his face, letting me know that he had heard this line of bullshit before.

"You're going to be fucking again, going to football games, eating Caesar salads. I'm even going to get your law license back."

Joe started laughing. "What an imagination," he said as he leaned back in his chair and lit up a cigarette.

Steve's affection for Joe was obvious, but, after Joe's chuckling subsided, he pulled his chair closer to Joe and got serious. Steve produced a cigar from his inside coat pocket, a fancy-looking stogie with a made-in-Cuba band on it.

"This is from two good ol' boys that you got a new trial

for three years ago because their court-appointed attorney never made a motion to suppress the evidence. Remember Cory Hallenback and Buford Potter?"

"Sure, I remember those guys," Joe responded. "I'm surprised they could get $20 together for this cigar—funny guys."

"Well," Steve said as he coughed on the smoke from Joe's cigarette, "not only did they pay for this cigar, but they also gave me a good chunk of $5 and $10 bills to be used to get you out of here."

Steve went on to explain that these two country boys had hit it big by smuggling marijuana into the swamps and creeks of west Florida that they had explored and fished since they were kids. "They're going to bankroll the whole effort. I'm dropping everything to work solely on getting you a parole."

Steve outlined the plan that he thought could accomplish the task. It involved lining up politicians across the state to endorse a parole. It involved psychological tests, job offers, favorable newspaper articles, and scholarly writings in prison trade journals about Joe's 19 years in Florida's prison system.

"Steve, tell Buford and Cory that I appreciate the concern, but this is just going to be a waste of money. I've been before the parole board almost every year I've been in here, and they're never going to let me out. You know what happens—if there is even a chance of one parole commissioner thinking I should get a parole, Bob Wenstrom gets right at his throat with a few of his newspaper buddies and the 'soft on murderers and criminals' articles start showing up all over Florida with me as the example of a killer who should never be let out. I'm tired of it, and it's the main reason I waived seeing the parole board the last two years. It's not even worth thinking about.

"I'm not naive enough to think we can muzzle ol' Bob down there in Palm Beach, but I do think we can counter him and then bury him a bit with our own newspaper people and the fact that he married your wife and just might have a personal interest in keeping you in jail."

"I don't want to bring Imogene into this," Joe replied, "because then the kids will be involved. I'm better off out of sight and out of mind right here."

"Look, it ain't going to be a love-in, but the time is right for the facts to come out and for you to get out of prison. You don't have to do a thing; just start writing me a chronological history of your life. One thing we don't want to do is have any of the facts wrong. When we get attacked from Wenstrom it is not going to be because we are putting out a fairy tale version of the history of your life."

"Steve," Joe answered as he cleaned his glasses, "I don't know about this. Wenstrom has that trust fund, and the only purpose of that money is to generate publicity every time I come up for parole."

"I know all about that. Look, we aren't going to dispute the crime. The bottom line is going to be that the average first-degree murder conviction with a life sentence in reality means the perpetrator does about 8 1/2 years till he gets paroled. You didn't do the murder, you're in on conspiracy, and you've been here 19 years. I'll have a book of statistics, I'll have testimonials from sheriffs and governors, I'll have analyses of your mind and character from noted shrinks, and I'll have job offers from some of the best-known law firms in the southeast. Joe, you old fuck, you're going to get out of here. Don't believe it if you don't want to, but I can do it."

After Steve left the law office, Joe ran the cigar under his nose a few times to savor the aroma and perhaps reflect for a few seconds on what it might be like to be a free man again.

"What do you think?" he asked with an anguished look on his face. "I don't even like to think of getting out of here; it just adds confusion and anxiety to every day."

"He sounds pretty confident he can do it," I answered. "Is Steve a shit-talker or does he have a good grasp on the reality of what can and can't be accomplished?"

"Steve's no shit-talker, but he's never been around the riot that erupts anytime the words 'parole' and 'Joe Peel' are uttered in Palm Beach County. Bob Wenstrom is a powerful, successful man down there, and he's not going to run and hide just because we might get an article or a TV clip questioning his motive for wanting me kept in jail. He did marry my wife years after I went to jail and we got divorced, but that's just one little item, and it will be quickly buried by the avalanche of articles and columns that Bob can get generated about the original crime I'm convicted of."

"But what about the fact you didn't do the crime?" I questioned. "Doesn't that mean something?"

"Very little. Legally, if you conspire to commit a crime, even though other people carry out the act, you are still as responsible as the actual perpetrators. After so many years of publicity, just about everyone in Palm Beach County that remembers the event will tell you that I was the one who killed Judge Chillingworth and his wife."

Joe had lit up the cigar and was leaning back in his chair enjoying the smoke. "I'll tell you the story of what happened," he said. "Then you tell me what you think about what Steve had to say."

Joe had grown up in the wealthy surroundings of Palm Beach, where some of the richest families in the United States would spend their winter months. He knew members of the Kennedy, Dodge, and Capone families, and Al Capone's boy Sonny was one of Joe's closest childhood friends.

"I grew up knowing the kids of these incredibly wealthy families. I'd be at the dinner table with Al Capone, and it seemed to me that what he'd done to get rich wasn't a whole lot different than what old man Kennedy had done. Al always said he just responded to what people wanted— he didn't argue about it or moralize, he just responded."

Joe enlisted in the army for World War II, came back from service in the Pacific to attend Stetson Law School, then returned to Palm Beach to start a practice. Joe married a beauty queen, had two kids, and was so highly thought of in Palm Beach that he was elected to the office of municipal judge only two years after he began practicing law.

His law practice was successful, he was making connections with the rich and powerful of South Florida, and he had a beautiful family. There was little doubt that he had a future in politics as one of the up-and-coming players in the Democratic Party.

His downfall began when he met a pair of petty criminals named Floyd Holzapfel and, through him, Bobby Lincoln. Floyd and Bobby were 1950s operators of the crimes and tricks that required no education or skills. Games of chance, moonshining, gambling, and fencing were about as high on the criminal ladder as these two aspired. Floyd worked the white part of town, and Bobby, who was black, handled the action in the black section of Palm Beach. Neither was doing particularly well in his life of crime; each was constantly in and out of Joe's courtroom, amassing a lengthy record of arrests, probations, fines, and county jail time.

"With me," Joe said, "I wasn't generating enough money with the law practice, and I was sure I could give Floyd and Bobby the protection they needed to start generating enough cash to make it worth the risk.

"We did pretty well; all I ever did was keep the fines low,

drop a few cases for lack of evidence, give probation instead of county jail time—that kind of stuff.

"The first white baby born in Palm Beach County was Curtis Chillingworth. His family was the most prominent in town, and he lived for the law. He guided me along from time to time and wanted to see me do well."

"Did he know about Holzapfel and Lincoln? Had they been in his court, too?" I inquired.

"If you were associated with the legal system in Palm Beach County you almost had to have heard the names of Holzapfel and Lincoln," Joe answered, "but these guys were rarely in his court. What got Chillingworth alarmed was just a bunch of rumors about the sentences I was handing out and then a situation when my secretary didn't file some legal documents on time, which botched up a divorce case I was handling.

"Judge Chillingworth called me into his office and told me that he didn't like what he was hearing and if there was any truth to the rumors then I had better rectify the situation immediately. This didn't happen overnight, and I was surprised that Chillingworth could have any idea that I was involved with Floyd and Bobby.

"Right about this time some other deals started to develop for me involving some land development on the west coast of Florida, and the opportunities were so inviting over there that it seemed stupid to risk the wrath of Judge Chillingworth to stay involved with the penny-ante game we had going in Palm Beach."

"Like, how much were you getting in Palm Beach?" I asked. "Thousands?"

"Yeah, over the years it would be well into the thousands," Joe answered without hesitation. "But even though this was 1950s money, and a few thousand could get you a pretty nice new car, it was still small change for what I thought I could make over on the west coast below Tampa.

"It was obvious to me that it was time to end my arrangement with Floyd and Bobby. So we had a meeting, and I told them that Chillingworth had wind of what I was doing and I was dropping out of our deal.

"We're sitting in my office and Floyd and Bobby are saying that things are going great—we're making more money than they ever thought they'd see in a lifetime. To me this was small-time pocket change, but those guys thought it was a fortune. At this point I should have thought that maybe they'd do something stupid to keep me involved."

"So, you never knew they were going to go out and kill Judge Chillingworth?" I queried.

"No," Joe replied. "What they said was, what if the judge left the bench or retired, then could we keep the partnership going? I humored them and told them that, yes, we could continue, but I knew Chillingworth wasn't leaving his position. He'd been there for 20-something years and would never retire.

"They never said anything to me about a plan to kill Chillingworth, but they had that look in their eyes that I should have picked up on. The look that said, 'Leave everything to us, we'll fix it so we can continue with the way things are.'"

"How did you find out they'd done something?"

"Chillingworth ran through his day like a fine-tuned Swiss watch. He was never sick, he always kept to his schedule, and anyone who knew him could probably tell you exactly where he'd be within five minutes during the course of his waking hours. So, at nine in the morning, when he didn't show up for his morning docket, the word flew around the courthouse that something must be wrong. At the judge's beach house investigators found some evidence of a break-in, and that's when it hit me that Floyd and Bobby had done something really stupid. Plus, not only could the judge not be found, but his wife also was missing. I knew it had to have been Floyd and Bobby. I think the bottom line is that if I had been more inquiring and forceful with them when I told them I was dropping out, they never would have done the killings. The only thing that kept them from getting caught right away was that no one ever found the bodies of the judge and his wife."

"What do you mean?" I asked.

"When I saw Floyd and Bobby a few days later, they told me they had tossed the judge and his wife into the Gulf of Mexico. They had weighted down the bodies, and they were sure they'd never surface. These guys thought they had committed the perfect crime; we could go back to business as usual, and now we wouldn't have to worry about Chillingworth probing into our racket."

"What if you had turned them in for the murder?"

"I thought about that pretty hard," Joe answered. "But no evidence had turned up linking Floyd and Bobby to the crime. They had actually done a heck of a job on the killing: there were no witnesses, no clues, and no trail. If I had turned them in, all there would be was me saying I heard Floyd and Bobby admit to the killing. Then it would come out about the protection thing we had going, and all three of us would go down with the ship. The only thing I could do was hope that Floyd and Bobby would keep their mouths shut and stay out of trouble."

"That didn't happen?"

"It never does. Floyd and Bobby were always going to be making their living doing criminal things, and I had no illusions about that—eventually, they'd get in some deep shit and try to bargain their way out of it by solving the Chillingworth case in return for leniency. And that's exactly what happened."

"Jesus, Joe," I said quietly. "You didn't do it. How did

you get the double life sentence when you didn't plan the killing or have anything to do with the execution?"

"Well, you've got to remember that six years elapsed before any information appeared about what possibly might have happened. Bob Wenstrom, the DA from Palm Beach, was under tremendous pressure to solve this case and make arrests. The newspapers and media were calling it the most sensational crime ever in Florida, and for six years the DA couldn't produce the bodies or charge anyone in the killings."

"Couldn't you come up with a way to leak information to lead the police to Holzapfel and Lincoln?" I asked, wanting to understand how a man who had nothing to do with the killings had ended up in jail for 19 years.

"There was no way to get Bobby and Floyd exposed without me being brought into it," Joe answered quickly. "Wenstrom never liked me, and I knew all along that in the back of his mind he thought I was somehow involved with Chillingworth's disappearance.

"What cracked the case for Wenstrom is what cracks the case any time more than one person is involved in a crime that goes more than a few months before being solved—people can't keep their mouths shut. Eventually the secret has use as a bargaining chip, and that's exactly what happened with Floyd and Bobby."

As I listened to Joe reflecting on the Chillingworth murders, I was absolutely certain he was telling me the truth about the way the web had been spun that ended with his conviction as accessory before the fact in the murder-disappearance of Judge and Mrs. Chillingworth. Joe and I sat in the law office five days a week hearing stories from hundreds of Florida's most notorious criminals who wanted legal help, and I hadn't heard anything even close to being as engrossing as the story Joe was telling me now. Joe paused momentarily as a guard walked through the visitor's room to use the bathroom and peeked in at us. Joe dropped his hand to hide his cigar from view, but the guard paid no attention to us, and once the guard had moved on, Joe continued.

"In 1961, it all came apart," Joe said and then took a long drag on the cigar. "Bobby was in the federal penitentiary in Atlanta doing time, I was having huge problems with the land development efforts in west Florida and being investigated by a million different agencies, and Floyd was implicated in another murder. I'm not sure how the story came out, but I think Floyd offered to solve the case for Wenstrom in return for sentencing considerations on the new murder and the Chillingworth killings.

"Once the story was told, Bobby jumped to protect himself, and I went from being a small-time crooked judge to the mastermind of a criminal empire headquartered in South Florida."

I wanted to make sure I understood everything Joe was telling me, and he didn't seem to mind the probing, exacting questions I was asking, so I interrupted him once again. "How? Floyd admitted to the killing, right? How did that involve you?"

Joe laughed at that naive question. He knew I had no idea of what had happened, and even he thought there was some joke in how he had ended up in the predicament that he had.

"Here's what happened. Wenstrom now has the notorious, infamous Chillingworth murder case solved. He knows who did it; he has a confession. But, really, all he has are two small-time locals who thought they could solve some problems by killing a district court judge. It wasn't supposed to happen that way. District court judges don't get murdered to protect a *bolita* game or a moonshining operation. District court judges only get murdered by big-time criminals: organized crime bosses or the heads of large-scale criminal conspiracies.

"Wenstrom meets with Lincoln, and, all of a sudden, a confession appears that has Bobby Lincoln saying he participated in the murder of Judge Chillingworth and his wife, but that I had issued the orders for and helped in the planning of the killing. A deal was struck: in return for his testimony saying that I had initiated and planned the murders of Judge and Mrs. Chillingworth, Bobby Lincoln would receive complete immunity from prosecution for the Chillingworth killings. Now who in his right mind wouldn't take that deal? You don't take the deal, you go to the electric chair; you do take the deal—saying Joe told you to do it—then you walk away.

"Then Wenstrom meets with Floyd Holzapfel. Now, ol' Floyd has bigger problems; he's got other murder cases floating over his head. Again a deal; this time Floyd confesses to the Chillingworth murders, along with a few others, but there is one addition to the confession. He says that I was the one who told him and Bobby to kill the judge. For this confession, Floyd is only going to get life in prison, not the electric chair, provided he will testify in court against me. Also, there is a little verbal sweetener thrown in that after 10 years or so, Floyd would be allowed to escape, and help would be provided for him to leave the United States and go to a country that doesn't have an extradition treaty with us. Again, who would turn down this deal—the electric chair or do 10 years and then away you go?"

Up till this point I was following Joe point by point. He had admitted he was no angel and was a crooked judge who wanted to make a lot of money any way he could, but this last bit was unbelievable: a planned escape of a convicted murderer agreed to by officials of the Florida judicial and prison systems!

"Wait a minute," I exclaimed as I sat bolt upright in my chair. "Wenstrom and some prison officials were going to set up an escape for Holzapfel? How did you know that?"

"Well, it wasn't written down in the plea agreement if that's what you're looking for. I've run into Floyd at the prison at Raiford a few times, and he told me that is what he was promised. I believe it, too. Floyd's an old-school con; I don't think he would have thrown my name into the pot unless there was something big in it for him. He knew that he'd never get a parole for killing a district court judge, so a death sentence or life in prison was about the same for him; but when they offered the escape opportunity, that got him off the fence and over to Wenstrom's camp to make a case against me.

"Wenstrom had the two admitted murderers both saying that yes, they had killed the judge and his wife, but that I was the one who had planned the killing and given them the orders to carry out the plan. In a nutshell, that was the whole case against me. The jury bought the testimony, and I was convicted."

"What about Holzapfel? Did he get to escape?"

"No," Joe replied, "but I believe the deal was set up. The prison officials probably backed off of the plan. It was the early 60s; there were Cuban commandos all over South Florida training for the Bay of Pigs. You had Kennedy having affairs with every hooker in Miami; Papa Joe Kennedy was always in the gray area of deals he was making; every politician in the state had side deals going—I have no doubt that what Floyd told me about the escape is true."

"Why? Wenstrom hated you that much?"

"He loved Chillingworth; he hated me—maybe he thought if he could bring me down, then, with a conviction like that on his record, he could get himself into the thick of the hierarchy of Florida politics. Maybe it was a combination of all three, plus some other things I don't even know about. Whatever it was, it happened.

"Once I was convicted, I was drained. I told Imogene to divorce me and get a new life for her and the kids. I knew I'd never be getting out of prison. When you believe that prison is the natural state of your existence, then you can deal with it pretty well and adapt to the reality of your situation. But when Steve comes in here full of confidence, that can affect you—even when you've been in here as long as I have."

"Then Wenstrom married your ex-wife?"

"Yeah, but it means nothing. The parole board isn't going to be concerned with that kind of information. I think it will all come down to what it has for the past 10 years when I come up for parole: publicity. Once the publicity starts, that puts the parole board in the spotlight, and these people like to remain anonymous. They don't want to see their names and pictures in the paper as having cast a vote in favor of paroling the convicted murderer of a district court judge."

The cigar was almost down to Joe's fingers. The story was over. "Come on; let's go to the chow hall," Joe ordered. "Jesus, tell me about this drug-smuggling stuff. If Buford and Cory can make money doing it, then you should have made billions."

Over the summer months, Steve Jamison was a constant visitor to the law library. Being a lawyer, he was allowed to visit at any time with his client, and he'd often appear with magazine writers or psychiatrists—anyone he thought could help in his bid to get Joe a parole.

The drama unfolded as predicted. Endorsements from prominent politicians, ministers, and even law enforcement officials were made public to counter the commentaries that appeared on television and the newspapers questioning the wisdom of releasing a person convicted of masterminding one of the most notorious crimes ever committed in Florida. Steve would provide Joe with good rumor after good rumor that he had heard from a friend of a friend of a parole commissioner, who had indicated, in strictest confidence, that he favored the Joe Peel parole.

Through it all, Joe tried to not let himself think that he might again be a free man; he thought in the end it would come down to what it always had—he generated too much publicity, and the parole commissioners would back off when the newspaper people and TV cameras came to see them.

Two things occurred in the Stephen Jamison-orchestrated parole attempt that had never happened before with Joe Peel. First, Steve got the state prison statistician to generate an in-depth computer analysis for the previous five years of the parole numbers and time served before parole of convicted murderers who were serving life sentences in Florida. The results showed that 234 inmates sentenced to life imprisonment had been released on parole, with the average time served before release being 9.13 years. These facts were used to counter the Wenstrom-initiated publicity about the original crime and had the effect of raising the possibility that the former DA of Palm Beach County was waging a personal vendetta against the man whose wife he had eventually married.

Second, Steve was able to get on record a written statement from the Florida Bureau of Prison officials favoring a parole for Joe Peel. Several of the hierarchy of the prison system commented on Joe's incredible record of serving 19 years without receiving a demerit, helping with riot prevention during racial turmoil, working with the Jaycees, and being a volunteer English instructor teaching inmates how to read and write. The list of good deeds acknowledged by

these men went on and on, with prison superintendent J.B.
Godwin stating, "Joe is not far from the cross, but he doesn't
talk about it—he lives it."

When the superintendent of one of Florida's toughest
prisons, located in the Bible belt of the central part of the
state, gave an endorsement stating that he just might have a
modern version of Jesus Christ locked up on his premises,
that created the momentum that resulted in Joe Peel getting a parole. But this victory was not one-sided—the
parole commissioners looked good because they didn't
parole Joe back into society; he was paroled to a federal
detainer that existed for his conviction for land fraud.

The parole commissioners were happy to get rid of Joe
and blunt the liberal allegations that they had turned Joe
into a political prisoner by not paroling him years earlier.
On the other hand, the parole commissioners weren't going
to have to take any heat for releasing him back into society;
that job would fall to the federal parole commission if it
decided to parole Joe from the nine consecutive two-year
sentences he had from the feds that were to run consecu-
tively to his life sentence from the state of Florida. When
Joe walked out of Lake Butler, he was still handcuffed and
was escorted by a federal marshal to the federal penitentiary
in Atlanta.

From the moment Joe checked into Atlanta, Steve was
working on a federal parole from the sentences for land
fraud convictions. However, by then 20 years of prison food
had taken their toll: Joe was diagnosed with stomach can-
cer. The legal maneuvering moved slowly, and it became
obvious that Joe would be dead long before the paperwork
came to an end.

After two years of Joe's steady physical deterioration,
the prison officials became convinced that he really was
dying. They consented to a humanitarian medical parole,

and he was allowed to leave the federal medical prison at Springfield, Missouri.

Joe Peel died nine days after release. But Steve Jamison and a score of others had helped to attain something that Joe thought was impossible: he hadn't died behind prison walls.

Rehabilitation and redemption are fancy words that are constantly used when experts discuss the purpose of prisons in American society. Superintendent Godwin was the prison official who made the astounding suggestion that it would take someone like Jesus Christ to have survived Joe's 20-year prison ordeal while still offering selfless service to any inmate who asked for assistance. However, fancy rhetoric aside, most inmates who came into contact with Joe Peel would say, when asked, that Joe wasn't the son of any god—he was one of them.

DANGEROUS JACK

T HE MOST MYSTERIOUS INMATE at Lake Butler was a charming, cold-eyed man named Jack Green. Jack was in the four-man group that had morning coffee with Joe, and he was a regular in the prison hobby shop where Joe did his leather work during the evening hours.

Jack wore his black hair slicked straight back and had a 48-inch chest stacked onto a 33-inch waist. He was in his early 50s, and he looked like it would be no problem for him to drop down and bang out a set of 100 pushups. He rarely spoke during the hobby shop conversations. He'd listen and laugh at the funny comments made about someone else, but no one ever made a comment that made Jack the butt of the joke.

There was an aura of danger about Jack, and my senses picked it up the first time I addressed him directly and asked what he was in prison for. He didn't answer, but the stare he gave me was more than adequate for me to grasp that I had better not ask him any future questions about his personal life.

By never commenting on his personal life before or during prison, Jack left a vacuum where rumor 119 assumed the form of facts. If a new inmate asked an old-timer who the fit-looking guy was walking around the jogging path with Joe Peel, you might hear anything, including; "That's Jack Green—he used to be a bodyguard for Elvis . . . he's a karate master and was Chuck Norris' sensei . . . he's a boss in the Mafia . . . he's killed a lot of men, both in and out of prison."

Jack had me worried right from our first meeting. He obviously wasn't trying to impress anyone with his criminal career, and he had no interest in being friendly. Thus, unless Joe was present, I avoided Jack's space. Whenever I even got near him, I felt like a college fraternity boy in the presence of an evil predator who might be sizing me up to be his next victim.

Jack didn't get any less intimidating to me until a few months after my Lake Butler arrival. My first conversation with Jack came on a Saturday during a visit with Karen and my mother. Mom was having a great time; she acted as if she was visiting her son at summer camp. She'd point out an inmate, and then I'd tell her why he was in prison.

The visitor's park at Lake Butler contained an indoor room, about the size of a tennis court, with doors that opened onto an enclosed courtyard. Both areas had picnic tables and chairs. Inmates and their visitors would usually start the visit outside until it got too hot, then move inside to get out of the noonday sun. Karen and I would do the opposite: we'd start in the visitor's room where we could get a table to ourselves and then move outside when everyone else began to move inside.

Karen, Mom, and I had moved outside even though it was so hot and humid that it felt like someone was standing two feet away and squirting a fine mist of hot water at your face. When I saw Jack come through the open glass doors that led to the courtyard, I turned my head so he was out of my field of vision. However, the folding chairs for the picnic tables were stacked next to the table where I was sitting, and when Jack approached to get two chairs for him and his female friend, I turned my head and acknowledged him with a quick "How's it going, Jack" type greeting.

Mom thought Jack was a friend of mine, and before he had time to pick up his chairs and move them to another table, she chirped up that she was going to get some Cokes and volunteered to get some for Jack and his friend if they would like to join us.

I had never heard of any jail house protocol involving behavior in the visitor's park with the scariest inmate in the joint, but it didn't matter because Karen, being friendly and outgoing also, quickly followed my mother's lead and arranged two more chairs so we were like a fivesome sitting at an outdoor table at the yacht club, waiting for the rum coolers to arrive.

I was surprised when Jack didn't decline, but joined us at our table. He introduced us to his friend, Susan, and I introduced Karen and my mother. The five of us started chatting about where we were from and what we did, and Jack sprinkled the conversation with a few funny stories about prison life.

Jack was charming. His girlfriend, who was an executive secretary, was beautiful, intelligent, and well-spoken. The last two hours of visiting zipped by, and after the fivesome broke up my mother couldn't wait to ask me what Jack was in prison for.

I told my mother that I wasn't sure, but the rumor around the inmates wàs that he was in for murder, maybe even two or three murders.

My mother gasped when she heard that, then wanted to hear more of the details, which I didn't have.

Karen's interest had also been piqued by Jack's rumored

crime. "I don't think so," she commented. "The only person who could be that charming and a murderer is Dracula."

It was some time before I was to learn exactly why Jack was in prison, and that knowledge—as did most of what I knew about other inmates—came directly from my appeals work with Joe Peel.

One afternoon, just Joe and I were in the law library. I was typing out parole appeals, and Joe was staring at his yellow legal pad. Usually, Joe would sit down, and his right hand would immediately begin writing while his left hand operated his cigarette and cup of coffee.

Finally, after 15 minutes of tapping his pen on the legal pad, he slid his chair over to my desk and placed before me a parole form issued from Tallahassee.

"Take a look at this," Joe said. "What do you make of the add-ons? Then compare it to the temporary form Jack got from the parole rep who did the initial interview."

I picked up the two forms and immediately noticed that the name of the inmate involved was Jack Green. The temporary computation form issued by the parole representative was very straightforward. For the salient score, there were points listed for prior convictions, prior jail time, and the use of a gun in a felony. On the other side of the matrix Jack's crime was classified as first-degree murder. The parole rep had computed the time that Jack needed to serve before he could be paroled as 13 to 16 years. On the same sheet, it was noted that Jack already had served 15 years, thus he was given a presumptive parole date of one year in the future.

However, the form assigning Jack a permanent parole date, issued from the commission in Tallahassee, had flashing red lights all over it. On this form, the computations of the interviewer were accepted, but below those figures was a section labeled enhancements. Enhancement #1 read: "Extreme violence used in the commission of the crime—

add five years." Enhancement #2 read: "Escape attempt—add five years." Finally, enhancement #3 read: "Threatened the chief of the Florida Bureau of Prisons, add three years."

The form then contained more computations where the 13 years of add-ons were tacked on to the one year still necessary to serve, giving Jack a permanent parole date that was 14 years into the future, meaning that the state of Florida wanted him to serve 29 years on his life sentence before he would be let out.

"Damn," I stated as I handed the parole form back to Joe. "What did he do to get 13 years of add-ons? No wonder Jack never alludes to what he's in for. Are we going to appeal this one and on what grounds?"

"Well, for the violence I'll probably question just what constitutes violence when a body is already dead. Then there's not much I can challenge about the escape—that's pretty cut and dried—but the threat against Harry Weber is purely a personal vendetta because Harry's mistress decided she liked Jack and wouldn't fuck Harry anymore."

"That's not Susan, the lady I met in the visitor's park a couple of weeks ago, is it?" I questioned.

"Yep," Joe replied. "Susan used to work here in administration, and Jack was my first typist in the law library. They used to meet in the ladies' rest room around the corner, until one of the other secretaries who knew about Susan and Harry blew the whistle. Harry went nuts when he found out that his sweet young thing was making a fool of him by falling in love with, and fucking, the most dangerous inmate at Lake Butler. Jack got barred from the law library, Susan got transferred out of Lake Butler and then fired from the Bureau of Prisons, and Harry became a joke when Jack got word to a newspaperman in Gainesville that he was worried he was going to be murdered by the guards because of the relationship he had going with Harry's mistress."

"You've got to be making this up."

"No, I'm not. Have you ever seen an enhancement for threatening the chief of the Bureau of Prisons? That's just Harry Weber's way of still trying to get back at Jack for all the embarrassment and grief he caused him, especially after the newspaper articles made the whole episode public."

"How long ago did all this happen?" I asked. "Was Jack nuts playing around with the head of the whole system's mistress?"

"About five years ago," Joe replied. "You think Susan looks good now, you should have seen her five years ago when she was in her late twenties. I'd be the lookout when they went into the bathroom. She was going to play with the paperwork to get him an early parole, and if that didn't work, I'm sure she would have helped him set up another escape."

"I don't get it. What's the big attraction with Jack? He's got a life sentence; why would she be involved in an affair with an inmate when she's already with the head of the whole system?"

"They're strange creatures, aren't they?" Joe laughed. "But Jack's always been able to charm the ladies. Do you know what he's in here for?"

"Murder of some kind," I answered, leaning back in my chair, knowing that Joe was about to embark on story time and I was about to learn about the mysterious Jack Green.

Joe told me that he knew Jack originally from Palm Beach. Jack was hired "muscle," and their paths would cross occasionally in connection with some schemes that Floyd Holzapfel and Bobby Lincoln were part of. Jack was a karate master, wasn't afraid of anyone, and got a reputation for being a guy in South Florida that you didn't want to have thinking of you in unfriendly terms.

"When Elvis played Miami, Jack was hired as a bodyguard, and they worked out together. When some of the big-crime guys had debts to collect, they'd go to Jack, and he'd take care of it. But what got Jack into big trouble was when he hooked up with Jack Murphy, and they branched out from the jewelry thieving 'Murph the Surf' was doing to some of his other schemes."

"I've heard of Murph the Surf—didn't he steal some famous diamond in Miami?" I chimed in.

"That's the guy," Joe affirmed. "He stole the Star of India diamond from a New York society lady whose husband owned CBS or something like that. Murph is over at Raiford right now doing a life sentence, but it's not for stealing jewels; it's for a murder he and Jack were convicted of—the murder of a couple of brokerage workers from San Francisco.

"Murph was the classic guy who figured if he could break into a house and steal something, then he might as well break into a rich person's house and steal something major. Jack knew people who would buy stolen jewels, and his reputation was such that everyone would pretty much do what they said they were going to do if he was involved. It worked well for them: Murph would steal the merchandise, and Jack would handle the fencing and the collection.

"By the time they took the fall, there was no doubt that the police knew that Murph was a major thief, and Jack was a midlevel hood who was on the verge of stepping up to a higher level of criminal activity. Murph loved the notoriety; his Murph-the-Surf-playboy-jewel-thief persona had him thinking that he was the next Cary Grant, and Hollywood would be his next stop. On the other hand, Jack didn't like people knowing anything about him; he wanted to stay unknown and low profile, which was kind of impossible if you were hanging out with Murph.

"What happened was, they went to San Francisco,

and while they were there, they met a couple of cute secretaries who worked in one of the big brokerage houses. They had a big time for a few days, and then Murph talked the girls into stealing a couple of hundred thousand dollars worth of negotiable bonds from the vault at the business where they worked.

"The girls took the bonds, and the four of them went back to Miami where they were living on a yacht Murph had gotten his hands on. The honeymoon lasted about a week, and then the girls started to talk about going back to San Francisco and returning what they had stolen. This didn't humor Jack, since he knew that the girls would immediately give the police Murph's and his name. The girls were going to have to die.

"They took the boat out for a spin up a waterway called Whiskey Creek. When Murph wavered on the plan to kill the girls, Jack looked at him and let him know that he didn't agree with Murph's new-found weakness. He was not going to change the plan.

"Jack killed the girls, and then when he couldn't get the bodies to stay submerged, he ended up cutting them up so no gases would stay trapped. Jack slit the bodies, thinking that would help them to stay submerged. That's what enhancement #2 on the parole form is all about—the way the bodies were mutilated."

"So Murph the Surf isn't in for jewelry theft?" I asked.

"He got some time for that, but he got the life sentence for the murders. They got caught right away, too. People had seen the four of them on the boat, seen them in San Francisco. They blamed each other, but both of them got life sentences, anyway."

Joe handed me the file that had Jack Green's paperwork in it. "You see that disciplinary report on the escape? It made Harry Weber look bad because he was the warden at the Glade Penitentiary then. Add to that Susan telling Weber to take a hike because she'd rather spend her weekends visiting Jack in prison than being with Harry and traveling about on official business. Finally, when Harry said he'd have Jack killed, Jack talked to the Gainesville papers, and Susan told them about all the taxpayers' money Harry had spent wining and dining her on bogus business trips— the answer is no, unless some national newspaperman or TV personality gets excited about Jack's parole situation, we aren't going to win this one. Steve Jamison or some other lawyer will have to take this one to court."

"You think he'll have a chance in court?" I asked.

Joe took the file back and leafed through it. "I doubt it. This is a situation the legislature was thinking about where they set up a special considerations procedure to keep inmates that scared the public with how ruthless they are in jail till they were almost dead. Jack's in his early 50s now, and they want 14 more years. I'm not sure I'd even want to run into Jack on the streets before he is in a walker. He knows Harry Weber is going to be able to keep him locked up, but every time Susan visits him I think he is so tickled that he made the chief of the Bureau of Prisons look like such a fool, that he doesn't mind the extra years he is going to have to serve. Susan's still waiting for him, and it drives Weber nuts."

TED BUNDY'S FAREWELL TOUR

BECAUSE INMATES AT LAKE BUTLER did almost all the prison labor and clerical work, it was almost impossible for anything of magnitude to happen without the prison population knowing about it in advance. For example, the prison bosses might think they were going to surprise us with a barracks shakedown, but we always had at least 12 hours to get any contraband we might have out of our lockers.

Thus, it shouldn't have surprised Colonel Dooly, the head of the prison, when the word got out days in advance that the man the Florida papers were calling the most heinous, psychotic, cold-blooded killer in the history of the United States was going to be passing through for a medical evaluation as he was being moved from a jail in the county where he had just been sentenced to Raiford and death row. Ted Bundy was coming to visit, and every permanent convict in residence was making plans to catch a glimpse of him so they could tell their grandkids that they had seen the beast in person before he fried in the electric chair.

Ted Bundy was a human mutant, a yuppie killer

who had left a path of dead female bodies from Washington State through Utah and Colorado and into Florida. He was never caught red-handed, but when the numerous clues were put together, police departments across the United States were sure that they had finally stopped the man they thought had committed anywhere from eight to 25 murders of attractive, mostly college-age women.

By the time he arrived at Lake Butler for a quick medical check, Bundy was one of the most recognizable names in the United States. He had represented himself during the trial that had garnered him a death sentence from the state of Florida, and during that period he was a fixture on the national newscasts. He had been on all the major magazine covers and his killing sprees had been the subject of several books. He was America's worst nightmare: a handsome, articulate, well-educated white man who could easily fit into the life-style and social settings of places as diverse as Seattle, Aspen, and Tallahassee. However, even all this scrutiny by the media couldn't define what Ted Bundy's problems were, and Ted admitted to nothing, proclaiming that he was innocent of all charges.

The breach of security revealing Ted Bundy's stopover emanated from the prison chaplain's office. The chaplain kept an appointment book in which he noted the time and date of interviews he was to conduct with death row inmates coming through Lake Butler. The chaplain had an inmate assistant, one of whose jobs was to type out a weekly appointment schedule. Most of the death row inmates weren't well known; they were just nondescript people who had committed a murder of passion or a murder for attempted economic gain and were on their way to jack up the numbers of the most-populous death row in the United States.

However, Ted Bundy was different. He had attained celebrity status, and the convict assistant noticed the name of Ted Bundy and passed it on as a conversational nugget to anyone with whom he came in contact. Within four hours of the word going out, it was impossible to find any permanent inmate at Lake Butler who didn't know that the infamous Ted Bundy would be visiting our humble prison.

Not only did the inmates want to catch a glimpse of Bundy, but so did the employees. Sergeant Wilkerson, who ran the mail distribution and was in charge of the law library, had his walkie-talkie on so he could monitor Bundy's progress through the checking-in procedure. Right before Bundy moved from the unloading area to the administrative area, Sergeant Wilkerson tapped on the glass of the law library window, and Joe and I walked the few yards to the double glass doors that led to the administration area. From that vantage point we would have a swell view of Ted and his minders as they moved down the corridor.

Bundy was wearing a blue prison jumpsuit, and his hands were cuffed in front of him as he moved down the corridor, flanked by an escort of three prison guards. The unusual part of the journey down the corridor was that all the doors that led into the hallway were open and three or four prison employees were packed into each doorway to glare at the heinous murderer. One secretary, who looked like she would have been high on the priority list as a Bundy preferred victim, snarled at him and said, "Welcome to death row, Ted. Just think, this is the last time you're going to be this close to a woman ever again."

I saw Bundy turn toward the attractive secretary and give her a wicked smile, as if to say, "Don't bet on it." Then he was gone, and everyone in the administrative offices returned to their jobs.

When Joe and I got back to the law library, he said, "Did you see the look on Miss Davis' face when she made that comment? I thought she was going to pull a 'Jack Ruby' on

him and whip out a gun and blow him away right there."
We had been back at work for about five minutes when I
looked up from my typewriter to see the Ted Bundy proces-
sion moving past the window of the law library and stop-
ping at our door. Colonel Dooly could see that we had no
inmate appointments going on so he opened the door and
told Joe that Ted Bundy wanted to see him. Joe said that
was fine, and a few seconds later Ted Bundy walked into the
law library office of Joe Peel and Associates.

Colonel Dooly never played any games with the law
library regarding inmate visits. When an inmate came for
an appointment, no guards ever entered with him for the
purpose of monitoring the conversation. Colonel Dooly's
policy was that a visit to the law library was covered by the
attorney-client privilege, and those same rules applied to
Ted Bundy. Once Bundy was in the office, Colonel Dooly
told him that he had only about 10 minutes before they had
to leave. The colonel then closed the door and stationed
one guard in front of the door and the other two in front of
the picture window. The guards could see in, but they
couldn't hear what we were saying.

Joe had never met Bundy but like everyone else had
seen him on TV. Joe introduced himself and then me as his
assistant. Ted's hands were still cuffed in front of him, but
we both made the effort to shake hands with him. Joe then
asked Ted if he wanted to talk in private, and Ted said he
just wanted to check on a few points. Joe arranged three of
the chairs in a half circle so our backs were to the window
and the guards couldn't read anyone's lips. We sat down and
Joe said, "What can I help you with, Ted?"

I was sitting to the right of Ted Bundy, who was in the
middle, and I could watch him as he was talking to Joe. I
first focused on his hands, the hands that were alleged to
have strangled over a score of victims. His hands were rest-

ing in his lap, and I didn't want to give him the wrong impression that I was staring at his crotch, so I raised my gaze to watch his mouth as he talked. Almost like a magnet, my eyes focused on Ted's teeth, the same teeth that had been rumored in some magazine stories to have bitten the nipples off some of his victims or to have taken a bite of flesh out of the ass of a girl he had murdered in a sorority house at Florida State University. I wasn't worried that Ted was going to snap around and bite off my nose; he was thin and had the grayed complexion of someone who hadn't seen the sun or fresh air for months—hardly threatening looking. However, I was spellbound to be so close to the appendages and body parts that had carried out the murderous impulses of someone so deranged that he had captivated the whole country with his deviant criminal behavior. In Vietnam, I had met Henry Kissinger and Gen. William Westmoreland, and I now had the same feeling being in the presence of the infamous Ted Bundy.

I watched Bundy's mouth move without listening to his words for at least five seconds, but then I realized that I'd better pay attention to what he was saying.

Ted asked Joe if he knew of anyone who could handle his appeals better than he—Bundy—could. We all knew that Bundy had fired several court-appointed lawyers and had handled his own defense in the Lake City, Florida, murder trial. "I'd recommend a lawyer out of Miami who does a lot of death row appeals," Joe advised. "I don't know the particulars of the case you made in your defense at Lake City, but if you're happy with the work you did, maybe you should continue with the appeals yourself."

"That's what I'm leaning toward," Ted replied. "The jury up there went for all the circumstantial evidence the prosecutor threw at them."

"Two things I think you should consider," Joe said as he got his legal mind working on Bundy's huge problems. "First, if you have no second guesses on how you handled your case and aren't kicking yourself for getting the death sentence—stay with doing your own work on the appeal because, secondly, I spent two years on death row, and if you're working your butt off on your own case, that can keep you sharp and help keep your mind off of where you are."

"How'd you get off the death sentence? Any suggestions?"

Joe offered Bundy a cigarette, which was declined, and then lit one for himself. "I didn't have a death sentence," Joe said after he had taken his first drag on the new cigarette. "They put me there to try to convince me to stop doing legal work for other inmates."

"Did you stop?" Ted asked.

"No, that's really all I had to live for. I wouldn't, and won't, stop doing that for anything."

Colonel Dooly knocked on the door and then stuck his head in. "We're on overtime. You all have to wrap it up in a minute."

Ted Bundy stood up. "If I need some help or advice, is it OK for me to get in contact with you—just check over what I'm doing?"

"Absolutely," Joe replied. "I'm helping Leroy Hayes with some of his appeals, and we're having no problem with getting the paperwork back and forth. Send me anything you have any questions about."

"Thanks," concluded Ted as Colonel Dooly opened the door, and Ted moved toward his waiting escort of guards, giving us a quick wave of his cuffed hands.

There was to be no legal magic in Ted Bundy's bag of tricks. He did most of the work on his conviction and death sentence appeals himself, and he lost all his appeals. He was executed by the state of Florida, and he took the secrets of his maniacal personality with him to the grave.

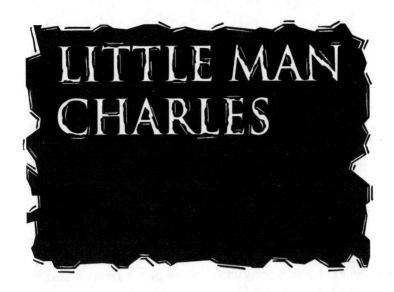

LITTLE MAN CHARLES

ONE DAY, AS JOE AND I WERE WALKING from the law library to the chow hall I glanced over at the temporary inmate dorms, where a long line of inmates waiting to buy cigarettes and candy at the transient canteen had formed. Everything looked normal, except for the person waiting in the middle of the line—he looked like a little kid. I told Joe to check the guy out. He looked toward the line and said, "Juvenile tried as an adult," after a quick glance at the 4-foot 6-inch black kid. "I'll get him a call-out, and we'll see if we can do something for him—see why he isn't at a juvenile facility."

It wasn't hard to get a call-out slip for the kid. Sergeant Wilkerson gave me a slip with the name left blank, then I ran it over to Jack Green, who worked as a food server at the chow hall, and told him to look for a 4-foot 6-inch black kid who looked 12 years old. When Jack spotted the kid coming through the food line, he gave him the slip, filling in the name because the kid couldn't write, and we had the kid at the law library the next day at 9 A.M.

Charles Jones was a comical figure in a world of   13 5

hardened convicts. At 4 1/2 feet and 80 pounds, his prison-issue clothes hung on him like a ridiculous fashion statement from a gender-confused Paris designer. His state-issue work boots looked like a clown's idea of footwear that might be worth a laugh, and the kid walked into the office wearing sunglasses and smoking a cigarette.

Charles had no idea why he had been called out or to whom he was talking. I got him seated and asked him his name, age, and where he was from; then I explained to him that Joe Peel was a convict who was also a lawyer, and we wanted to see if we could help in some way.

Charles told me he was 15 years old and lived in Liberty City, which I knew was the black ghetto in Miami. Joe quit writing and turned to face the kid while tamping down a cigarette, getting it ready to smoke.

"Hey, man," the kid said in a voice that hadn't seen puberty yet. "Give me a cigarette."

Joe gave the kid a smoke and then lit it for him. "You in a gang?" Joe asked while sizing up the failure of Florida's social system sitting in front of him.

"Fuck no," Charles answered. "I don't want to fuck up my life with no gang shit."

"You're in for drugs, armed robbery—just what is a 15-year-old kid doing in an adult prison?"

It took only three questions for the kid's gangster attitude to wear off and expose a child who was barely a teenager and scared shitless. He removed his sunglasses, and I could see that his eyes were brimming with tears. Then the tears started falling down the cheeks of a kid so cute that he could have been cast on the *Bill Cosby Show*. He wiped his eyes with his sleeve, and Joe handed him a Kleenex so he could blow his nose, while explaining to Charles that he wanted to help because a 15 year old didn't belong in an adult prison, no matter what he had done.

Charles showed the first trace of a smile and mumbled, "You got that right."

The kid's instincts were good. He figured he had a guy who wanted to help him in Joe Peel, and he told us that he was in prison for murder; he had killed both his grandparents when they wouldn't give him five bucks to go to the toy store.

"Did you live with your grandparents?" Joe questioned.

"Yes."

"What about your mother and father?"

"They are both dead. My dad beat my mom and she died, and then he got killed in prison. My grandparents were my parents."

"Jesus," Joe said as he exhaled and contemplated for a moment the horrendous nightmare the kid had already been through. "Were your grandparents good to you?"

The kid started to nod his head as the tears began to form again. However, this time he made no effort to wipe his eyes. He started sobbing and then pulled his feet up into a fetal position on the swivel desk chair he was sitting on.

Neither Joe nor I was equipped to handle Charles' problems. Joe told him that we'd contact the clerk and get the sentencing memorandum, and write to his public defender to see if there were any legal avenues we could pursue. However, these were fancy words to a 15 year old who couldn't read or write, and they weren't quelling his uncontrollable sobbing.

Charles needed a mother immediately. Someone who would hold him in her arms and tell him that everything was going to be OK. Joe told me to go over to the infirmary and see if one of the free-lady nurses would come over to help Charles.

However, as I was walking out the door, Mrs. Branson, who was a secretary to one of the prison officials, came walking by to use the ladies' rest room. Joe was on good terms with Mrs. Branson. He had written up some legal documents for her when she was going through a divorce, and she would often come by the law library just to flirt. Joe had even said that she wanted him to follow her into the ladies' rest room so she could repay him properly. Now, I would have thought that a guy who had been locked up as long as Joe had would have jumped on that offer. Plus, Mrs. Branson wasn't that bad looking, in a Southern hooker sort of way. She had a trim body, crowned by a wild nest of black lacquered hair, and the deep facial lines, yellowed teeth, and stained fingers that come with 40 years of chain smoking. But that wasn't what bothered Joe, who had probably matched her cigarette for cigarette over his lifetime. The problem was that she was "the man," a prison guard, and as such could cause him way more harm than the good one quick fuck could accomplish.

Joe politely put off her innuendo that he could have her if he wanted, and it almost became a challenge to her femininity to figure out why Joe wasn't responding. She even started wearing dresses to work instead of the brown pants and brown shirt that were the uniform of all prison employees with guard status.

Mrs. Branson saw Charles sobbing in his chair and asked me what was wrong with the nigger midget. I explained to her that he wasn't a midget, but a 15-year-old kid who told us he was sentenced to life for murdering his grandparents.

Mrs. Branson wasn't known for being nice to any inmates besides Joe. Once she had almost thrown Karen out of the visitor's park because she claimed Karen and I were rubbing legs under the table. And she didn't seem overly fond of blacks since "nigger" was the only word she ever used when talking about black people, unless a black prison employee was present. Thus, it was surprising when she entered the law library, sat down next to Charles, and pulled him over so he could cry on her shoulder.

As Mrs. Branson soothed Charles, he gradually began to regain his composure. After the sobbing stopped, one of his hands gravitated up to Mrs. Branson's prized hairdo, and he began running his hand along her hair.

"Your hair feels like my grandmother's," Charles said, thinking he had made a new friend.

Mrs. Branson, upon hearing Charles' comment, immediately disengaged from her mothering mode. The fact that a teenage murderer had compared her beautiful, lacquered black hairdo to that of an old "nigger" lady from a South Florida ghetto was an appalling thought.

"All right, Charles," Mrs. Branson said sternly as she reverted to being a prison guard. "You're in prison, boy, and you've got to leave the administration building."

As she led Charles out of the law library, Mrs. Branson looked back at Joe and asked him if he knew what kind of sentence Charles had gotten. Joe shrugged his shoulders and opened his palms, indicating that he had no idea what the kid was facing.

"I'll see if I can get you a copy of his file" were Branson's closing words, as she left with a wave to Joe and escorted Charles back to the prison yard, where the transient inmates at Lake Butler spent their days.

The next morning Mrs. Branson came by the law library, and I almost didn't recognize her. Her trademark, shellacked, Southern white trash hairdo was gone, replaced with a natural mid-length cut that actually had independent movement to it.

Along with the file for Charles Jones, Mrs. Branson had brought Joe a cup of coffee. Joe remarked how much he liked her new hairdo and how well it went with the beautiful dress she was wearing. She ate up the compliments and gave Joe a bit of head-and-eye movement that seemed to indicate that now would be a fine time for them to visit the ladies' rest room. However, Joe didn't respond, so she told him that she'd be back in an hour to pick up the file.

I was amazed to see the length of Charles Jones' criminal record. There were more than 50 arrests, starting when he was 9 and ending with the murder of his grandparents when he had just turned 15. The list included robberies, armed robberies, assaults, assaults with deadly weapons, and car theft. The record showed that Charles had been in and out of foster homes and juvenile detention facilities and was a constant problem for the social workers in Liberty City.

However, the most appalling information in Charles' file concerned the killing of his grandparents. There were several letters to the Dade County Social Services from the grandparents begging the agency to give them custody of their grandson because they thought they were best suited to take care of him and turn his behavior around.

The last document was the sentencing memorandum from the judge who had sentenced Charles. The judge called the killings, which were done with a kitchen knife while the grandparents were asleep, the most brutal he had ever seen during his 30 years on the Florida bench. He further indicated that there was not an iota of evidence that Charles had shown any remorse for what he had done, nor was there any possibility that this person could or should be allowed to live in civilized society again.

Rather than give Charles the standard first-degree murder sentence of life in prison, which according to Florida law meant the convicted person had to serve 25 years before being eligible for parole, the judge gave Charles a sentence of 300 years in prison and noted in the paperwork that Charles could not be considered for parole until he had served one-third of his sentence. Thus, the judge was making it very clear that he never wanted Charles Jones to be a free man again. The judge's last comment was that the only reason he didn't impose the death penalty was because, considering the age of the defendant, he didn't think the sentence would survive the appeals process.

We saw Charles one more time before he got shipped out of Lake Butler. His classification officer brought him over so Joe could explain Charles' sentence to him. The classification officer, Mr. Wills, said he had explained the numbers to Charles, but he didn't think he understood.

Charles was waiting outside the door as Joe told Mr. Wills that he didn't like being put in the position of having to explain to an inmate how hopeless his situation was. "I'm kind of the last hope some of these people have," Joe said, "and I want to offer a chance that maybe something can be done to help them out. Telling a kid he's got to do 100 years before he can even be considered for parole is going to take all hope away from this kid right now."

Mr. Wills agreed with what Joe was saying and explained that he had gone over and over the sentence and what it means, but the kid wouldn't believe it till Joe Peel told him that was the truth. "He can't read the sentencing order," Mr. Wills said. "He thinks I'm lying to him."

Mr. Wills was a good guy, and both Joe and I felt sorry for him in this situation. He had helped my wife during a visitor's check-in when she was trying to bring in a copy of *The Murder Trial of Judge Joe Peel* by Jim Bishop, which had been written more than 10 years before and was out of print. Karen had found it at a used-book store in Fort Lauderdale and brought it so Joe would autograph it.

While searching Karen's purse, the guard on duty noticed the book and said that she couldn't bring it in. Mr. Wills, who was supervising the check-in of visitors, came over and said he'd take it in, then take it back out and give it to her after visiting was over. When he returned the book to Karen, he told her that if she found another copy, he'd like to buy it. The next week Karen returned with another copy of the book, which Mr. Wills bought and then had Joe autograph. After that, Karen always got treated well during visitor's check-in, and Mr. Wills would often come by the law library just to shoot the shit with Joe and me.

Joe relented and agreed to talk to Charles. When Charles entered the law library this time, he wasn't wearing sunglasses, and he exhibited some of the manners that his grandparents must have taught him before he killed them. He looked even thinner than when we had seen him 10 days earlier, and he refused the cigarette Joe offered with a barely audible, "No, thank you, Mr. Peel."

With Charles looking so frail and being polite in his mannerisms, whether you were an inmate or a prison employee, you couldn't help but feel sorry for what awaited him for the rest of his life, regardless of the crimes he had previously committed.

"Charles, I've gotten to look at your file," Joe said, "and I'm not going to tell you anything but the truth as far as I see it. After I saw your file, I wrote a letter to the lawyer that handled your case to see what his plan was for postconviction remedies. You've got a tough situation, but I think there might be a chance for some relief down the line."

"Mr. Wills told me I'll have to serve 100 years before I can get out," Charles stated with the one thought that was dominating his thinking. "One hundred years, man, nobody lives that long, do they?"

"The way the sentencing order reads, what Mr. Wills is telling you is true. However, a sentence like this is so rare that it might be able to be declared cruel and unusual punishment. There might be a racist element to the sentence.

Also, there's the question of trying you as an adult in the first place. So I think there are quite a few possibilities for an appeal."

"OK," Charles said, "100 years. Well, at least then I won't have to serve 300 years, will I?"

Joe and Charles' public defender from Dade County exchanged several letters regarding ideas for postconviction relief for Charles Jones. An appeal was filed attacking the legality of both the sentence and of trying a 15 year old as an adult, as well as the racial implications of the sentence. The public defender had reviewed all the sentences handed down by the judge in first-degree murder cases and found that black defendants received significantly harsher sentences than white defendants.

However, after all the appeals were ruled on, there was no change. Charles would be doing his prison time as an adult, and he would be doing 300 years with no parole possible until he had served 100 of those years.

After the appeal process was over, the public defender in Dade County tried to convince the sentencing judge to remove the stipulation that Charles would not be eligible for parole until one-third of his sentence was served. If that could be accomplished, then Charles would fall into the matrix of parole guidelines, which could have him eligible for parole in 18 years.

The judge's answer, while not an outright yes, left a ray of hope that Charles wouldn't be in prison for the rest of his life. The judge said that at present he would not remove his stipulation, but, if after serving 25 years Charles had produced a clean prison record, then—and only then—he would consider lifting the stipulation.

Whether you're talking 25 years, 100 years, or even 300 years—it was more time than a teenage kid could comprehend. As it turned out, it didn't matter, anyway. Charles was sent to one of the gladiator schools for "adult" prisoners under age 26, where he got involved in one of the gangs. Three years later, he was killed in a knife fight over a $10 football bet he had made.

Charles had killed his grandparents because they wouldn't give him $5, and he had been killed over a $10 bet. However, Charles Jones was not remembered around Lake Butler for the brutal killings he committed, his size, his age, or the disproportionate sentence he received. Little Man Charles was lionized by the inmates as the kid who caused Mrs. Branson to terminate her shellacked hairdo, and, even though that wasn't quite enough to snare Joe's sexual interest, it did make her a whole lot better to look at and the air in her vicinity much safer to breathe.

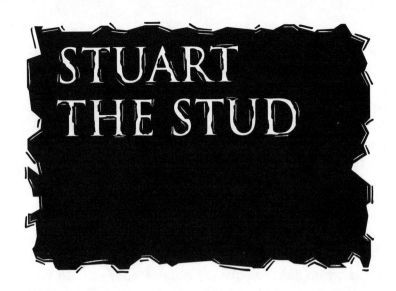

STUART THE STUD

Aт Lаке Butler, there were no prison
industries where an inmate could earn
spending money. Thus, if an inmate didn't
have money given to him by his family or wasn't
able to make wood and leather objects that could be
sold through the prison hobby shop, then he had to
resort to a hustle to acquire cash.

It was against the prison rules for one inmate to
pay another inmate for goods or services, but this
rule was unenforceable. It was capitalism at work—
if a need existed, it would be supplied by an
entrepreneurial inmate. Nowhere was this more
apparent than in the black market goods and services that sprang up around cigarettes.

Almost all the inmates at Lake Butler were smokers. One sociological observation of which I am dead
sure is that if, by chance, all smokers disappeared from
the face of the earth, then almost all the criminal ele-
ments of society would be gone. We might lose a few
lawyers and type-A New Yorkers in the group, but
that's a small price to pay for eliminating the criminal
element of all countries worldwide.

At Lake Butler, an inmate was allowed to draw

no more than $15 a week from his inmate account. Cigarettes were a dollar a pack at the canteen; thus, if someone was puffing down the average two to three packs a day, toward the last two days before an inmate could get more money, he was looking at either a cigarette or a money crisis.

It was around this supply of and demand for tobacco that the inmate economy was based. At the top rung were the few guys who had a steady source of money from their family and who didn't smoke (of which I was one). We had disposable income, and I was constantly being offered a 100 percent return on my loan for a week at a time.

Next in the economic pecking order were people who had a hustle going that was generating more money per week than they could smoke up. Again, this was another source of capital to be invested at a 100 percent return per week.

After these two groups, everyone else was pretty much in the same boat: either they smoked away all the money they had, or they didn't smoke because they didn't have any money.

Joe and I had the opportunity to generate more money than any inmate hustle that existed. We had the knowledge and expertise to generate legal work and parole appeals that could drastically cut an inmate's time in prison. However, this was set in stone—no money for legal work. Joe wouldn't even accept a pack of cigarettes from an inmate for legal work, and this applied whether he had something to smoke or he was dry.

I didn't want to be involved in any loan schemes for my excess money, but what I would do is buy a few packs of cigarettes and stockpile them to give to Joe when I noticed he didn't have a pack in the pocket of his shirt. Without tobacco, Joe was like all the other addicts: he'd get less productive in his writings at the law library, and we'd quickly fall behind. When Joe had his cigarettes all lined up to chain-smoke for the day, then he was like a well-oiled legal machine banging out the paperwork.

Even with helping Joe out with his tobacco habit, I still had plenty of money to participate in other inmates' hustles that made my life in prison a bit more genteel. The big-ticket items (meaning they cost more than a dollar) were drugs, booze, and sex. A joint rolled so tightly that it resembled a toothpick cost a buck, a cocktail made out of whatever was available in the kitchen that would ferment cost a buck, and a blow job from a convict wearing a dress and wig cost two bucks. However, these were the recreational diversions available for purchase; the quality-of-life hustles were much cheaper.

One dollar a week to the inmate who handled laundry distribution ensured that a clean T-shirt, boxers, socks, and towel awaited me on my bunk at 5 P.M. when I came back from my afternoon run. Fifty cents a week paid for a twice-weekly changing of my sheets, and 25 cents a week to Buttonhole Sam (so named because he had been shot right between the eyes, and the way the scar healed made it look like Sam had a buttonhole sewed on his face) employed him to be the first in line for the morning canteen, where he'd buy me a morning newspaper. A pack of cigarettes a week bought me one fresh cherry tomato a day, and I even had money left over to indulge in a pint of ice cream a day, join with Joe to play the football lottery, and get Joe an emergency pack of cigarettes when the nicotine withdrawal set in.

There were two indicators that Joe was going into withdrawal. First, his everpresent pack of Marlboros would be missing from his shirt pocket, and, second, I'd see him over at Stuart the Stud's bunk buying homemade cigarettes, just one of the many items that Stuart sold at his after-hours canteen.

Stuart the Stud was the major shit-talker in my dorm. He was an average-looking white man in his mid-30s with curly black hair. Stuart usually was surrounded by a couple of younger inmates, and if you listened to the conversation dominated by Stuart's New York-accented voice, you would invariably hear Stuart making references to *his* Rolls-Royce, *his* yacht, *his* beach-front home, and *his* Rolex watch. Stuart wanted everyone to know that he was rich, very rich, and if you acted properly when you were around him, then you too just might be able to share in the good times and high living, which would occur when he got out of the joint.

Stuart would lose $100,000 in a weekend at Las Vegas—no problem. He only dated women who had a certified beauty title before their names. He was wrongly charged and convicted of masterminding a limited-partnership fraud involving shopping centers, and there was no way he wouldn't win his appeal. Stuart had confidence in the shit he was talking and had even started showing off some letters to back up his claim that he was good friends with the rock star Alice Cooper, and that he was working on bringing Alice and his band to Lake Butler to play a concert for the inmates, which would be videotaped and then sold to cable television.

My reasoning was, if Stuart was so rich and famous, why was he running an after-hours canteen? The regular prison-operated canteen was positioned in the corridor that connected the four dormitories where permanent inmates were housed. The canteen closed precisely at 7 P.M., and if you hadn't bought your desired evening snack by then, you missed out or you had to deal with the after-hours hustlers with their inflated prices. The usual guys sold the standard candy bars, soda, sandwiches made from food stolen from the kitchen, and coffee packets. However, Stuart had introduced a new item: cigarettes that he and a hired underling made themselves.

This added another tier to the tobacco pyramid: if you couldn't afford a brand-name pack of cigarettes, you could, for half the price, buy a pack of Stuart the Stud's hand-rolled clones.

Stuart would buy the tobacco and rolling paper from the canteen, then he and his hired roller would retreat to the farthest corner of the dorm, squat down so the dorm boss couldn't see, and start production. Once the cigarettes were rolled, they were inserted into an empty pack—ready and waiting for buyers who couldn't afford $1 a pack but didn't want to roll their own or chew.

Stuart's cigarettes acquired the slang name of "studs." Soon every after-hour canteen operator was offering his own version. As these homemades caught on, cigarette sales at the legal canteen dropped off, and the word went out to the dorm bosses that they were to crack down on the illegal canteens, especially the inmates who were making and selling studs.

I'd see Stuart lurking behind the bunks at the rear of the dormitory, like a mouse keeping his eye out for the cat, to make sure the dorm boss wasn't in the area. If the dorm boss did appear, then Stuart would pass off the tobacco to one lookout, his rolling papers to another, and the three of them would go different ways to avoid the bust.

Joe said that the studs had a horrible taste and he hated to have to smoke them, but they were definitely better than some of the stuff he had tried when he had no money.

Stuart never asked Joe or me about legal proceedings, which seemed kind of funny since he claimed he had one of the highest-priced criminal attorneys in Florida working on his appeal. Usually someone who knew Joe would touch base just to make sure that their outside attorney was following through for them, but Stuart never did. Furthermore, Joe knew that Stuart had seen the parole representative and had asked Stuart how it had gone. Stuart answered that it didn't make any difference because he was going to win his appeal, and then he changed the subject.

However, one day before Stuart's right to appeal the parole findings expired, he showed up at the law library, gave Joe a free pack of "studs" as part of his buy-nine-packs-and-get-the-10th-one-free promotion, then showed Joe his parole paperwork.

"You won't tell anyone about this, will you?" Stuart remarked as he saw Joe smile while reading the page.

"No, this is between us," Joe answered, "but if you want us to write an appeal, you're going to have to tell the truth. Is that understood?"

Stuart nodded his head and went on to explain that he was in prison for selling fake insurance policies to little old ladies. He had no money and no attorney working on an appeal, and it looked to him as if he had gotten a parole date that was only three months before the date that he would max out his sentence.

Joe and I had seen this situation before where inmates don't want early parole. Often an inmate who had been around the track knew that he didn't want to mess with parole officers, weekly check-ins, and no-notice searches from parole commission employees. For these people who knew that they didn't do well in a parole situation, it made sense to just stay in the joint until they maxed out their sentences, and then walk out the gates without having to deal with any outside supervision. I'd seen a guy refuse parole and stay inside the joint for an extra nine months just to avoid that kind of transition supervision.

In Stuart's case, the difference was only three months, but his motivation to stay in wasn't his fear of screwing up with the parole people; it was that he claimed he was making $150 a week from his after-hours canteen, and that was more than he could earn in some minimum-wage job he'd have to have for the time he would be on parole.

"Jesus, Stuart," I said. "What could the difference be? Twenty bucks a week? Wouldn't you rather be out of here, back with your family?"

Stuart's response was pragmatic: "I don't have any family, plus in here I'm getting room and board for free so I'm banking all the profit. Out there, I'd have to rent a room, pay for food—every penny I'd get from flipping burgers would be gone. I stay here for that three months, I can walk out of here with a few thousand bucks."

"What if you get caught with the money?" Joe queried. "You know if they catch you with more than $15 they'll confiscate it."

"I'm not worried about that. I get what I don't need out of here every week. It'll be there when I max out. Can you see any reason why I shouldn't stay here till I max out instead of accepting the parole?"

Joe had no reply other than to suggest that he'd get an extra three months toward what he was going to do for the rest of his life, plus he might be able to get laid a few more times than life behind bars offered. But Stuart didn't buy those arguments—prison was an economic opportunity that provided much more than he'd make with a minimum wage job on the outside.

Stuart didn't lie to Joe and me when he was telling us about his situation, but he did have one last whopper for the prison officials.

Florida law enforcement and prison officials were the subjects of a great deal of negative newspaper stories centering around such subjects as drug offenders posting $1 million bonds and then failing to appear or white-collar criminals getting picked up by Learjets after they were turned loose from prison. The Florida legislature reacted to these sensational stories by passing a law right before I entered prison that any prisoner who had assets or income would be charged a per day cost of incarceration based on his ability to pay.

This law was handed to the Bureau of Prisons to implement, and it decided the best way to do this was to require each prisoner to fill out and sign a net worth statement before he could be released on parole. Then, based on that net worth statement, an inmate would be charged a room-and-board figure that he had to pay before being released.

The statute, as passed by the legislature, was very clear that a net worth statement had to be signed by all inmates, but what wasn't clear was which state agency was going to be responsible for sleuthing out the assets of inmates who might be lying on their net worth statements. Joe and I thought that this new law was nonsense. Not only had no agency been designated to enforce the discovery of assets, but no money had been appropriated to hire state workers to do the tough work of figuring out whether any inmates owned property, had bank accounts, or had outside sources of income that could be attached to pay for their incarceration. Given this, Joe advised anyone who asked to list nothing that concerned bank accounts or property and to sign the form.

Sergeant Wilkerson, our law library supervisor, was the prison official in charge of getting every permanent inmate's signature on a net worth form. Sergeant Wilkerson was an easy-going guy who had retired from the army after 20 years and then started working for the prison system to supplement his military pension. As a supply sergeant in the army he had seen and played a lot of tricks himself, and he had no delusions that any convicts were going to be stepping up to write a check to the state of Florida to the tune of $36 a day for their room and board in a prison facility.

However, one day Sergeant Wilkerson stopped by to chat with Joe and me and remarked that he had a permanent inmate who Colonel Dooly thought was going to pay the room-and-board fee.

"This guy is worth millions," Sergeant Wilkerson told us. "He's got a Mercedes, a house on the beach in Fort Lauderdale, apartment buildings, securities, bank accounts—he even listed gold jewelry worth $50,000."

"And he's a perm at Lake Butler?" Joe queried, trying to guess who he'd run across who was that wealthy.

"Yeah, I'll even tell you who it is since the colonel is getting interviewed right now by the press about what a success this new law is for the taxpayer to get inmates who can afford it to pay for their prison cells," Sergeant Wilkerson said. "Stuart Hays. You guys know him?"

"The Stud," Joe and I said in unison. "He's the biggest bullshitter in Lake Butler."

"I think a news conference would be a bad idea," Joe remarked.

"Too late. They've got a few politicians down from Tallahassee, whooping it up how this is going to help keep the prison budget down."

The news conference was too big for the colonel's office, so it was moved to the visitor's park. Joe and I could see and hear the whole proceedings. First, the legislators talked about the success of the statute, then the colonel remarked on the great job the prison administration had done to implement the statute. It appeared that Florida had outwitted the criminals by making them pay for their own incarceration.

When the press was allowed to ask questions, a young reporter for the *Miami Herald* asked if inmate Hays had paid his $13,000 bill yet.

The politicians looked to Colonel Dooly for the answer,

and he remarked that the bill hadn't been paid yet but would have to be paid before the inmate would be released on parole.

The news conference concluded with the *Herald* reporter asking if Mr. Hays was going to pay in cash or write a check? Everyone laughed and then left the visitor's park.

Stuart the Stud was enjoying the publicity. The lies that the prison authorities believed seemed to validate the lies that he had been telling to any inmate who would listen, and Stuart was a big man on campus.

Unfortunately, the *Herald* reporter stayed on the story, and he wanted to bring up a photographer for another story on Stuart actually signing over the $13,000 cost of his prison stay to the state of Florida. Stuart said that was fine, but all his bank accounts were dry so he'd have to give the state the title to his Mercedes.

By this time, Colonel Dooly was feeling some pressure from his boss to capitalize on this great opportunity for favorable publicity, but Stuart wasn't coming through. First, he couldn't find the title to the car, then he couldn't get any securities released from his brokerage house, and, finally, Stuart said that he'd sign over his percentage of the profits from the Alice Cooper prison concert to the state of Florida.

The *Herald* reporter smelled a rat and did some investigations into the vehicle registration and property records and couldn't find any evidence that Stuart possessed what he claimed on his prison net worth statement.

Colonel Dooly threatened to cancel Stuart's parole unless he came up with cash, check, or money order to pay his prison room-and-board bill. Stuart said he was doing the best he could, but what he really needed was a week's furlough to Miami to find the paperwork.

The colonel canceled Stuart's parole date. The *Herald*

reporter wrote a story stating that the legislators and prison officials had been conned by a convict, concluding with a quote from Stuart that if the prison officials would just work with him on the Alice Cooper concert, then everyone could make some money.

Stuart insisted till the day he maxed out his sentence and was given $50 and a bus ticket to Miami that he wanted to pay his incarceration bill. He even went so far as to give the guard who drove him to the bus station his Rolex watch to give to Colonel Dooly so he could sell it and apply that money to his incarceration bill. Of course, the watch was fake, but the guard who kept it had a couple of days where he thought he had lucked into an $8,000 watch—till he took it to a pawnshop in Gainesville to turn it into cash.

GUARDING THE DRUG TRAFFIC

PEOPLE LIKE STUART COULD DO ALL RIGHT for themselves making and selling "studs" or vending Baby Ruth candy bars after normal canteen hours were over. However, the really big money to be made from inmate entrepreneurial efforts revolved around illegal drugs.

To old convicts like Joe Peel and Jack Green, marijuana and cocaine were a ridiculous waste of money. "The couple of times I tried marijuana, it just made my throat sore, like smoking cheap chewing tobacco," Joe had told me, "and cocaine just made my nose a little numb. What is the big deal with this stuff?"

For Joe and Jack the best diversions from the reality of prison centered around a good batch of prison "buck," usually brewed up by kitchen workers who could get their hands on fresh fruit and vegetables before they were baked, mixed, or boiled. At Lake Butler the buck was popular only because it was all but impossible to smuggle in bottles of real liquor.

With 500 to 700 transient inmates housed at Lake Butler at any given time, the authorities tried 157 their best to keep these new inmates, many in the big house for the first time, from being relieved of any money they might have brought with them from the county jails by perms hustling whatever they thought they could sell.

The authorities couldn't stop the selling of studs to these new temporary inmates, but they did do a great job of keeping the making of buck to a minimum and keeping bottled liquor out of the prison. Every permanent inmate who had a visitor (temporary inmates weren't allowed to have visitors unless they had been there four weeks, which few ever were) was strip-searched when he left the visitor's park, and every inmate who worked outside the prison walls was patted down, or randomly strip-searched, when coming back into the prison.

However, as in all prisons, there was one weak link that the Lake Butler authorities couldn't control: the employees of the prison. Lake Butler contained nurses, a dentist, a doctor, secretaries, classification officers, a chaplain, and an assortment of other free people necessary to run a hostile fort holding 1,000 people who didn't want to be there. However, most of these employees didn't deal with the inmates in anything other than a controlled setting. It was the guards who were responsible for keeping the inmates under control and supervision, and among people who worked at a prison, the guards had the lowest status and the lowest pay.

Being a prison guard required only a high school education, and even that could be waived if the applicant was part of the close-knit prison community in Starke, where almost all the employees of the complex of prisons in the area lived. In Florida, a guard started out at about $14,000 a year, and, if he had a wife and a few kids, that meant he lived below the poverty line and was eligible for food stamps and other social services, as befits the working poor.

Along with the pay, a guard had a job that had no status within the prison itself, incurring nothing but contempt from the inmates and a wary eye for thievery and human rights abuses from the guard administrators.

For a guard, it wasn't much different than being the lion tamer at the circus. You had the club and were the authority figure, but the lions, tigers, and panthers were eyeing you. The question wasn't whether they would turn on you, but when—and who would it be?

Before the war on drugs began depositing its prisoners in massive numbers into Florida's prisons, there was a total "us versus them" mentality. There was little that any guard admired about the armed robbers, thieves, murderers, and tricksters that made up the bulk of the state prison population. A lot of these convicts were on the serve-three-years-then-commit-crimes-for-a-year-before-you-get-caught program. These convicts had nothing to offer, and the guards despised them.

However, when the POWs from the drug battles began showing up, some of the guards began to change their attitudes. The drug criminals were an economic force in prison. As a group, they had the most disposable income to spend to make their prison stay more tolerable. For these captured warriors, the desired contraband was not some potatoes mixed with sugar and left to rot in a blocked-off toilet for a few weeks in order to produce an effluent with an alcoholic content. Marijuana and cocaine were needed inside the prison walls, and guards who could smuggle the stuff in had the opportunity to earn up to three times their monthly prison salaries.

The best part for the guards who chose to bring the contraband inside the walls was that it was so easy. A guard who searched a truck before it was allowed into the prison would stash two ounces of marijuana he had paid $60 for in the truck, then clear it through the sally port gates. Once the truck was at the unloading spot, the same guard would retrieve his marijuana, pass it off to the inmate buyer, who would pay $200—a quick and safe 200 percent-plus profit for the guard.

Once the inmate had the two ounces, he would cut it with chewing tobacco and then roll the mixture into a cigarette that was so tight that it was about the diameter of a kitchen match.

A good roller could make 500 joints from the marijuana-tobacco mixture, which would then go to the pushers for $.75 a piece, and move on from there to permanent inmates for $1 or transient inmates for $1.25. Thus, $30-an-ounce marijuana outside the walls quickly became worth $250 by the time it was sold to the ultimate users.

With a turnover of 500 to 700 transient inmates a week, there was always a ready market of people who had to have a drug of some kind to lessen the initial feeling of shock from really being in a penitentiary.

Almost everyone could scratch up a dollar or two to buy a few "pinwheel" joints, as they were called. But cocaine was a different story. Whereas an ounce of crappy marijuana cost about $30 outside the walls, an ounce of cocaine was more like $1,500. This was big money to inmates who had to be wary if they had more than $15 in their possession. Thus, only a few inmates had the resources to play the cocaine game, and these people tended to group together in a buyers' syndicate.

With marijuana, there might be three or four guards who were bringing in the evil weed to inmate buyers, and the total weight of all the stuff being brought in by the various sources was probably about a pound a week. If any more came in, sales would slow down, which didn't do anyone any good because the middlemen and pushers would get very nervous about having to keep the stuff in their possession for longer times. On the other hand, the cocaine market in the prison could only support about an ounce of the white powder a month.

The head of the syndicate that financed the cocaine buys was the man who occupied the bunk right above me. Patrick Leahy was a burglar from Miami who had spent 20 of his 35 years on the planet on the three-in/one-out plan. He was a fast-talking street hustler who had grown up in New York but had then gravitated south to Miami to relieve the nouveau riche of the drug trade of some of their ill-gotten material possessions. Patrick was a handsome Irishman with a devoted wife of 15 years. Whenever Patrick had to go back to prison to serve a sentence, he and his wife would work as a team to find a guard to bring cocaine into the joint. Once Patrick had the goods, he'd do the usual cutting, then sell the half-gram "threads" for $60 a piece.

Patrick wasn't an idiot. He kept his mouth shut about what he was doing, but his hustle was happening right under my nose, and I quickly figured it out.

Every Saturday, without fail, Patrick's wife would arrive for a visit. She'd bring up a quarter-ounce of cocaine packed into a tampon. After her visit with her husband, she'd drive her car over to a local grocery store where she would meet up with a female guard who worked at Lake Butler and whom they paid handsomely to bring the cocaine-loaded tampon into the prison. Patrick's wife would give the guard the tampon plus a $300 fee to make the delivery.

On Monday morning, Patrick cleaned the windows and mirrors in the visitor's park and law library. As he was cleaning, he was also waiting for the female guard to use the only ladies' rest room in the administrative building, which was the one in the visitor's park. The female guard would use the rest room and then leave. Once she had left, Patrick would take his cleaning equipment, prop open the door to the ladies' rest room and begin cleaning the mirror. It only took him a second to retrieve the tampon that had been deposited in the trash can.

On Fridays, he would reverse the process. While cleaning the ladies' room, he'd throw a pocket-size package of Kleenex in the trash can. At 1:58 P.M. he'd finish the bathroom and move on to the windows so he could watch his contact enter the bathroom at 2 P.M. and pick up the package of Kleenex, which contained the money that was to be given to his wife the next afternoon. The guard was getting $300 a week for her delivery services, and Patrick's wife was taking home $500.

Patrick had a gut feeling that Joe and I knew what he was doing. One Friday afternoon, after he had made his drop-off, he caught Joe and me in the law library by ourselves and asked if he should stop or change his procedures. We said we didn't know what he was talking about.

"I don't do it so much for the money," he said as he offered Joe a cigarette. "It's kind of something my wife and I can do together that keeps us feeling like a team. Plus, I don't lose that edge; you know, keep those senses and instincts alert so when I get back on the street I haven't lost anything."

The big worry of the people involved in the drug business inside the joint was not so much that of guards catching them in the act of selling to another inmate, but rather snitches seeing a guard-inmate transfer of some kind, thus causing the guard to get fired and closing off a hard-to-come-by supply line. This was a big loss when it happened, but it was nothing when compared to the economic aberration in the marijuana trade that occurred when Johnny Jeff Jennings arrived to take over the swing shift as the floor boss of the dormitory I lived in.

The new dorm boss was only in his mid-20s. He had the accent of a north Florida native, but didn't have the beer gut, crew cut, and constantly pissed-off demeanor that all the other dorm bosses had. In fact, Mr. Jennings looked like he worked out, wore his hair in a long perm, and wore glasses.

All the other dorm bosses didn't do much but sit in their cages, read magazines, and watch TV. Just about the only time they'd leave their steel cages was to make the required inmate counts or walk over to the canteen for a cup of coffee. However, right from his first day on the job, Mr. Jennings was different. He'd be out among the inmates, asking people their names, where they were from, then shootin' the shit about whatever the inmates wanted to talk about.

This "get-acquainted" period was quickly followed by the beginning of Mr. Jennings' "small-favors" era. Once he knew who inmates were, he told them not to call him Mr. Jennings, but rather Johnny Jeff, that was unless another guard was around, in which case Boss Johnny Jeff would be OK. Then, rather than make inmates wait till the 7 P.M. mail call, when the dorm boss would walk through the bunks taking an evening count and handing out the day's mail, Boss Johnny Jeff began passing out the mail to individuals right after he came on duty. He'd turn the TV on early so the blacks could watch *Soul Train*, and he took the fear of a bust out of the after-hours canteen operators by occasionally buying a candy bar from them.

Everyone liked Boss Johnny Jeff. He hassled no one, the card games could go on with no worries, the dope smokers didn't have to lie under beds to share their pinwheel joints, and the buck drinkers could enjoy their evening cocktails in the TV room without fear that the dorm boss was going to come by and randomly sample the cold drink can they were sipping from to see if it contained alcohol.

Boss Johnny Jeff was one of the boys, especially to the 15 or so white inmates who were about the same age as he. Boss Johnny Jeff hung out with these guys. He brought them in hard-core porn magazines, and that was quickly followed by presents of marijuana cigarettes.

The guys Boss Johnny Jeff was yucking it up with were post-jitterbug chronologically; however, their mental maturity wasn't that advanced. They couldn't seem to realize that they had a great thing going and they could preserve it only by not talking about it. There was no way they could keep quiet about the fact that not only were they getting marijuana from a guard, but they were also getting it for free.

The temptation to be a big shot and pass this secret was just too great. Word quickly reached the inmates, whose marijuana importing and sales business made them a comfortable inside-the-joint income, that there was new competition in the joint and Boss Johnny Jeff's price couldn't possibly be undercut.

There was no possible solution to this problem except to prime the snitches, get Boss Johnny Jeff's marijuana giveaway compromised, and then get back to business as usual.

When I saw the dorm laundry guy, who delivered clean socks and underwear to my bunk, walking around doing his daily chores with a fat marijuana joint stuck in his mouth, I figured it wouldn't be long before Boss Johnny Jeff was soon to be Ex-Boss Johnny Jeff. But Boss Johnny Jeff was smarter than I, or the snitches schooling about to gain information, gave him credit for.

Everyone assumed that Boss Johnny Jeff was bringing in marijuana for his buddies to sell and that he was reaping some good money to supplement his dorm boss salary. However, this wasn't the case. Boss Triple J was only handing out individual joints for personal consumption and had no intention of being anything more than a good guy helping his convict buddies get through the day a little more easily.

The buzz around the dorms was unmistakable: Boss Triple J was under surveillance and was going to get arrested. But that never happened. He immediately figured out that some of the guys he was blessing with free joints were compelled to tell everyone they knew about their good fortune, and he ended his marijuana giveaway.

The snitches couldn't provide anything concrete to their contacts, and the guards who really were smuggling in dope for sale couldn't catch him in the act so they could get him busted. The marijuana trade went back to normal, and the only difference was that the guys who spent their evening hours hanging with Boss Triple J got no more free joints to smoke.

Boss Johnny Jeff Jennings took Joe and me into his confidence when he showed Joe an article he had cut out of the Gainesville paper about how Florida was using some of its National Guard troops to fly helicopter surveillance looking for marijuana patches. Boss Triple J wanted to know if Joe thought that would hold up as legal probable cause for law enforcement to get a search warrant.

I researched the current cases in the Florida and federal case books and turned them over to Joe. Joe took a look and told Triple J that, in his opinion, a search warrant based on air surveillance would probably hold up in court.

What Boss Johnny Jeff was really excited about was not being a dorm boss, it was growing marijuana. He knew I had smuggled grass from Colombia, and he wanted to know the nuts and bolts of how it worked.

In a private conversation, Boss Johnny gave me a phone number and told me that when I got out I should call that number and he might have some work for me. He had grown up in Starke, and a couple of his relatives were guards. He knew that if a prison guard ever got arrested, the authorities would make him do his time in a federal joint because of the chance that he'd get killed by some inmate who recognized him from his prison guard days.

"I know enough about prisons to know guards have to almost kill somebody before they're going to get time," Boss Triple J said, "but if I do I definitely want to be at a federal camp."

"That's correct thinking," Joe added, "but what are you doing that's illegal?"

Boss Triple J didn't answer that question till the day he quit being our dorm boss and left the state of Florida Bureau of Corrections. "The crop's harvested and sold," he told me. "I got about 300 pounds out of these three small patches I planted on some land around here. Great stuff and I got tons of seeds for next year."

Boss Johnny Jeff went on to say that the guy who bought the whole crop was from New York. He owned some farm-land in upstate New York, and they were going to be part-ners, with his seeds and the other guy's land to grow a crop next summer.

"Call the number I gave you next fall, because this guy's sales are mainly in California. You could fly the stuff out for us."

"I'll do that," I answered. "Tell me, why were you a guard? Was it to avoid jail time if your growing operation got busted or to make contacts inside the joint for sales and transportation?"

"Both," he said. "This is a great place to recruit a crew. I think some of these old boys will work out real well for me."

I never called Johnny Jeff Jennings when I got out of the joint, but I have no doubt that he did very well in the marijuana business. He's the only criminal I've ever run across who gave so much thought to how to make his prison years as painless as pos-sible and then do something about it *before* he got caught.

SOME GAY BOYS DRESS UP, SOME DON'T

MUCH OF WHAT THE MEDIA FIND fascinating about life behind bars centers on the sexual tension prevalent in a single-sex living environment. Animal studies have shown that after a few weeks of living exclusively with males, laboratory mice will turn homosexual and start trying to fornicate with their fellow males. There is a homosexual culture in prisons, but it isn't quite the meshing of gang rapes and an English boarding school that the media would like you to believe.

There are only three viable options for an inmate who has decided that homosexual sex in the joint is better than no sex at all. The first is to become a predator homosexual and force himself on the object of his desire. However, this act is violent and is certainly not the way to find a companion to snuggle and share a relationship with during his prison years.

A second choice is to court and woo the one he's infatuated with until his truelove consents to a proposal of homosexual love behind bars. With these first two choices, definite male/female roles exist. Often, the male role player doesn't even think that 167 he's in a homosexual relationship, but rather considers himself a heterosexual who had to alter his orientation so he could have a sex life while in the joint.

The third possibility for a sex life behind bars involves inmates who already know they are homosexual before they enter prison, and those who realize it and come out of the closet while they are locked up. These people exist in any prison in the world. Not only do they exist, but this group of admitted homosexuals has the best social life in the joint. For these guys, the sexual games and preferences they liked on the outside can move right behind the bars with them.

Everyone entering a penitentiary for the first time has the fear that he might find himself in a rape situation. But the odds that any inmate would be singled out for a predatory homosexual attack are minuscule. Even if you enter the joint looking like Tom Cruise, the predators who might have access to you are not going to be leering within striking distance, watching your every move and poised to pounce for your asshole at the first opportunity.

You enter prison worrying about protecting your asshole, and immediately you get more worried because of the language you hear directed at you from other inmates. This is a verbal initiation that is tailored to make a new inmate think his worst fears are true.

When I was getting processed into Lake Butler, two black guys had the job of taking an inmate's street clothes and boxing them up and marking them so they could be returned when the inmate was released. Everyone handing in clothes to these guys got a sizing up and verbal comment on how long they'd last before they'd be sucking dicks. For example, the guy in front of me in line elicited the comment, "We're going to tell Mahmoud about you."

When the skinny, 30-year-old white guy made the mistake of asking who Mahmoud was, he played right into the act as far as the two black guys were concerned.

"Mahmoud," one of the black guys said in dead seriousness, "he's one of them Black Muslims in D-dorm. You'll recognize him; he's about 6 foot 6, maybe 250—a *big* guy."

"Yeah, so what's he got to do with me?" the white questioned. "I'm no Black fucking Muslim."

"Well, if Mahmoud likes you, then he'll be stroking into your chitlins and finish up by letting your brains get a taste of the mix. You dig?"

The white guy looked worried as he walked away. I was next, and I got the following appraisal, "You're pretty big, slim. That's good because the niggers with them horse dicks, they can't get it all the way in with some of them little-bitty-sized white boys. I'll bet you can take 12, maybe 14 inches."

This pre-greeting to Lake Butler was followed by the assigning of bunks. At this stage, you'd hear inmates within hearing distance asking each other who the new fuck boy was or if they knew where the sissy was from.

This was the welcome that awaited a new inmate who didn't have some homeboys in residence who could immediately vouch for him being a good guy. I just smiled when I heard the comments. Nate from the county jail had told me that you didn't need to worry unless someone actually tried to get physical with you, that the talk was all just playing with your mind to see how you'd react.

However, the talk did cause the guy in front of me at the clothing checkpoint to panic. He and I were assigned to the same dormitory, and as I sat on my bunk that first evening trying to figure out which guy was Joe Peel, I noticed a big black guy approach the bunk of my check-in mate.

The black guy had curlers in his hair with a nylon stocking covering them. All he was wearing was a pair of boxer shorts so it was easy to see his incredible physique. I adjusted my position on the bunk so I could hear the conversation about to take place.

The new guy four bunks away from me was arranging his below-the-bunk locker. His shirt was off, revealing a con-cave upper torso and hairless skin that had him looking a bit like a plucked chicken hanging in a butcher shop.

"I'm Mahmoud; Latrelle said you wanted to see me."

"Fuck no, man," the white guy said.

"Oh" was all the fierce-looking guy in curlers said as he turned and walked away.

As soon as the man in curlers had left to go back to his own bunk, the white inmate grabbed a T-shirt, threw it on, and double-timed it to the dorm boss' cage.

Five minutes later, a guard escorted the white guy back to his bunk where he grabbed his shoebox full of possessions and disappeared into the world of protective custody, never to be seen again.

As the guard led him out of the dorm, they walked right past where Latrelle, who had been one of the men checking our clothing, was standing.

"Guess who works in protective custody?" Latrelle whispered. "Mahmoud. He'll be coming for those chitlins tomorrow."

As soon as the area was clear of the guard and his charge, Latrelle started laughing, then calling his homeboys over to hear the story. Meanwhile, Mahmoud just went about his business of working on his jerrycurls; he had no idea that Latrelle had set him up to be the heavy in his "worst nightmare" jailhouse joke.

Homosexual innuendo in prison was nothing more than playground shit-talking. It lasted about a day, and that would be the last you heard of it—that is unless you were a homosexual and wanted to make contacts in the gay social life that existed in the joint.

Since almost all the permanent inmates at Lake Butler were in their late 20s or older, we didn't have any December/June romances going on. However, we did have a few inmates who would do the standard prison drag dress-up routine. Lake Butler was strict about what the dress-up boys could and could not do to project their sexuality. For example, no makeup or nonissue prison clothing was allowed.

The dress-up boys got around the makeup rules by constantly plucking their eyebrows and other facial hairs to achieve a macabre look as if they had just come from the undertaker's. Eyelid tattoo work did a great job of resembling eye shadow, and some of the boys would make a homebrew of human blood and candle wax that sufficed as lipstick.

The clothing restrictions were circumvented through creative tailoring. The boys would modify prison-issue pants to look like fashionable bell bottoms, alter their shirts to resemble halter tops with shoulder pads, or revamp their tennis shoes into platform high heels.

The dress-up boys were a tight-knit social clique and probably the only social group in the prison that was integrated. Black, white, or Hispanic didn't mean a thing to this group; the only trait that counted was that an inmate wanted to be one of the girls.

On weekends or after work hours, these guys would put on a pair of short shorts to show off their shaved legs and they'd strut about doing their comedy act. They always seemed to be in a great mood, and they were at their funniest when they'd be teasing around with the guards, asking them if they were getting enough sex at home.

It was impossible not to notice the dress-up boys around the prison grounds. They tried to stand out, and they did. However, even though I'd been at the prison a few months, I'd never talked to any of them . . . that is until Burton Jeters paid Joe and me a visit in the law library one day.

Burton was the most effeminate of the dress-up boys. He was a white man in his late 30s who was sent to prison for burglary. He and a partner were caught breaking into the upscale shops on Worth Avenue in Palm Beach, Florida, where they would steal women's clothing and accessories.

Joe Peel and Burton went back 10 years in the Florida prison system. Burton had been in and out of prisons, not only for burglary, but also for prostitution, drugs, and fraud. Therefore, when Burton Jeters sat down to talk to Joe about some legal matters that he thought needed litigating, I stopped working on the parole appeal I was writing so I could participate in the conversation.

Burton, with the seriousness of a *Roe* vs. *Wade* defender in front of the U.S. Supreme Court, began laying out the incredible miscarriage of justice that had befallen him at sick call.

"Here's the story, Joe," Burton began in a newly acquired New York lisp he had picked up and perfected from one of the other dress-up boys. "I was cutting hair at the beauty salon when I got these horrible cramps in my stomach. It was time for my monthlies, but I'd never had them like that before."

"Wait a minute," Joe interrupted. "What's a monthly?"

"Joe, I was having my *period*. I had menstrual cramps, and they were severe. I told Boss Dugan what was happening, and he told me to go to sick call."

"So they gave you some pills, and you went back to work?" Joe interjected, trying to speed up the drama in Burton's story.

"Yes, but my complaint is that the nurse wouldn't give me a medical so I didn't have to go back to the salon and cut hair. I was in pain, and she enjoyed seeing me suffer. You know what she did? She gave me a Kotex and told me to stick it up any hole that existed below my waist."

"Did you go back to the barber shop?"

"Yes, I did," Burton answered. "Boss Dugan said that if I left, he'd write me up, so I had to stay there, on the verge of fainting for the rest of the day."

"OK," Joe said. "Why don't you just write up a beef form about the nurse? I don't think this is something you can sue the state about."

"Then what about next month? I'll get the nasty cramps again, and I'll just have to go through the same thing. I want sick call to acknowledge that some of us do get cramps, and if they're bad enough, we should be excused from work."

"I see your point, Burton," Joe replied. "I'll write a memo to Colonel Dooly, and we'll see where the paperwork takes us, OK? Now, how's everything else going?"

With the problem of Burton's monthlies on the back burner, Joe wanted to hear some of the gossip making the rounds in the dorms. Burton filled us in on who was fucking whom, plus how Boss Dugan had given him a pair of black satin bikini briefs in thanks for some sewing Burton had done for Dugan's wife.

"And I just found this out," Burton continued. "Tim who runs the commissary, he's using that storage room back there for orgies every night after he closes. He's going to get caught—everybody but everybody is dying to go."

For the first time since Joe and Burton started talking, I had a question. "You mean Tim Wyatt? I didn't know he was a dress-up boy."

"Joe, your friend here doesn't know much, does he?" Burton said in a snippy voice. "Tim does not dress up."

"He lives two bunks up from me," I added. "I've never seen any of your group hanging around."

"Oh, is that so," Burton retorted. "See if you can grasp this point—you don't have to dress up to like to fuck."

Joe didn't like the way Burton was acting toward me, and before Burton got too bitchy, Joe wrapped up the gossip session so Burton would leave, and Joe and I could get back to work.

As soon as Burton had gone, I asked Joe if we had a file on Tim Wyatt. "Did you know he was gay?" I asked. "He only lives 15 feet away from me, and I had no idea."

"Do you know what he's in for?" Joe asked as he glanced at Tim's file.

"Selling pornography," I answered.

"It's a lot bigger than that," Joe continued. "Tim's lawyer is an old law school classmate of mine. Tim and his partner own a string of bookshops, clubs, strip joints, and even a mail-order facility. He probably sells more dirty magazines and movies than anyone in the state outside of the Miami-Fort Lauderdale area."

"So what's he doing in here? I thought there was First Amendment protection to sell that stuff."

"There is," Joe replied, "but Tim got caught up in the politics of a Florida law passed a few years ago to keep porno shops out of neighborhoods that didn't want them. This case could end up at the U.S. Supreme Court, but I think he'll win it before it has to get that far."

"I'm still surprised that he is a homo," I said. "Living that close to him, you'd think it would have been obvious."

His homosexuality might not have been obvious to me, but what was obvious from the first time I met Tim Wyatt was that he was one of the few people in the joint who had money to spread around. I thought the constant flow of goods and services being delivered to his bunk was because he was an economic engine. I never guessed that all his visitors were to a degree entwined with the homosexual social world, of a non-dress-up-boy nature, that existed behind the bars of Lake Butler.

Tim was a white man in his mid-30s, who wore glasses
and combed his hair forward in a Julius Caesar cut to try
to cover up the fact that he was getting very thin on top.
However, the regal characteristics stopped with his
appearance. As a personality, Tim was quick, slightly arro-
gant, and sarcastic. Until you got used to his conversational style, it was like talking to a road-weary stand-up
comic who believed he should be a star on network television rather than having to play comedy club one-nighters
to support himself.

Tim wasn't happy about being in prison. He felt he was
being made an example of by a bunch of Bible-belt politicians from Jacksonville, and he was right. All he had to do
was sign an affidavit that he would close his stores within
the Jacksonville city limits and that he would not sue the
city, and he would have been released immediately.
However, Tim and his partner had decided to fight the case
in the courts. Tim was doing the time, and his partner was
on the outside paying the lawyer's bill.

The job of running the inmate commissary at the permanent dorms was the only job assignment inside the joint
that paid an inmate worker a salary. The prison system had
tried every possible arrangement regarding the inmate commissary. When guards ran it, they were caught stealing.
When inmates ran it, they were caught stealing. Finally,
they had decided to select an inmate who was one year
short of his sentence and to pay him a salary, figuring these
two precautions would eliminate any reason an inmate
would have to steal from the state.

However, it didn't make any difference. Accepting the
job of inmate commissary clerk was like becoming an NBA
head coach: you had the job for awhile, and then you were
fired in disgrace. No inmate had lasted at the job for more
than two months, and the termination ritual was always the

same. At 7 A.M. a sign would be put on the door by a guard that the commissary was closed for a spot inventory. The guards would go through the stock, checking things off on their computer sheets, and about 15 minutes later the ex-inmate commissary clerk would be led away in handcuffs. Within a day, a new inmate would be offered the position, and the commissary would begin the cycle all over again.

However, the prospect of running the commissary was more than most convicts at Lake Butler could resist. Not only did you have the cash take, in the neighborhood of $700 a day, passing through your hands, but you also had the merchandise under your control. Therefore, between the weekly stock inventory, you could sell items on credit. The credit terms were standard jailhouse loan rates—100 percent interest a week. Everyone who took that job figured he could outsmart the prison officials. He could make the salary, cover the bad debts from people who didn't pay off their loans, and make a couple of hundred bucks a week extra from the good loans. The money was there, the work environment was good, but no one could pull it off . . . that is until Tim Wyatt took the job.

When I showed up at Lake Butler, Tim's job was sorting books in the library. He and I became friendly, not only because our bunks were so close together, but because I was in the library every day looking for books to read. We'd talk about books, plus exchange magazine reading material that was sent in to us by mail. Tim was a smart guy and well read, and I liked hearing his sarcastic slant on prison life and the personalities of some of the guards we were in daily contact with.

Tim took the commissary job two weeks before Burton Jeters gossiped to Joe and me about Tim's sexual preference. Before he took the commissary job, the goods and services he was buying were the standard laundry service, bed making, and after-hours canteen snacks that just about everyone who didn't smoke much and generated $15 a week in income could afford.

However, after Tim took over the commissary, the activity around his bunk increased dramatically. From the moment he woke up to the time he fell asleep, he was like a queen bee with drones of worker bees buzzing about him. His coffee, orange juice, and first cigarette of the day were delivered to him in bed. When he was done with his beverages, he went to the latrine where a special chair was set up so he could be shaved by another inmate. He didn't go to the chow hall anymore since all his meals were delivered to the commissary. Furthermore, he had become a patron of the arts in the hobby shop. Tim had Joe Peel and the other three master leatherworkers creating anything he or they could think of that would be neat to make out of leather. Not only were Joe and the guild making wallets, purses, and belts for Tim, but also scrabble boards with leather letters, backgammon boards, chess boards, monopoly boards, picture frames, cowboy hats, and even a hand-tooled leather vest with a pornographic motif. He was spending so much money, and so conspicuously, that after about two weeks, Stuart the Stud began a pool to bet on how many more days Tim would last before he was arrested for theft of state property and carted away from the commissary. No one thought Tim was going to make it more than two weeks beyond the startup of the pool.

The guards knew something was going on, and at least once a day Tim would be stopped and searched to see if he had more than the allowed $15 on his person. Tim would empty his pockets, then undergo a pat-down, but he was always OK.

Not only were the guards baffled, but so were the inmates, because Tim refused from the start to give any credit at the commissary. He might do a little favor, like hold back a newspaper or a pint of chocolate ice cream, but if the favor involved money—forget it. Tim was running a no-tricks-allowed commissary. The game had changed, and a lot of the inmates who needed that end-of-the-week commissary loan to get their items were unhappy about it.

On day 24 of Tim's rein as commissary clerk, the auditors showed up. At 7 A.M., the closed-for-inventory sign went up, and a crowd formed around the commissary door expecting to see Tim being led out in handcuffs. However, at 7:30, the auditors left, and Tim opened the dutch doors of the commissary, ready to do business. He had survived the audit and still had his job.

What Tim was doing was simple. Every morning the commissary received 20 morning papers: 10 from Gainesville and 10 from Jacksonville. These papers were dropped off at the administrative building, shrink-wrapped in plastic. At 6:30 A.M. Tim would pick them up, and at 7 they would be available for purchase.

Tim and his partner knew the person who distributed the Jacksonville newspaper. Twice a week, Tim's partner would insert a $10 bill between pages 29 and 30 of each of the 10 papers marked for delivery to Lake Butler Reception and Medical Center. The papers would be wrapped in plastic and were not opened till Tim prepared them for sale at the commissary. This was bringing Tim in an extra $200 a week for comfort and life-style enhancements.

Tim had no desire or need to steal from the inventory or charge inmates outrageous terms of interest. The guards never guessed that Tim would be bringing money into the prison via the commissary. They kept up the pressure because they were sure he had somehow invented a new way to cook the books to cover up what he was taking.

But smuggling in money was not the only need that the commissary job allowed Tim to fill. He had sexual needs that had been curtailed since he entered prison. A quickie blow-job was possible in the back of the library, but the group orgies that he preferred were impossible because there was no place private enough that a four-man orgy could be pulled off without the risk of getting caught.

However, this lack of privacy problem ended when Tim took over the commissary job. Adjacent to the commissary was a storeroom for excess inventory, and Tim controlled the only key, other than Colonel Dooly's. The warden didn't want his guards to be tempted to steal, so he issued no keys to anyone who worked in the dorms. If there was theft from the commissary, then it would have to come from the inmate commissary clerk because he was the only other person in the building who had a key.

Now, Tim not only had plenty of whip-out cash that had every dress-up boy and homosexual sucking up to him, but he also controlled the one room in the dorm area where a sexual act couldn't be ruined by a guard barging in unexpectedly.

The commissary closed at 7:00. At this time of night, there were only the four dorm bosses in the H-shaped complex that housed all the permanent inmates. Usually, these bosses stayed in their cages and watched TV. Once in a while, a boss might stroll over to the hobby shop or hang around the corridor by the commissary, but that was rare. Thus, from 7:00 to 9:00, when the supervisor arrived to run the last count of the day and make sure everyone was on their assigned bunks, inmates could easily move about the building without attracting any attention from the guards.

Right after Tim shut the dutch doors of the commissary, he would begin letting guys in one at a time to the adjacent storage room. Tim had from 8:00, by which time he had finished the accounting he had to do to close out the day's commissary receipts, to 8:45 to kiss, hug, grope, suck, and

fuck with the other inmates he had invited to his back-
room soiree. As the host, Tim would offer the party goers
cigarettes, coffee, and ice cream so everyone would relax
and get in a silly mood.

I was in the hobby shop most nights, and if no one
was running a lathe or grinder we could hear the giggling
and laughing coming from the storeroom. Burton Jeters
had told us that Tim's parties were the height of chic, and
if he didn't get invited at least once a week he would get
so depressed that he wouldn't even want to wear his
black satin bikini! Tim knew some of the boys were
beginning to bitch about a lack of invitations, and he
knew that people in the hobby shop could hear the party
sounds coming through the shared wall, but he was having too much fun and didn't think anyone really cared
about what he was doing in the storeroom.

The end came three months after Tim had started running the commissary. Once a month, usually in the evening,
Colonel Dooly would show up unannounced at the permanent dorms. He might audit a GED class, play some horse-
shoes, or hang around the commissary and let inmates voice
their complaints to him.

On this particular evening, the prison warden chose to
drop in at the hobby shop. Colonel Dooly was a fair guy, and
he was genuinely liked by the inmates. He had come up
through the ranks, starting as a guard about the time Joe
Peel entered prison. He knew the three major inmate beefs
centered around food, mail, and visiting privileges, and by
keeping the inmates happy in these areas, he was assured
that his prison would run relatively smoothly.

At 8:15 the hobby shop was a busy place. The leatherworkers were tapping on their leather, the woodworking
guys were using the lathes and sanding machines to make
chessboards and inlaid boxes, and painters were working

on canvas to create oil paintings of inmates and their families from Polaroid snapshots that could be taken in the visitor's park.

When the warden walked in, the activity came to an immediate stop, for the hobbyists expected him to be followed by an escort of guards coming to arrest someone for a violation of a prison rule. However, this night there was no one else, just Colonel Dooly coming in to hang around and see what everyone was working on.

Joe took the lead and welcomed the colonel to the hobby shop. Colonel Dooly was offered a cup of coffee, and then he just moseyed about the room, making small talk with the workers about the projects they were creating.

When Colonel Dooly got to the woodworkers, he noticed that they were making some scale-model airplanes out of oak. I had contracted for these to be made, and we were having fun creating one-inch-long jet engines to go on a Learjet fuselage. The finished products were obviously homemade, but they had a folk art quality about them that made you want to pick one up and examine it, applauding the detail of the carver's work.

Colonel Dooly did just that. He was play-flying a DC-3 through the air, and asking Cowboy Ned how he got the model balanced so nicely. So the colonel could hear his answer, Cowboy Ned shut off the lathe and sander he had been using, and suddenly the room was quiet enough that everyone could plainly hear the laughter and conversation coming from the adjacent commissary storeroom.

"Tim," said a voice from next door in a New York lisp, "why don't you dip that one-eyed party animal in this glass of root beer, then put it in my mouth, and I'll make you a root beer float."

It was impossible not to surmise that a group orgy was in progress on the other side of the wall, and those of us in the hobby shop hoped that the colonel was having so much fun flying the wood aircraft that he somehow wouldn't pick up on what was being said in the adjacent room.

"What's going on in there?" the colonel remarked to no one in particular as he brought the DC-3 in for a landing on the workbench.

Cowboy Ned got the sander running again, but it was too late. The colonel put down his cup of coffee and left the hobby shop to investigate the voices he had heard on the other side of the wall.

The colonel had the only other key to the storeroom besides Tim's. No one in the hobby shop had a chance to even bang on the wall to let the party goers know the warden of the prison was about to crash their event. Within seconds, the colonel had opened the dutch doors to the commissary and then opened the door to the storeroom.

The freeze-frame first look Colonel Dooly got was like something out of a Picasso mural. For the night's festivities, the regular white light bulb in the storage room had been replaced with a low-wattage red bulb that provided just enough light to silhouette how the bodies of the four participants were linked together.

Burton Jeters was giving Tim a blow job, while each was being fucked in the ass by two other guys I didn't know. The four had the wide-eyed look of a startled teenager caught in her bedroom with her boyfriend by parents who weren't supposed to be home for several more hours.

Tim's sex organ immediately wilted and fell away from Burton's mouth at the same time that the two other guys were pulling their dicks out of the sodomy holes. The colonel just stood there taking in the sight as everyone from the hobby shop regrouped in the corridor to see what was going to happen.

"Colonel Dooly!" exclaimed Burton as he was pulling up his

pants. "Looks like fun, doesn't it? We'd love for you to join us, but you have to use a condom—we practice safe sex here."

A howl broke out from the gallery behind the warden, and even he smiled at Burton's ad lib. Then he got on his walkie-talkie, and within five minutes the goon squad had arrived to take Tim, Burton, and the two other inmates away in handcuffs.

The authorities always threatened to take a violation of the rules to an outside court; however, unless the arrest was for assault with a weapon where someone was hurt or killed, they never did. Thus, Tim and Burton found themselves being sentenced to 30 days in the hole.

The hole was a 4 x 8-foot cement cell. The occupant received only beans and water, and he slept on a piece of Styrofoam one inch off the cockroach-infested floor. The one light bulb was on all the time, and no TV, radio, or reading material was allowed. All the occupant could do was talk to the people in the cells next to him.

Tim had only been in the hole two days when he got the good news. He had won his appeal and was to be released from prison immediately.

However, even though Tim was out of the joint, that didn't mean he was going to just forget the embarrassment that Colonel Dooly had caused him by intruding on his storeroom orgy. Like clockwork, on the fifth of each month, a package would arrive in the mailroom addressed to Colonel Dooly. In this package would be the new monthly editions of 23 pornographic magazines that Tim's company sold in its stores. Sergeant Wilkerson, who ran the mailroom, told Joe and me that the note that accompanied the magazines was always the same: "Colonel, if you can fit this over it, then it's party size." A condom was taped to the note, and it was signed "Fondly, Tim."

GREASING THE WHEELS

W HEN YOU LIVE YOUR LIFE AS AN OUTLAW, two of the fairy tales you most want to believe in are, one, that no matter how red-handed you are caught, there are lawyers for hire who *never* lose a case and, two, if you somehow do happen to be convicted (as unlikely as that might be) that there are judges who can be bribed so that you'll never have to go to prison—which stands in blatant, though widely ignored, contradiction to the first fairy tale. The key is to know who these lawyers and judges are and then have enough cash on hand so that the wheels of justice can be properly greased to turn in your favor.

By the time I entered prison, I had attained some firsthand experience in dealing with these "magic men" who were so smart and so well connected that they supposedly never lost a case.

Bribes and payoffs had worked perfectly in my smuggling group's missions to Colombia, Jamaica, and the Bahamas. It was part of doing business, and we were happy to pay. A few thousand dollars paid to a Bahamian customs man Mike Buff knew got us the patrol boat schedule for the U.S. Coast Guard cruising in Bahamian waters. A $5,000-payment to 185 the customs people on Caicos allowed us to land, refuel, and proceed without filling out any documents or flight plans. Plus, during a fouled-up mission in a DC-3 to Colombia when the Colombian army detained Gene and me for unlawful entry, it took our in-country man only 10 minutes and $8,000 for it to be decided that there had been some mistake and that we were free to leave the country with our prized airplane. As long as it was just illegal drugs we were dealing in, there never was any problem in paying for the services we needed or buying our way out of any unexpected problems.

Mike was convinced that if we ever got caught by U.S. law enforcement we'd be able to buy ourselves out of any situation, just as we had been able to do in the drug-source countries we operated in. I didn't agree with him, although I hoped he was right. I couldn't buy that the American justice system was so corrupt that we could count on being able to stay out of prison based on which lawyer we hired and how much money we were able to pay out in bribes.

As it turned out, Mike and I got to test our opposing views on the bribability of the U.S. justice system within a year of starting our smuggling enterprise, when we were caught with the 1,200 pounds of marijuana in Stuart. This was one occasion when I truly did not want to be able to say, "I told you so."

But 27 months and $40,000 dollars later, Mike's theory had been proven wrong: Melvin Kliner's appeal magic hadn't worked. Mike fled, and I was going to prison for a crime I had committed—what a concept!

Once in prison, I thought it would be almost impossible for an inmate to be involved in a bribery attempt. However, that was not the case. I had direct knowledge of two attempts to bribe state employees. The first was an attempt to pay off a district court judge to reduce a sentence, and the second was my own effort to bribe one of the seven members of the Florida Parole Commission to get me an early release.

Hal Huppman checked into the permanent inmate dorms at Lake Butler with a big reputation and an even bigger ego. Hal was the self-described "mogul of marijuana," who boasted that he was the biggest grass smuggler in the United States. *High Times* magazine got wind of Huppman's claims and did a profile on him in the magazine that portrayed him as a criminal prince who liked the notoriety because he was sure that a majority of Americans were 100 percent behind what he was doing.

Getting a favorable piece in the nation's number one magazine that advocates the fun and harmlessness of illegal drugs while you are an active smuggler does not show good judgment. It didn't take long for the mogul of marijuana to take the big fall, and when it happened the tens of millions of marijuana smokers in the United States did not march on the county courthouse where he was being tried and demand his release—perhaps a bit of amotivational syndrome?

Hal got nailed for conspiracy to import and distribute marijuana. He was given a nine-year sentence, and right after he was sentenced, he expressed his newly gained knowledge that, in retrospect, maybe it would have been wise to avoid the publicity until after he had retired from being a smuggler.

From the day Hal arrived at Lake Butler, he made it clear that he was too rich and too important to have his life disrupted by a nine-year prison sentence, which meant he would have to serve three years before even being considered for parole. He confidently told Joe and me that he had the best attorneys working on his case, and if his appeal didn't produce his release, he had contacts and had made big political contributions to the governor of Florida, which could get him a full pardon.

Hal was so confident of his connections to the governor that he implied that not only was he buying his way out by way of a political contribution to the governor's campaign, but if you were a friend of his and believed his bullshit, then you, too, might be getting a pardon.

This kind of rhetoric wasn't unheard of at Lake Butler. A lot of people made up stories that involved convoluted plots about how "their people" were owed big favors by the governor, an appeals court judge, or a parole commissioner, and how this was going to result in an early release for them. Whether these stories were fabricated to make the teller feel like a big shot around other convicts or just to have something to believe in that spelled release at the end, I never knew, but often a whole cult developed around one of these fairy tales, and you'd have a score of guys sitting around waiting for their pardons from the governor to arrive in the legal mail.

However, when Mogul Hal stated that he was taking names to get on the governor's pardon list, there was more of a frenzy to sign up than with any of the other shit-talker's scripts. Hal was a heavyweight smuggler; *High Times* reported that he was worth more than $10 million, and a lot of guys thought Hal had inside knowledge of something big. They got on Hal's pardon list and believed it was going to happen for them.

Ironically, there was one person of judicial influence who was thinking very hard on how to get Hal out of his prison sentence, but his interest was independent of Hal's lawyers, powerful contacts, or the governor's office—and it had nothing to do with altruism or justice. This proposal was being generated for one reason and one reason only—money. This "broker," Judge Jefferson Davis Hunt, wasn't about to make his offer through Hal's attorneys; instead, he opted to go through a contact who would offer him total deniability in case his plan was exposed—inmate Joe Peel, who was an old law school classmate of Judge Hunt's.

Judge Rex Shoudt had been the district court judge who had presided at the trial and sentencing of Hal Huppman. The trial was routine as far as a conspiracy trial went, and the evidence was overwhelming for conviction. The state had informants, taped conversations, and telephone calls, and the jury was only out one hour before it brought back a guilty verdict. Hal could have received up to 20 years or as little as three. Therefore, the nine-year sentence was close to the middle range and an entirely appropriate sentence.

The Huppman trial had been Judge Shoudt's last; he was retiring from the bench. Any legal matters still dangling in Judge Shoudt's court were assigned to another judge in the same district. The new judge assigned to handle the leftovers from Judge Shoudt's court was Jefferson Davis Hunt.

It's always surprised me why so many Southern judges have these grandiose names that incorporate Confederate heroes. Not only did Judge Hunt have the name of one of the major risk takers in American history, he also shared a problem with his namesake—he was broke.

Judge Jefferson Davis Hunt was on his third marriage, with significant alimony going to the first two Mrs. Jefferson Davis Hunts. He had two kids at expensive eastern universities, and he was a regular on the casino junkets that went from Tampa to Atlantic City. Judge Hunt was mortgaged to the hilt, but no bank wanted to foreclose on him since his more than 20 years of service on the bench had made him a pillar of the community.

Judge Hunt had seen the articles about Hal Huppman

and heard the rumors of what Hal was paying his attorneys to handle his appeal. Furthermore, the judge knew some of the boys close to the governor and had heard off-the-record comments on how much Mogul Hal was spreading around in Tallahassee as he fished for some favorable treatment. The judge now controlled Huppman's case at the district court level, and he had an idea that might work out for everyone involved.

Florida law stated that a person had 60 days from the time of sentencing to file a motion with the sentencing judge asking for a sentence reduction. The judge would then set a date for a hearing, the defense would argue for a reduction, the state would oppose the reduction, and in 98 percent of the cases the sentence would remain the same. A reduction-in-sentence motion was standard legal procedure, and the reduction was rarely ever granted.

By the time Mogul Hal became a permanent inmate at Lake Butler, all he had to show for the hundreds of thousands of dollars he had spent on legal fees and political tribute was that he only had to spend a week at a transition prison before being assigned to Lake Butler. Thus, on the day when Judge Jefferson Davis Hunt visited the law library of ex-judge Joe Peel, there were still 20 days remaining on the legal calendar wherein a motion for a reduction in sentence in Hal's case could be entertained.

Judge Hunt was at Lake Butler as part of a three-man judiciary panel investigating the classification process of assigning inmates to permanent prisons. There had been so many complaints by inmates and their families about South Florida residents being assigned to prisons in the northern part of the state that the head of the Bureau of Prisons requested the governor to assign some non-Bureau people to report on the complaints to prove that there was no bribery or favoritism taking place.

The panel was conducting interviews in an office down the corridor from the law library, and during a break a tall, slender man wearing a three-piece suit strolled over to the law library and knocked on the door.

When I heard the knock, I looked up from the motion I was typing and, seeing a three-piece suit waiting, immediately sprang up and opened the door. We had attorneys and dignitaries drop by all the time, and when a free man showed up, Joe didn't want him to have to wait for even a second. When Joe looked up from his writing, he jumped up to greet the visitor.

"J.D.," said Joe, "what are you doing here?"

"I'm here for the day with a governor's panel," replied Judge Hunt as he shook Joe's hand. "Good to see you haven't quit smoking; there aren't many of us left these days."

Judge Hunt pulled out a pack of Marlboros and offered one to Joe and me. "Judge Hunt, this is Ken Gross," said Joe. "The judge and I went to law school together at Stetson."

"Nice to meet you, sir," I answered.

Whenever Joe had a free-man visitor I would always excuse myself so he and the visitor could talk privately. I'd go out the door and get a drink of water, and if the visit wasn't of a business nature, Joe would open the door and motion that it was OK for me to come back in. With Judge Hunt, the door stayed shut, so I bought an RC Cola from the vending machine and sat down at one of the tables to wait for the judge to conclude his meeting with Joe.

I could see in the large picture window that the judge and Joe weren't joshing around with each other. Joe was reading a letter the judge had produced from his inside coat pocket, and after he finished, he took off his glasses and began cleaning them with his handkerchief—a sure sign that a serious matter was under discussion.

After about 10 minutes, Joe and the judge shook

hands, and the judge left the law library, giving me a quick wave as he padded back to his meeting in the administration building.

When I went back in the law library, I left the door open because we had call-out appointments beginning in 10 minutes. Joe was sitting at his desk puffing on a cigarette and looking at the ceiling. When I had sat down at my desk and was ready to resume my typing, he got up and closed the door so we could have a private conversation.

"I've seen a lot in 20 years in this place," Joe began. "When I was over at Raiford, Warden C.D. Masters said he'd get me an immediate parole if I'd sell out the inmates who had asked me to represent them when they took 10 guards hostage after they couldn't take the horrible conditions any more. But what just happened, I think, takes the cake."

"Are you going to tell me?" I asked.

"If I tell you, you're not going to believe it anyway," Joe said with a teasing smile on his face.

"Come on, you know I'll believe whatever you tell me."

"All right," Joe continued. "Did you see that letter Judge Hunt handed me? He did that because he was afraid of even whispering to me while he was in the law library, because he thought the place might be bugged."

"You think we're bugged in here?" I interrupted.

"No, Colonel Dooly told me he'd never allow that, plus Jack knows his way around listening devices, and he takes this office apart once a month looking for microphones. Anyway, J.D. was so nervous about the words he had written that I thought he was going to collapse when he handed me the proposal to read."

"Let me guess," I injected. "He's going to get you a parole?"

"Not quite," Joe replied. "Judge Jefferson Davis Hunt wants me to set up a bribe."

"You're kidding?"

"I couldn't possibly make this up. He's got it all spelled out on the paper I read. He wants $500,000; if it is paid, he'll cut Hal Huppman's sentence from nine years down to three years. Furthermore, he wouldn't remark against the earliest possible parole date for Hal; Hal could be out of prison in 10 months."

"What's he need you for?" I questioned.

"Because we're going to do the motion for a reduction in sentence from here."

"What?" I exclaimed. "How about his fancy attorneys and political connections?"

"J.D. doesn't trust them," Joe explained. "If the attorneys win a new trial on the appeal, or Hal gets a pardon from the governor, that's fine with J.D. However, since J.D. now has control of the case at the district court level, he's the one who will rule on a reduction-in-sentence motion. All he's offering is to take Hal down to the minimum-sentence area, but that would still have him out of prison way before a successful appeal."

"Won't it look funny to have us filing this reduction-of-sentence motion instead of his lawyers?" I asked.

"J.D. has been thinking about this for a month. It wouldn't be that unusual for Huppman to ask us to file the motion. If he was ever questioned about why he had the motion filed out of the law library, he could say that his lawyers told him they wanted $20,000 to handle the motion and that it probably wouldn't be successful. Thus, why wouldn't Hal ask us to file the papers since we don't charge anything? Then when it's time for the hearing on the motion, J.D. has a lawyer friend he trusts who would appear to represent Huppman and argue for the reduction. Of course, the state would oppose, but a few months later J.D. would quietly issue a ruling reducing the sentence to three years."

"He'd reduce the sentence based on the standard bullshit we write—first offense, hardship to family, nonviolent crime, that stuff?" I asked.

"That's what J.D. wants to see," Joe confirmed. "The more we have to say the better, plus a few testimonials as to Hal's outstanding character from some of the politicians he claims owe him favors. We've got 15 days to get the motion filed. If Hal wants to pay the bribe, he has about four months to meet Judge Hunt's demands."

"So, if Hal doesn't do it, then Hunt just denies the motion. It sounds like this could work," I remarked. "If you arrange this deal, is there anything in it for you?"

"J.D. and I go way back. He said he'd help me behind the scenes with a parole, and if I got out, he'd give me $50,000. He's a good guy and going through some tough times. Let's talk to Hal and see if he's really got a half-million in whip-out cash to get himself out of three years of real jail time."

Joe met with Hal Huppman the next day in the law library, and, once again, I waited in the visitor's park, sipping an RC.

Joe explained the deal to Hal, including the terms of payment, which the judge would not negotiate—the full $500,000 must be in the possession of his trusted attorney friend, who would represent Hal at the motion hearing, before Judge Hunt issued the ruling that would reduce the sentence to three years. The judge wanted the money delivered in cash, and Hal couldn't mention or discuss the deal with the attorneys he had on retainer. Hal had four months from the date the motion was filed to get the money delivered. If the money wasn't in place or any word leaked out in the good-ol'-boy legal grapevine about what might be happening, then Judge Hunt would simply deny the motion for a reduction in sentence, and his jurisdiction involving the case would be closed.

Hal loved the idea, but, even to a mogul, a half-million dollars is a lot of money. He was concerned about what his recourse would be if he paid the money and then the reduction in sentence didn't happen. Joe told him that trust had to be a factor here; you don't get receipts and contracts for performance when you are bribing a district court judge.

Joe and I got the ball rolling by filing a motion for a reduction in sentence for Hal Huppman. I wrote the standard paragraphs about how this was a first-time offense, no weapons were used, no violence was involved, the wife and children were suffering, and Huppman's asthma was complicated by being in prison. However, Hal was not able to produce the glowing testimonials from political figures around the state that Judge Hunt wanted to supplement the motion. This was our first indication that maybe Hal was just a mogul in his own mind and the beef wasn't there to back up all the shit that came out of his mouth.

The whole plan collapsed when Hal failed to get any money to Judge Hunt's contact. Judge Hunt did not want to visit Joe again at Lake Butler, but he did send his contact to inquire what was going on with the half-million that Huppman had indicated would be no trouble to assemble.

When Joe brought up the payment situation to Hal, he heard one of the classic tales of prison woe that have existed since man first began locking his fellow man behind bars. Hal claimed to have given his wife of 10 years his power of attorney, and she had traveled to the Cayman Islands, Nassau, and Panama to assemble the money from the foreign accounts he had. However, he had just found out yesterday that she was filing for divorce, and it looked as if she had cleaned him out of all his money. He was broke.

Hal wanted Joe to see if he could convince the judge to go ahead and grant him his sentence reduction. Then, once Hal was back on the street, he'd immediately start smuggling again and pay Judge Hunt the first $1 million he made. In other words, Hal wanted to reverse the situation—he wanted the judge to trust him to pay off the money after the sentence reduction had been approved and he was released from prison.

Once more the judge's friend visited Joe at Lake Butler. Even though Hal had offered to double the size of the payoff, Judge Hunt would not accept the deal. When the hearing was held on the motion to reduce his sentence, no one was there to represent Hal Huppman, and Judge Hunt issued an immediate ruling denying the motion. For good measure, Judge Hunt clothed his ruling in language stating vehemently that drug criminals would never be coddled by his court, that they had to pay a steep price for what they were doing to the children of America. The state's attorney was so impressed with the passionate statement by Judge Hunt that he asked whether it was OK to release the speech to the newspapers.

The ruling was printed, along with a profile of the outstanding record of the law-and-order judge, Jefferson Davis Hunt. Judge Hunt didn't get his bribe money, but his impassioned rhetoric on the drug issue made him one of the most influential judges in Florida with law-and-order politicians. As for Hal Huppman, he got no pardon, he lost his appeal, and he had to serve three years and six months before he received a parole.

Before parole guidelines came into effect, the word best suited to describe the parole system for Florida was capricious—it was hard to explain or predict. Seven appointed parole commissioners held the ultimate power over most of the 30,000 inmates in the state system because their approval was required before an inmate could be released on parole. Generally, an inmate could count on being released after serving between one-third to one-half of his sentence, but the final decision rested with this board of seven people. If they wanted, they could have a person out of prison in as little as six months, no matter what the sentence.

I've always been amazed at how cheaply elected officials, at all levels of government, could be bought for a specific agenda. Five hundred dollars to a state representative in Kentucky was enough to buy a vote to sponsor off-track betting, according to an FBI sting operation. A $50,000 campaign contribution was enough to get a U.S. Senator to attend a meeting where famed savings-and-loan swindler Charles Keating pleaded his case for special legislation to get the feds off his back. If elected officials were constantly being bought for such paltry sums, surely the moderately compensated parole commissioners, a position that offered such an excellent opportunity for bribes, were accepting money to make sure an individual got an early parole.

There was never much of a buzz among the inmates about people who were getting out early because of a successful bribe of a parole commissioner. Joe said that this was because 98 percent of the inmates had been represented by only a public defender and, once the plea bargain was made or the trial was lost, that was the end of any contact these people had with their lawyers. According to Joe, it was the good-ol'-boy network of lawyers that was the conduit to discreet early paroles. Most of the people in the state legislature were lawyers, most of the lobbyists were lawyers, and most of the higher officials in government were lawyers—these people were practically interchangeable parts. A lawyer in private criminal practice might run for the state legislature and win; he'd serve a few terms and then go back to private practice. After a few years of this, he might be appointed to an office in state government—he was then in the network. The convicts whose private attorneys knew the paths in this maze were the ones with any chance to get early paroles—provided they had cash.

The three lawyers I had contact with weren't part of this lawyers' network. Joe Peel had been locked up too long; Stephen Jamison was too young; and Melvin Kliner was too flamboyant to be part of the back room, pat-on-the-back or wink-of-an-eye, mutual favors network. However, I had my shot at bribing a parole commissioner from the state, and it happened because a friend of a friend worked for a lawyer who was part of the good-ol'-boy fraternity.

During the two and a half years between my getting busted and having to check into prison, I moved back to my mother's house in a suburb of Chicago. While I lived in Highland Park, one of my best friends, and the person I most enjoyed being around, was an ultrafun, ultrasmart, and ultra-attractive woman named Kimberly. Through Kimberly, Karen and I met Dusty. Together, Kimberly and Dusty cut an eclectic social path through the under-30s world of Chicago nightlife that I sporadically participated in.

A few months before Karen and I headed to Florida for me to begin serving my time, Dusty's marriage broke up, and she opted for a change of weather and surroundings and moved to South Florida. When Karen arrived in Fort Lauderdale to live with her sister and brother-in-law, Dusty was the only person besides her immediate family she knew. Dusty and Karen would get together a couple of times a month to have some fun. Often, this fun would commence on a Friday afternoon when Karen would pick up Dusty at work; Dusty was a secretary/bookkeeper for an attorney.

Most important to this story, however, was Dusty's role in introducing Karen to two people who promised to help me get early release.

As previously discussed, the Florida Department of Corrections rules stated that an inmate had to go before the

parole board within six months of his date of incarceration.
After I had served five months, Karen arrived for our weekly Saturday visit with exciting news.

"You're going to be getting out soon, very soon," she
said with the conviction of someone who truly believed
what she was saying.

"What's happened?" I asked excitedly. "Did Kliner get
the appeals court to change the verdict?"

"No, nothing like that," Karen replied.

"Then what? What's going on?" I asked, hoping that
Karen had the first piece of good news about the legal outcome of my case on the tip of her tongue. I was ready for
good news.

"Well," she purred as she looked me in the eye, "I visited
Dusty's psychic yesterday, and she said that you would be
getting out before eight months. That means you only have
three months to go if it's the worst-case scenario."

"A psychic," I half laughed, covering up my disappoint-
ment that the hoped-for good news was a bunch of nonsense. "You can't really believe that bullshit?"

"Hey, you believed that bullshit Kliner told you about
winning your appeal. I think my psychic is at least as credible
as Kliner was, and she certainly won't make things worse."

I could tell that Karen was slightly offended at my dis-
missal of her news from the psychic, and I definitely didn't
want to ruin our visit by chastising her for throwing money
away on something as foolish as a fortune-teller.

"Well, you're right about that," I said. "Your psychic
can't do any more screwing up than Kliner did. Did she happen to say just how my release was going to come about?"

Five days after Karen had told me about her fortune-
teller, I received a letter from her in which she cryptically
stated that the psychic had been right, and she would tell
me the details on our next visit.

The next Saturday, Karen filled me in on the details of how I was going to be getting out of prison, possibly as soon as two weeks after I saw the parole board. Karen informed me that this piece of good news had also come by way of Dusty—not from her psychic this time but rather from her boss, attorney Charles Winters.

Charles Winters worked out of a two-attorney office, and he had hired Dusty to handle the books and be his office manager. Charles was in his 50s, and he had the look of a middle-aged man whose tennis and golf game were right up there in importance with his legal career and his family. With his well-groomed appearance and Brooks Brothers suits, Charles was in direct contrast to Melvin Kliner. In fact, Charles was one of a disappearing breed of South Florida lawyer: the stately, well-spoken, considerate, father figure who returned his phone calls and didn't dwell on the word "I" as in "*I* will win your case, or *I* can cause magic to happen."

Charles Winters fit perfectly the pattern of how a network attorney's career functioned, as described by Joe Peel. Charles had served three years in the state legislature after having worked five years in the Dade County District Attorney's office, and had been in the private practice of criminal law for eight years. When he'd had enough of the legislative life in Tallahassee, he returned to Fort Lauderdale and resumed his law practice. Only this time it was different; he knew most of the players and inside power brokers in South Florida and Tallahassee. Charles was one of the guys, but he was not amused by the back-slapping, whiskey-drinking, cigar-smoking group who thought that was the way you had to act to get deals done. Charles was a gentleman, a regal good ol' boy.

Dusty had discovered something in Winters' books that she didn't understand. The problem involved escrowed money that had come into the office and then most of it had been withdrawn in cash, leaving a fee for the office that she couldn't reference to any cases or clients that the office had handled.

Charles trusted Dusty so he told her that the escrowed money went to a lobbyist he knew in Tallahassee, where it was used to pay for favors from the parole commission. Charles kept a small percentage for himself as the middleman in the deal.

Charles and Dusty decided the best way to account for the middleman fee was to simply attach it to a fictitious client as a retainer. That problem solved, Dusty asked Charles if her friend's husband could be helped with his prison sentence.

"I'd never met Charles," Karen said. "I'd seen him when I picked up Dusty a few times, but she'd never introduced us. Anyway, yesterday Dusty had an appointment set up, and he can do it. He can get to a parole commissioner and get you an early release."

Karen had tears in her eyes, and I knew she wasn't kidding around. "How?" I questioned. "How can anyone get around the parole guidelines?"

"I don't know," Karen explained, "but I believe Charles. He's so different from Kliner you wouldn't believe it. He didn't make any promises; he just told me how it works and what we have to do."

"You really believe him?"

"I do," Karen said. "He has a close friend who used to serve in the Florida legislature. He wouldn't tell me his name, but referred to him as Mr. H. Mr. H. is now a lobbyist for a bunch of companies in Tallahassee, and he's close with some of the people on the parole commission."

"What's it cost?" I asked, figuring this service wasn't going to be cheap.

"Five thousand dollars, total. Charles said that when I give him the money, he escrows it in his office account, and no money is released to Mr. H. till you've been released. If you don't get released or something screws up, Charles gives me the money back."

"Once we give him the money, then what happens?" I queried, thinking that there had to be some catch. Five thousand dollars sounded too cheap, and Mr. H. sounded too good to be true.

"Once Charles has the five thousand, he tells Mr. H., and Mr. H. goes to the parole commissioner he deals with. After you see the parole board at Lake Butler, the paperwork goes to Tallahassee for review, and that's where the commissioner gets you a parole date that should have you out within a month after seeing the board. Once you're out, Charles gives the money to Mr. H., and he then pays off his commissioner."

"Do they know that I see the board in three weeks? What am I supposed to do when I go in?"

"I told Charles when you're slated to see the board. He said you don't have to do anything, just keep your record clean and don't get any disciplinary infractions. Whatever they tell you is irrelevant; it's going to be taken care of in Tallahassee."

I was skeptical of the whole thing. The new parole guidelines system stated specific parameters for when I would be getting a parole. Unless there was something I didn't know about, the earliest I could get out was after 11 months of time served and the latest was after 15 months. I didn't see how anyone could wave a wand and reduce me to seven months; that's exactly what the new system was supposed to prevent.

"You want to give Charles a try?" I asked. "It sounds like we can't lose. If he gets me out at seven months, that's great; and if his plan doesn't work, we get our money back."

"Dusty went back in the books for the last three years, and she found three other times when money has been escrowed and then paid out in cash. She's right there to watch what's going on. Charles said I could bring the money in cash or a check, either way he puts it in his account."

"I'm not going to get my hopes up, and neither should you," I counseled. "Remember Kliner and his influence with the appeals court bullshit? Damn, out of here in under two months . . . that would be great!"

"I'm going to see Charles Monday after work, and I'll give him the money. Then, I think I'll go back to Dusty's psychic and get an exact date for your release."

We hugged, and I had to break it off when I noticed a female guard pointing at us and shaking her head. "If we got a disciplinary infraction now," I said as we broke up our clinch, "that would be a disaster. Tell Charles that we're on the program."

Besides paying $5,000 to Charles, the other part of the deal was that I couldn't mention our bribe attempt to any-one. I wanted to run the plan by Joe to hear his opinion. I didn't like keeping a secret from Joe, especially involving such a conversational nugget as the bribe of a parole com-missioner, but I could certainly understand that Winters and Mr. H. would want no one else but Dusty, Karen, and me to know that the fix was in.

Meanwhile, my call-out to go before the parole board came right on schedule: at the six-month and two-day mark of my time served. The parole board at Lake Butler consist-ed of a representative of the parole commissioners, an inmate's assigned caseworker, and a prison official.

When I walked in for my parole interview, I was imme-diately surprised to see an attractive woman sitting between my caseworker and the assistant warden of the prison. Even though Ms. Henry was firm and all business in her introduction, there was still the initial impression that she was someone I would have wanted to get to know if I had met her during my college days.

I was asked to take a seat facing the three authority figures, and we quickly established that the information Ms. Henry had regarding classification of crime, sentence given, and time served was correct. My caseworker added that I was employed in the prison law library, had joined the Jaycees, and had taken a college credit course offered by the local junior college. Then the prison official confirmed that I had a clean disciplinary record and that he was lowering my custody status from medium security to minimum security.

Now it was Ms. Henry's show. It was up to her to pronounce a verdict on how many months I would have to serve before being paroled.

Ms. Henry looked at her notes. "Mr. Gross," she began in a tone that had a bit of the how-did-this-happen-to-you inflection in it. "You're as clean as I see. This looks more to me like a résumé for a Fortune 500 company than for a parole date—college grad, air force officer, Vietnam pilot, Distinguished Flying Cross. I trust you never plan on involving yourself in criminal activity again?"

"Absolutely not," I said when it was obvious by her pause that she wanted me to affirm her statement.

"Good," she stated. "It says here that you were caught with 1,200 pounds of marijuana in your airplane. You fall into the category of between 200 and 2,000 pounds in your possession. I'll tell you what—your guidelines are between 11 and 15 months, your 1,200 pounds is just about in the middle of 200 to 2,000. How about we set your parole date at 13 months? With the time you've already served, that will put you out in the middle of February. How does that sound?"

Ms. Henry's reasons for the release date she proposed sounded rational. She looked at me as if she expected me to say "thank you" and leave the room, but I knew that the fix was in with the commissioners and decided to take a shot and see if I could get her to go for the 11-month date.

I answered cautiously, "That sounds good . . . I don't know if it shows on your paperwork, but my wife and I were married a month before I entered prison, and we've never spent a Christmas together. If you could put me at the low end of the matrix, we'd be able to be together for Christmas, and that would be a great way to start off our life after prison. Would that be possible?"

"Is this your first wife?"

"Yes," I said.

"Your wife has stuck by you while you've been in prison?"

"Yes, she rides the church bus up here from Miami every weekend to visit—10 hours each way," I added.

Ms. Henry looked at the prison official. "Any objections?" she asked.

The prison official shook his head indicating it was OK with him. "We'll call this an early Christmas present from the state of Florida to you, Mr. Gross. I'll drop you down to 11 months. That will put you out on December 16. Will that be enough time for you to get in the holiday spirit?"

"Absolutely," I exclaimed. "This will be our best Christmas ever."

As I left the room, I was thinking, "Five years from the judge in Martin County, then Kliner says figure 18 to 30 months, then Joe Peel says it's going to be 15 months tops, and now we're at 11 months, with the biggest surprise still to come."

I immediately went to the law library and showed Joe my presumptive parole date. "That's great," he said with a broad smile on his face. "This is the way the system is supposed to work. I'm going to have to start looking for your replacement."

I knew how the parole process worked. After all, Joe Peel and I were probably the legal experts on handling parole date appeals involving the new system. However, Charles Winters and Mr. H. said the new system didn't make any difference with regard to how they were going to get me an early parole.

While not telling Joe exactly what the situation was, we did go through the regulations to see what ways were possible to get an inmate released below the guidelines. The only way that looked possible to get a below-the-guidelines release was if he was credited with an act of heroism while in custody. An act of heroism was defined as saving another inmate's life or an act of bravery committed while protecting prison employees from possible harm. That was the only way, and I didn't see how Mr. H. was going to get me out from behind the prison gates before I had served 11 months.

I wrote detailed letters to Charles Winters, which Karen carried back to Fort Lauderdale, explaining what had happened with my parole interview and how the process proceeded from that point. I concluded these letters by asking for a hint of what Mr. H. was going to do to bypass this parole process. But, actually, I wasn't worried. I believed that Winters and Mr. H. had to know something of what they were talking about, and if the situation developed that all they were able to do was to protect my 11-month decree given to me by Ms. Henry, then that would be fine and still worth the $5,000 escrowed with Charles Winters.

Winters and Mr. H. assured Karen that the 11-month date would not be raised in Tallahassee and that they expected me to get word that I would be getting out well before that date because of their efforts.

The way the process worked was that the date you

received from the parole representative during your interview was called your presumptive parole date. The seven parole commissioners in Tallahassee then had to approve this date. Once the date was confirmed, you received a letter stating that your parole date was now permanent and that the only way this could be revoked was if you were involved in a disciplinary infraction.

In all the parole interviews we had monitored, Joe and I had never seen a first-time offender have his presumptive parole date elevated in Tallahassee. However, when I received my official letter from the Parole Commission in Tallahassee, I was not happy with what I saw. I was quasi-expecting to see a date that would have me out of prison well before December 16. Charles Winters and Mr. H. had said all along that I'd find out my good fortune before they did, and this was the only document I could imagine that would accomplish what they said was going to happen. When I looked at the envelope, I was sure that even if the date wasn't before December 16, at least Mr. H. had preserved the date that Ms. Henry had given me. Thus, I was appalled when I opened the envelope and saw that my permanent parole date had been elevated to the top of my matrix guidelines—I had been upped to 15 months.

Karen was crushed, Charles Winters was upset, and Mr. H. said it was all a mistake. At first Mr. H. blamed the change of dates on his parole commissioner contact who had died in an auto accident between my interview with Ms. Henry and my getting a permanent date from Tallahassee. Then he said that he would handle the details with a different parole commissioner that he had paid off before but hadn't used in a few years. His new line was that I should go ahead and file an appeal and he would represent me in front of the appeal board.

However, as Karen would pass me messages from

Charles Winters and Mr. H. about what was happening, it became clear that neither had any idea of how the process worked. Charles kept reassuring Karen that Mr. H. had produced before and knew what he was doing. Mr. H. would call Karen and tell her that everything was all taken care of, and I would hear that I would be getting out any day now. Meanwhile, I was just about sure that I had been slimed by another shit-talking member of the Florida bar—good ol' boys or not, these guys couldn't fix a traffic ticket and certainly not a parole date. I was going to be doing 15 months.

Charles Winters didn't even wait till after the hearing on my appeal of my elevated parole date to give Karen back the $5,000. He told her that even if for some reason my parole date was lowered again he didn't think it would be because of anything Mr. H. had done and that she should just keep the money. But the date wasn't lowered; it stayed at 15 months. Fifteen months was certainly something I could live with, although it was a disappointment after you had turned over money and heard former state legislators practically guarantee that a bribe for an early parole date was the easiest payoff that there was in Tallahassee.

After the bribe attempt fizzled, I told Joe Peel about the conspiracy to bribe my way out early.

"I'd accept any bribe that was offered to me back when I was the municipal court judge," Joe explained. "Some bribes I knew I couldn't do anything about, but I'd take the money anyway on the chance that something would happen that would cause the case to be favorably decided. That's what your situation sounds like to me. On the other hand, are you sure this wasn't a case of Winters trying to act like a bigshot around Karen and her friend?"

"I don't think so," I replied. "Karen has always said that Winters has been nothing but a gentleman and that he's as upset as she is that Mr. H. didn't produce."

"Then this Mr. H. sounds like the prime bullshitter in this deal," Joe said. "I doubt he has any idea of how the new system works up in Tallahassee."

"I agree," I answered. "I once mentioned the name of chairman of the parole commission to him in one of my letters, and he told Karen that he had never heard of him."

"It's too bad this didn't work out," Joe added, "but I'm even sorrier that the date Ms. Henry gave you didn't stick. There was no reason for that date to get changed. But you're lucky in one respect."

"What's that?"

"You got your money back," Joe laughed as he blew smoke in my face. "I've never heard of a guy actually getting his money returned after a failed bribe attempt. I think that shows all those lawyer jokes you hear are out of line—there is *some* integrity in the profession."

BIG JIM NOLAN

T HE LAKE BUTLER RECEPTION and Medical
Center had a strict dress and grooming code
for all inmates: permanent inmates were
required to wear white pants and shirts, transient
inmates wore blue uniforms, all inmates had to keep
their hair cut short and their faces clean shaven. If
an inmate had money, he was allowed to buy one
pair of athletic shoes from the canteen; if not, he
was issued a pair of military-style brogans.

Once the facial hair was cut off and the studded
leather jackets removed, even the most threatening-
looking humans would revert to an appearance of middle America when they donned their prison whites.

The one item of apparel that the prison officials
could do nothing about, however, was tattoos. To
punks like Leroy the Jitterbug, having tattoos was a
sign to their friends that they were going to devote (or
already had devoted) considerable effort to pursuing a
life of crime. For many inmates in the state joint, the
pursuit of an outlaw life had resulted in skin that
looked like an old brick wall in a run-down neighborhood that had 30 years of graffiti etched in or painted
on the bricks.

211

Almost all the tattooed inmates sported the crude, amateur jailhouse variety done by other inmates. Chimpanzees spend hours each day grooming their fellow party members, and to a certain extent that is the function that tattooing has taken on in prison—it is a form of social interaction with other inmates.

The faded blue, primitive tattoos that a majority of the inmates had pricked into their skin chronicled a life that had included a lot of jail time. Whether at the weight-lifting iron pile, the gym, or the shower room, this ancient art form was evident on the arms, legs, chests, backs, and buttocks of these outlaw warriors who wore their ink markings as soldiers wore their medals.

Once in a while you might see an inmate with a professionally done tattoo, but these were rare—except for the members of the two most feared groups in the prison, the Hell's Angels and Outlaws motorcycle gangs.

In Florida, these two gangs were much more than a group of guys who liked to dress up in leather, look mean, and ride Harley-Davidson motorcycles. The Outlaws and the Angels were vying for market share in the same business enterprises, much like Coca-Cola and Pepsi. For the two motorcycle gangs, their business revolved around the production and distribution of amphetamines and designer drugs, as well as control of the majority of biker bars/strip joints that existed all over South Florida. From these two main businesses sprouted all sorts of peripheral income producers, such as prostitution, motorcycle theft rings, and protection rackets. The gangs hated each other, and they were in a constant state of war inside and outside the prison walls.

At Lake Butler it wasn't hard to figure out if an inmate was a gang member and to which gang he belonged; the first time a man removed his shirt, his tattoo was there for all to

see. If you were an initiated, hard-core member of the Hell's
Angels or Outlaws, it was expected that you'd proudly have
your affiliation etched into the skin on your back. These
weren't small tattoos, either; they covered the whole back
from the top of the shoulder blades down to the taper of the
waist and displayed the gang's name, the chapter location,
and the gang's crest.

No one but other gang members or gang member
wannabees hung out with these guys. It wasn't that you'd be
afraid that they'd pull a shank and stick you as much as the
prevailing thought that once you became friendly with one
gang, you'd then be targeted by the other group as a potential adversary. Unless you wanted to be part of the life
behind bars of an affiliated gang member, and the scrutiny
that brought from the prison officials as well as the other
warring gang, it was best to stay clear of everyone who had
the huge, professionally done tattoos covering their backs.

No one knew exactly how many hard-core members
there were for each group. The law enforcement estimates
coming from the various task forces in South Florida that
were trying to deal with the violence estimated that the
Outlaws had approximately 2,000 members and the Hell's
Angels about half that. Whatever the total, the tally at
Lake Butler was four Outlaws and three Hell's Angels, who
circled each other like two bison vying to win the breeding
rights to a herd of cows.

I had nothing to do with either bunch. They had all
been represented by private attorneys, and none ever
showed up in the law library to request legal services. These
men stayed to themselves and didn't even ask Joe or me for
opinions on their parole interviews. The gangs' respective
lawyers handled everything. Whether I saw them lifting
weights or in the chow hall, each gang always seemed to be
huddling together, and whether they were planning an

escape or an attack on their rivals, I didn't know and didn't want to. They had almost no interaction with any inmates who weren't part of their gang.

Once Joe and I began limiting interviews with inmates to the morning hours, Joe's afternoons were when he produced most of his work. If we didn't have any distractions, Joe could put in a strong two hours and produce enough legal work to keep me typing for the rest of the day and keep us from falling behind.

Right after lunch on a brutally hot July day, Joe and I were getting settled at our desks after the quarter-mile walk from the dorm. The air conditioning had just finished the job of removing the moisture from our necks and faces, and Joe had fired up his first postlunch cigarette, signaling that he was ready to create legal brilliance. He was barely into his first paragraph when he left his desk to use the inmate's bathroom in the visitor's park.

Since our office was air conditioned, we always kept the door shut. When the door opened, I looked up from my typing, expecting to see Joe returning from the bathroom. Instead, I saw an inmate wearing the white state-issue uniform of a permanent resident enter the office. I had never seen this man before, of that I had no doubt. He was definitely the largest and tallest permanent inmate at Lake Butler—either white or black. I am 6 foot 4, and this man had a good five inches on me. His frame carried at least 350 pounds, and not much of it hung over his belt. He had red-brown hair, and no jailhouse tattoos were evident on his Popeye forearms.

"Where's Joe?" the man asked, not wasting any time with small talk.

"He's not here right now," I answered, hoping to get the man to move on before Joe returned and the whole afternoon's work schedule went down the drain.

"How 'bout I wait for him?" the man said, leaving little doubt that it wasn't going to be my choice whether he stayed or left.

"You can't," I said, "unless you have a call-out. If you get caught in here without a call-out, they'll write you up. If you need a call-out, go through the dorm boss."

"What kind of bullshit is that? Are you on the chain gang, or are you a hack?" the man asked, looking very displeased at the information I was giving him.

I was going to launch into a further explanation of why he couldn't wait in the law library for Joe, when Joe opened the door and entered. Joe smiled broadly and embraced the big man. "Jesus, Jim," Joe said, "what are you doing up here? The last I heard you were in Fort Lauderdale on a murder charge."

"Not *a* murder charge," Jim replied, "a *triple*-murder charge. Three Hell's Angels bit the dust, and they tried to pin the thing on me. A year and a half I've been in the Broward County slam, but I beat the charge—a hung jury on the first try and then a not guilty on the retrial."

"Great," Joe laughed. "You lead a charmed life. If it's not guilty, then what are you doing up here?"

I was listening to a conversation between Joe and a man charged with a triple murder. "You were charged with killing three guys?" I asked, betraying an attitude that the man was talking shit to impress Joe.

Jim picked up right away that my tone of voice and inflection might be slightly mocking. He turned away from Joe and looked down at me. With a quick move he grabbed my shirt collar from the front and lifted, bunching the shirt and pulling the underseams into my armpits.

"I don't know you," he scowled, "but let me tell you something: so far I've killed 12 men, and when I get out of here, I plan on killing a whole lot more—just hope you're not on my list."

He released his grasp on my shirt and gave me a slight shove back. Joe immediately stepped between us. "Joe, who is this asshole?" Jim questioned.

I was shaken. I had popped off like a veteran wiseass, and, what's more, I'd done it to a guy who outweighed me by at least 150 pounds and about whom I knew nothing.

"I thought you two had met," Joe said. "Jim, this is Ken; he's been with me in the law library for five months now."

Jim eyed me like he'd give me another chance for a first impression if I was a part of Joe's team. "You just pissed off Big Jim Nolan," Joe continued while chuckling to himself. "Jim's the head of the Outlaws motorcycle gang in Florida."

Jim stuck out his hand, and I shook it. Big Jim went on to explain to Joe that he had been acquitted on the triple-murder charge—which he had done—but the one count he had been found guilty of was using profanity in the presence of a law enforcement officer. It was a felony count with a maximum of five years, for which no one in the history of Florida criminal law had ever been sentenced to much more than six months in prison. However, when the judge saw Big Jim beating a death-penalty sentence that he was sure Jim was guilty of, he slapped him with five years for the profanity charge. Big Jim had just checked into Lake Butler to serve five years for saying "fuck you" to a police officer.

"How much time is this 'fuck you' going to cost me?" Big Jim asked. "Every lawyer I talk to says that you're the expert on this parole guidelines deal."

"We'll write the clerk down at Broward County and get a copy of your sentencing order," Joe replied. "We'll have it in a week, and then I can tell you exactly where you stand. But my guess is that you're not going to be here long."

After Jim left the office, Joe could tell that I was still worried about having incurred the wrath of the Supreme Allied Commander Czar of the Outlaws motorcycle gang.

"Don't worry about it." Joe said. "Big Jim won't even remember this happened the next time you see him."

"You don't think I'm on the death list with the other enemies of the Outlaws then?"

"No chance," Joe laughed. "Big Jim and you will be slapping each other's backs the next time you see him."

Joe was right. That evening Jim showed up in the hobby shop and quickly became the life of the party. He knew Joe and Jack Green from previous prison stretches, and Jim would sit around playing his guitar while Jack painted, Joe pounded on leather, and I conferred with some of the woodworkers who were making me scale-model aircraft of the smuggling airplanes I had flown.

The evening camaraderie was broken when a guard, whom no one knew, entered asking which one Big Jim Nolan was. When something like this happened, it usually meant that an inmate was going to be led away in handcuffs and taken to the hole for violating a prison rule.

Big Jim casually put down the guitar he was fiddling with, stood up, and announced his presence to the guard he towered over.

"Are you missing any of your personal possessions?" the guard asked.

Jim said that during the check-in procedures yesterday, someone had stolen his wallet.

"How much money did you have?" the guard wanted to know.

"I think is was $300."

The guard held up a wallet and handed it to Jim. "A couple of black kids gave me this. It's got $290 in it. They said to tell you that they didn't know whose wallet they had stolen and they don't want any trouble with the Outlaws. They spent $10 before someone told them the mistake they had made, and they'll get that money back to you as soon as they can."

"That's good," Jim remarked. "Tell them it's good to find out that at least a few of the black punks in here have a brain."

Everyone in the hobby shop laughed at Jim's retort, even the guard who was impressed that he was dealing with a man of such notoriety that the convicts who had stolen his wallet had immediately realized their error and returned it, with its small fortune, to its owner.

"It must have been stolen before you had a chance to turn all but $15 over to your inmate account, right?" the guard prompted. "You do know that it is against prison rules to have more than $15 in currency in your possession, don't you?"

"You bet, boss," Jim said. "Thanks for bringing it back."

The guard gave Jim $15 and said he'd take the rest of the money to the accountant and make sure it got in Big Jim's account.

Two days later one of the thieves handed Joe an envelope and asked him to give it to Big Jim Nolan. Inside was a $10 bill. Big Jim Nolan, the king of the Outlaws, had arrived at Lake Butler and was being accorded the proper respect to a man who carried one of the baddest reputations in Florida.

When we received Big Jim's sentencing document from the clerk of the court in Broward County, Joe and I quickly saw that Big Jim was barely going to have any time to recruit new Outlaws members from the inmate population before he would be right back on the street.

We got an immediate call-out to Jim, and Joe told me to explain the parole situation to the man who 10 days ago was about ready to make me into chum for my improper attitude. This time when I spoke, Jim was all smiles: I was the bearer of good news.

Jim was in a great position. He had received a five-year

sentence, and the judge had checked the box where the Department of Corrections was not allowed to parole Jim until he had completed at least one-third of his sentence. However, he had been denied bail from the time of his arrest for the murder charges to the time he was sentenced for the profanity charge. Those 17 months that he had been locked up counted toward time served for the profanity sentence.

When I crunched Jim's background into the parole matrix, the time served to parole for a profanity conviction was only six to nine months, even for a man who had as high a salient score for the probability of parole failure as I had ever seen. Jim was eligible for an immediate parole: he would be on the street in two to four weeks after his interview.

The problem was that once an inmate had showed up at Lake Butler, he had to wait six months for his paperwork to be shuffled and to get his name in the system and on the list for his parole interview. For Big Jim to have to wait this extra time was a violation of rights and would in fact make him have to serve at least six months more than was required. Jim understood completely what I was telling him, and our recommendation was that he have his attorneys hightail it up to Tallahassee and demand that he be given an immediate parole hearing.

Jim agreed, and two days later his attorney paid Joe Peel and me a visit in the law library to be briefed on exactly how the parole system worked and what he should do in Tallahassee to get Jim an immediate hearing. This lawyer was on a $100,000 a year retainer from the Outlaws, but he knew little about how the new parole system worked. The most impressive thing about him was that he had taken Big Jim's suggestion that he stop and see the men in the law library at Lake Butler to discuss what the legal strategy should be.

The Tallahassee meeting with the parole commission

went perfectly, and two weeks later Big Jim was sitting in front of the same Ms. Henry with whom I had conducted business a few months before. She pronounced Big Jim eligible for an immediate parole and told him that as soon as her findings were turned into a permanent date that he would be released—probably in about three weeks.

During this waiting period, Big Jim could have won the most congenial trophy in the Miss America Pageant. He was a regular in the hobby shop, played guitar in the prison rock 'n roll band, and he and his girlfriend would hang out with Karen and me in the visitor's park on Saturdays. The only time you could catch a glimpse of the mean side of Big Jim Nolan was when he was anywhere near any of the Hell's Angels; he knew that they knew he had killed three of their members and that he was number one on their death list. Whether he was killed in or out of prison wasn't a question the Hell's Angels were debating.

It seemed a bit like jailhouse silliness to me the way the Angels and Outlaws circled each other, but it wasn't. No matter how cleaned up these guys were in their short haircuts and white shirts, they were still wearing leathers and living for the glory of riding their snarling Harleys into combat against the hated enemy. For these guys, there was no R&R or end-of-tour; they had the tattoos on their backs, and they were in the battle till the day they died.

The mail Big Jim received back from Tallahassee was obviously politically motivated. We were all expecting to see a permanent parole date set that would have Big Jim walking out of Lake Butler on the Tuesday after he got the letter. However, the parole commissioners had chosen to disregard Ms. Henry's opinion of where "verbal abuse of a police officer" belonged in the matrix, and instead of agreeing with Ms. Henry—who had put Big Jim's crime in the "nonviolent assault" category—they had upped his crime to the "violent assault" category. When combined with his salient score, this raised his parole window from nine months to 21 to 24 months. And, of course, the commissioners had set Jim's parole date at the top of the matrix—they wanted 24 months from him.

Joe explained the appeal of the parole date process to Big Jim, and the success we had had in getting miscarriages of the matrix corrected. "Even if we can't get this corrected on appeal," Joe told Jim, "we'd take this into court. But the problem would be that it would take at least a year before we'd get into a courtroom, and you'd be long gone."

"Could I get any money from them?" Big Jim wanted to know.

"Probably not," Joe said. "The parole commission would argue that it was an honest interpretation of the rules. Of course, if you were still in prison on the charge, you'd be released immediately."

Big Jim had been unimpressed with his attorney's lack of knowledge about the parole system, and he didn't want to spend another $10,000 hiring a new lawyer who probably didn't know close to what Joe Peel did about the parole system to handle an appeal that, at best, might produce parole five months earlier. Big Jim asked us if we'd handle his parole appeal from the law library. That was our job—Joe Peel and Associates had the case.

Writing parole appeals was my specialty. Not only was Big Jim a special friend of the law library, but in the outside he was also the führer of the Outlaws army. If I could win Big Jim's appeal for him, in the world of mutual favors, which Big Jim was very big on, I would then be holding a "payback" of immeasurable value.

The facts of the appeal were simple: the legal definition of "violent" was based on physical harm; therefore, since words can't cause physical harm, the correct category for

Big Jim's crime of saying "fuck you" to a police officer was in the nonviolent grouping.

I agonized over every word. I wanted to portray the outrage inmates in the system feel about the way the parole commission capriciously put people in the incorrect classification for the crimes they were to be paroled from. I hammered the commission with phrases on how they were deliberately trying to circumvent legislative intent and undermining the efforts of the judiciary to bring justice to people for the specific crimes they had committed.

My opinion was that anything less than forceful words would cause the parole commissioner who was reviewing the appeal to just skip over the effort. If Big Jim was going to lose, at least he was going to lose not as a meek, pleading petitioner, but as an aggressor, who knew he was being fucked around and demanded that things be made right.

Joe toned down some of my language, and the appeal was in the mail four days after Big Jim had received the letter from Tallahassee upping his term to 24 months. The appeal would take from three to four weeks, and that was extra time that Big Jim would be at risk for a retaliatory attack from the Hell's Angels.

Big Jim could have requested protective custody, but that idea never entered his mind. The thought of the czar of the Outlaws motorcycle gang running to a prison official because he was scared the Hell's Angels were going to attack him was repugnant; besides, Jim was too big and strong to be brought down by one man using standard prison weapons. If the Angels were going to kill Big Jim Nolan while he was in prison, it was going to have to be a coordinated attack by all the Hell's Angels against all the Outlaws.

When two such groups become sworn enemies, the only thing that can end such dislike is for a new entity to appear on the horizon that alters the balance of hatred. At Lake

Butler, this entity appeared in the form of a most unlikely inmate: a scrawny, tobacco-chewing, Southern white trash, Ku Klux Klan member known as Orville the Dog Boy.

The position of "dog boy" was an anachronism of prison life. The dog boy traditionally had run the kennel and trained the dogs that were used to track escaped inmates. If an inmate accepted the offer by the prison officials to become the dog boy, he was usually given a few extra favors. These might include extra good time plus being moved into a housing situation away from the other inmates because an inmate who trained dogs to track down other inmates became the most hated snitch in the joint.

Lake Butler still had a dog boy only because one of the assistant wardens liked to breed and raise bloodhounds. Orville took the job not to get any special favors, but because he loved animals and playing around with a bunch of cute puppies each day was a lot more fun than working in the prison laundry with a bunch of blacks, whom he hated. Most of the inmates didn't even know Lake Butler had a kennel, and because the assistant warden's hounds had never been used to chase anyone, Orville wasn't given quarters; he lived in the dorm like any other permanent inmate.

Prison officials who liked visiting the kennel to see the bloodhounds were nostalgic for the old days when men did hard labor on a chain gang and didn't come into prison to be rehabilitated. These old-time guards remembered the days when men would spend years working on tunneling under a perimeter boundary or chipping away at a cement wall to get into the heating ducts—not like the new generation of criminal who might have so much drug money stashed away that he could hire a helicopter to fly right into the prison yard to pick him up. The chain gang and bloodhounds kind of went together, and the puppies that Orville raised were always in demand as pets.

No permanent inmate at Lake Butler ever gave serious thought to tunneling under the double rows of 20-foot-high fencing topped with razor wire. There was a much easier way to "escape": keep a perfect prison record and push for a prison job that allowed you to work outside the prison walls. Just about every inmate would get a drop in classification from high to medium security within five years, and once they were dropped to medium, they were eligible for jobs that allowed them to walk out the gates at 7 A.M. and came back in at 4 P.M. This was the way to escape; there was no sense in trying to scale a fence and become target practice for the bored-out-of-their-minds prison guards who manned the towers. Inmates intent on escaping waited until the officials trusted them enough to let them walk out the prison gates to work at the power plant, water treatment facility, or sewage pools, and then they would not return for the evening meal.

One such escapee was Earthman Flowers, a Hell's Angel who didn't fit the mold. Earthman was only 5 feet 8 inches and looked almost sickly. He got his name because he would smoke only marijuana to get high, and he wouldn't wear leather garments because he disapproved of the killing of any living thing for food and skins. The Earthman loved riding his motorcycle, though, and he had the big Hell's Angels tattoo proudly etched into his back.

When the Earthman escaped, it made the prison authorities look so bad that they made up a story for the local newspapers to make it look as though Earthman had executed a brilliant plot to tunnel under the fences, through the two-foot-thick anchoring foundations, and escaped into the wilds of central Florida. However, Earthman really escaped by driving one of the assistant warden's vehicles away—after the assistant warden had given him the keys.

One Friday afternoon, Earthman was in charge of a Jaycee car wash to raise money for a scholarship to a deserving son or daughter of an inmate at Lake Butler. Everyone who wanted his car cleaned would leave the keys with the secretary in the administrative building. Earthman would pick up the keys, go out into the employee parking lot, get the car, and drive it to the wash area. Earthman had a medium-security clearance, and he was approved to go outside the walls for this Friday afternoon car wash project only.

What the prison officials didn't know was that Earthman, who had served two years of a nine-year sentence and still had a couple of years to go to parole, was tired of the prison food, which didn't cater very well to his vegetarian needs, and was scared to death that if something happened to Big Jim Nolan he would be the likely choice for retaliation from the Outlaws.

Earthman's daring escape was as tricky as taking one of the cars he was asked to wash and driving it to Gainesville, where he dropped it off and was picked up by his wife.

After the successful escape, the Earthman picked right up where he had left off, hanging out with his Hell's Angels motorcycle buddies. He stayed on the street for two months before he was turned in by another Hell's Angel who was looking for some sentencing favors from the Broward County judiciary.

When Earthman was brought back to Lake Butler, the assistant warden whose car he had stolen had a great idea. The assistant warden took the shirt Earthman had worn back to Lake Butler and gave it to Orville and told him to whip the dogs into a frenzy for that scent.

Orville took the shirt and held it under the dogs' noses while he played rough with them and shouted encouragements that they were going on a manhunt.

By the time the assistant warden brought Earthman down to the kennels, the dogs were worked up and hoping for a chase. The warden told Earthman to go ahead and make a run for it, but Earthman just stood there not sure what the warden was wanting him to do. He soon figured it out when the assistant warden opened the gate to the kennel and five adult bloodhounds came tearing after him.

The force of the dogs leaping at Earthman immediately knocked him to the ground, and the dogs swarmed all over him. All Earthman could do was cover up in the fetal position and hope the warden called off the dogs before they killed him.

The assistant warden let the dogs bite and tear at Earthman for three minutes, and then he had Orville pull them off and get them back in the kennel. What was left of Earthman wasn't pretty. He was bitten up and down his legs, arms, neck, and buttocks, and in some places the flesh had been pulled completely off, leaving patches of bloody meat exposed.

Orville was pissed that his dogs had been used to chew up another inmate, but he had to keep his mouth shut or he thought he might be the next chew toy for the dogs. The warden knew he had let the "bite-the-inmate" practice for the dogs get out of hand, and he called for an ambulance to take Earthman to the prison hospital.

That night, Big Jim Nolan made the command decision that was in essence the offering of a olive branch to the Hell's Angels and was the first act in what became a peace plan to end the Outlaws and Hell's Angels gang war—Big Jim and his Outlaws beat the shit out of Orville the Dog Boy as a show of compassion to the Hell's Angels for what had happened to Earthman.

The attack occurred right after the evening meal as Orville sat in the TV room watching an after-school cartoon show. In front of 10 other inmates and the dorm boss,

Big Jim and three other Outlaws walked over to Orville, pulled him off his chair, and started kicking and pounding on him.

Orville was outweighed on this fight by about 1,200 pounds to 135. There was nothing he could do but get in as tight a ball as he could and wait for the blows to stop.

A prison assault isn't like a hockey fight where the referees try and get between the combatants. No one tries to break up a prison fight; inmates don't want to be involved in something that isn't part of their business, and a dorm boss doesn't want to risk being stabbed. The first act a dorm boss takes when he sees a fight breaking out is to get himself locked into his protective cage, then he gets on the phone and calls for the goon squad. Once that's done, all a dorm boss can do is sit back and enjoy the fight until the goon squad arrives to break it up.

Big Jim and his cohorts had been in enough prison fights to know that they wanted to have their work finished by the time the goon squad showed up. Thus, they pounded on Orville for about three minutes (the same amount of time that the dogs had chewed on Earthman), then they got off him. The worst cuts Orville suffered came from kicks to his head, and he lay motionless in a small pool of blood. Meanwhile, Big Jim calmly changed the TV channel from the cartoon show to the network newscast, and he and the other Outlaws sat down on folding chairs to await the arrival of the prison goon squad.

Five minutes later, Orville started to stir and make noises that indicated he had suffered an ass-whipping but was going to live.

Orville's movements were immediately followed by the arrival of six men clad in flak jackets, helmets, elbow and knee pads, and protective groin belts much like those a boxer wears during training sessions. The goon squad carried sticks and stun guns, and they were ready to do what they found exhilarating—wade into inmates and kick ass.

However, when the goon squad charged into the TV room, accompanied by a flurry of growls and metal-on-metal cracks of their nightsticks, they found only Orville groaning on the floor and four Outlaws sitting on chairs with their hands clasped above their heads, waiting to be handcuffed.

There was nothing the goon squad hated more than to get all dressed up and pumped up and then not be able to swing their nightsticks and feel the contact as bones were broken and skulls fractured. But with 50 inmates watching, the goon squad couldn't risk smacking Big Jim and the boys around as they sat there in total submission—at least not till they got them to the hole.

The Outlaws were handcuffed and led away. No one did anything to aid Orville until a stretcher arrived from the prison hospital, and then he was loaded up and taken away. As soon as everyone was gone, inmates strolled back into the TV room as though nothing had happened.

Within 10 minutes of the attack, everyone in the dorms knew what had happened—including the Hell's Angels. Ten minutes after that, a call had been placed to the leader of the Hell's Angels in Fort Lauderdale telling him of the amazing act Big Jim Nolan had led to avenge what had happened to Earthman Flowers. The healing process had begun between the two gangs.

As soon as Orville was cleaned up by the prison nurses, the assistant warden visited him to tell him that he had a "get-out-of-jail-free" card: all he had to do was testify in court that Big Jim had been part of the assault team.

The assistant warden and every other prison official at Lake Butler knew that Big Jim had gotten lucky with his triple-murder charge, and they wanted to tack 10 more years onto his profanity sentence by getting an assault-with-intent-to-inflict-physical-harm conviction.

However, Orville let the warden know right away that he would not cooperate with any prosecution of the Outlaws. Orville had less than a year to go, and it wasn't worth it to him to get out a few months early and then have to worry about an Outlaws member beating up on him or his family for the rest of his life.

Naturally, no inmate who witnessed the attack would cooperate as a witness, and that left only the dorm boss who could identify Big Jim. Orville went as far as to advise the prison officials that if he was subpoenaed to give testimony, he would say that he didn't know who attacked him but he was sure it wasn't Big Jim Nolan.

When the prison officials realized that they couldn't go to court with just a dorm boss saying that Big Jim was the attacker, they forgot about the idea of an outside prosecution and issued an in-house disciplinary infraction to Big Jim that got him 60 days in the hole.

After a week, Orville was released from the prison hospital, and his praises were sung for the rest of his stay at Lake Butler for being a standup guy and not snitching on Big Jim. Both the Hell's Angels and the Outlaws told him that they didn't blame him for Earthman's chewing and if he wanted to go back to being the dog boy, that was OK with them.

The warm and fuzzy feeling between the motorcycle gangs didn't stop at the walls of Lake Butler. A new era of working out their differences without violence spread throughout South Florida, and the Angels and the Outlaws became an even stronger force in organized crime.

It was in this budding era of motorcycle gang rapprochement that I experienced the most glorious moment of my prison years. Big Jim had been in the hole for 10 days when we got the word in the law library that we had won the appeal of his parole date. The commission had agreed with my argument that Big Jim had been put in the wrong category. They reinstated the parole date that Ms. Henry had given him and ordered him released immediately.

The order was received in the warden's office at 10 A.M. At 11, Big Jim was let out of the hole, and at 2 P.M. he was escorted out the prison door to be picked up by his girlfriend, who had lead-footed it down from Jacksonville in Jim's red Cadillac.

However, before Big Jim walked out the prison gates, he stopped by the law library to give Joe and me a hug and a handshake. "I won't forget this," Big Jim told me. "If you ever have any problems, you let me know—I owe you."

It wasn't money or a material thing, but having the Supreme Allied Commander Czar of the Outlaws declare that he owed you a big favor had to be something priceless.

Unfortunately, that was the last I ever saw of Big Jim. He was stabbed to death in the parking lot of a biker bar within two years of leaving Lake Butler. But I still carry the business card he gave me showing the crest of the Outlaws motorcycle gang with his name and phone number on it. On the back of the card was written "I owe you a big favor, Lake Butler Prison parole appeal," and it was signed, "Your amigo, Big Jim Nolan."

It was probably best that I never made the call to ask Big Jim to repay the favor. However, if I had called, I'm sure he would not have let me down.

CRIMINAL KIDS WITH WEALTHY PARENTS

M OST PEOPLE LIKE TO DOMINATE a conversation by talking about their two favorite
topics: themselves or what they know.
Very few individuals can take in a conversation as a
listener; this is as true in prison as it is in the world
outside the walls. I've had people I barely know tell
me about the intricacies of their financial worth and
how they've cheated the IRS out of thousands of
dollars, and I've listened to people in the joint give
me a play-by-play description of crimes they've
committed that they've never been prosecuted for.
Everybody likes to talk; the question is, is what
they're saying true?

While I was in the Martin County jail, Nate
briefed me on all the things to be careful about with
other inmates. He told me that it was foolish to
believe much of anything another inmate would tell
you because 99 percent of it was lies. The world of
prison, according to Nate, was going to be one
where most everyone who tried to be friendly with
you was doing so with an ulterior motive.

By the time I left the county jail and was moved
to the BTU of the state prison to await assignment 2 3 1

to a permanent prison, I was wary of anyone who even said the word "I" to me.

"It's not the physical attacks that you have to watch out for," Nate warned me. "You'll see those from a mile away. It's the guys who want to be friendly. They'll be the ones trying to take your money or fuck your wife. They'll be the ones trying to get you to tell them some secret about your criminal life, and then they'll snitch you out. Just remember one thing—there's no such thing as a secret in the joint; if you want to keep something a secret, don't tell anybody."

I don't know if someone passed this knowledge on to Nate or if he made it up himself, but it was obvious from my first couple of days at BTU that most inmates didn't share his philosophy. Often it would take no more than five sentences before an inmate I never met before would be telling me the criminal history of his life. Bullshitting was the way most inmates passed their time.

All prison conversations between two people who didn't know each other began with two exchanges: where are you from, and what are you in for? From this simple dialogue, each person would cautiously explore other conversational avenues so he could size up the other to see if there was enough interest to go to the next level of a prison friendship. If someone asked me what I was in for, I honestly stated that I got five years for possession of marijuana. I had no desire to impress anyone with the fact that not only was I in possession of the weed, but I was also smuggling it, and not only was I smuggling it, but I was flying it in with aircraft as large as a DC-3. I knew that kind of bragging would indicate to other convicts that I had money, and that would pique their interest to try and figure out whether there was a way they could take some of my money away from me.

This is not to say that I didn't feel tempted to talk a

bunch of shit and develop a following. I knew I could have let a few people in on my flying and smuggling background and in a few days have a group hanging on my every word on how to fly in the cocaine and marijuana, which was by far the most lucrative criminal activity in the United States.

However, becoming a big man in the joint was only a fleeting thought. I knew that Nate was right about keeping my mouth shut and doing my time as a voyeur: listening to others while I remained a nonentity.

There had been no phones in the cell block at the Martin County jail. Once I got to BTU, this situation improved to where one pay phone was available between 9 and 11 A.M. and 1 and 3 P.M.—for 700 inmates. After the morning and lunch count had cleared, a horn would sound, and everyone who wanted to make a phone call, usually 40 to 50, would run out to form a line. At precisely 9 A.M. and 1 P.M., a guard would turn the key that activated the phone line, and then he would sit there the whole time with a stopwatch to make sure no one talked beyond the allotted five minutes. The calls had to be collect, and they were tape-recorded. If no one was at the number you called or if the person wouldn't accept your collect call, you lost your place in line.

The Florida prison system had a rule that an inmate could not receive a visitor until he had been in the state system at least six weeks. The reasoning was that the state needed that time to verify visiting lists and get the paperwork in order to ensure that felons and ex-convicts wouldn't be cleared in for visits with other inmates. Another reason was that because all inmates went to BTU to await assignment to a permanent prison, BTU, with its limited visiting facilities, wouldn't have to take money out of its operating budget to provide the overtime for guards to monitor visits that were less than secure. However, the flow of inmates through BTU was so backed up that many inmates were finding themselves still waiting for assignment at the six-week mark, and that meant BTU had to allow them a weekly visit until they were shipped out.

Karen and I wrote letters to each other every day to maintain contact during the first six weeks. To supplement the letters, I would stand in the line and hope I could place a phone call on Sunday morning, a time when I knew Karen would be home.

It didn't always happen that I'd get to make the call. Sometimes the phone line would go dead, or the guard would get upset with the behavior of the inmates in the waiting queue and cancel the rest of the calling period. On the other hand, even if you did get to place a call and the other party accepted the charges, it wasn't exactly an intimate phone conversation. The guard and 50 other inmates in the queue and milling around were listening, your conversation was being tape recorded and timed, and you had to shout to be heard above the background noise of the yard. But once a week it was worth it just to get the chance to hear Karen's voice.

Central north Florida can be as cold and dreary as Chicago during the winter months. Not only was this Sunday in February cold and gray, but it was also windy with a steady, pelting rain turning the yard into a sea of mud. The weather was so lousy that after the morning count cleared, only 10 of us dashed for the phone line.

When I placed my call, Karen immediately answered and accepted the charges, and we started right in talking about the major problem of the day: the status of the charges that Sheriff Hall in Martin County had threatened to hang on me for failure to appear (way back when I first entered the prison system), and what my asshole then-attorney, Melvin Kliner, was doing about it.

This was as depressing a moment as I'd experienced in prison—standing outside in ankle-deep mud, getting pelted by freezing rain, and putting the burden of having to deal with my big-reputation, high-priced attorney onto the shoulders of my wife of eight weeks. She ended the conversation by telling me not to worry about anything, she'd get the problems solved. But I hung up the phone feeling like shit. I had created a huge mess, and the responsibility for cleaning it up fell on Karen. This was not the ideal way to start a marriage, but the continual problems we were facing brought us closer together than we'd ever been. Actually, it was more like I was doing the time, and Karen was facing the problems.

When I went to open the door back to the dorm, I found that it had been locked from the inside to prevent anyone who had gone into the yard from coming back in and tracking mud all over the newly cleaned floor. That meant there was no way I could get out of the rain until the noon meal. The only shelter in the yard was provided by the wall of the dorm buildings. The eaves of the galvanized roof extended a foot beyond the wall, and I found a section where the mud hadn't formed yet. I plastered my back to the wall and watched the rain roll off the roof about three inches in front of my face.

I was standing there, in my soaked prison blues, freezing, mired in mud, with a veil of water blocking my view of a miserable, gray day, and I thought that all I would need was a roll-your-own cigarette dangling from my lips to pose for the perfect album cover for a country-and-western singer crooning such songs as "Doin' Time," "Jailhouse Tattoos," and "The Boss Don't Care, I'm Just a Number to Him."

I'd been hugging the wall, trying to stay dry, for about 10 minutes when I noticed a teen-aged-looking inmate finish his five-minute phone call and dash over to where I stood.

He ducked through the curtain of water running off the gut-
terless overhang and braced his back to the wall right next
to me.

"Hey, I couldn't help but overhear your phone call
when I was in line," the kid said. "Is Melvin Kliner your
attorney?"

"Yeah, he is," I answered. "How did you know that?"

"You said his name about 10 times during your phone
call. It sounds like he's screwed you around."

I was surprised. I didn't realize that I had been talking so
loudly that people waiting in the phone line could hear
everything I was saying. Then again, since I could hear
what the people ahead of me were saying into the phone,
there was no reason to think that others wouldn't hear what
I was saying.

I glanced over to get a better look at who I was talking
to. I had seen him standing in the phone line before. He
looked like a college kid: 6-feet, athletic build; thick, black,
curly hair; and wearing a pair of expensive running shoes.

"How do you know Kliner?" I asked.

"He's my attorney, too. It looks like you and I must be
the only two cases he's ever lost."

This was the point at which I normally would have
drifted from a conversation, but the kid next to me watching the rain roll off the roof was well spoken and had a
polite manner, so I stayed under the overhang for the next
level of "getting to know your fellow convict."

My first question brought the information that the kid's
name was Barry Abrams and that he was from Miami. My
next question was the standard: "What are you in for?"
Barry's quick reply was "drugs." Therefore, not only did we
have the same attorney representing us, but we were also in
for the same type of crime.

Barry wanted to know what got me locked up, and he

got my possession-of-marijuana answer. Three minutes had gone by, and we knew each other's names, where we called home, and the type of crime we were in the joint for. This was the point at which my flow of information ended and I'd shut up and listen.

Barry told me that he had gotten 12 years for cocaine possession, and not only had Kliner fucked him, but his family was going to try and sue Kliner for legal malpractice in how he had handled the case.

We spent the rest of the morning sitting under the overhang talking about Melvin Kliner. The fact that we both had Kliner as an attorney indicated one thing: we both had money, or access to it.

Over the next couple of weeks, I'd see Barry in the yard everyday, and we'd talk about the rumors floating around BTU. There were always rumors about the parole system, how to get assigned to the permanent prison near your home, early releases due to overcrowding, and jailhouse-lawyer motions an inmate could write himself to sue the prison system. It seemed that every convict in the joint knew of a friend of a friend who was fucking his classification officer in her office when he went in for progress reports, or knew how to file a motion against the prison system that would have it so worried that it would give you an early release. These were nothing more than prison folk tales, kind of like the ones in the outside world where a friend of a friend had given his date a dose of "Spanish fly" and she had fucked herself to death on the gearshift knob of his Corvette—just little stories that keep going around and around with a life of their own.

After hours of walking around the yard, playing Ping-Pong, and sitting on the grass taking in the late winter sunshine, Barry had pretty much told me his whole story. He was 19 years old, and the last two years of his life had been a bad dream. He didn't try to cover up the fact that his parents were wealthy and that one set of his grandparents was superwealthy. Barry told me that while in the last two years of the exclusive prep school he had attended in Miami, he and a couple of his classmates had started using, and then dealing, cocaine. It had ended when one of the kids he was dealing with got caught by his parents, and the parents had made the kid go to the cops and implicate everyone else. It sounded to me like all the kids had wealthy parents, who had all scrambled for the best drug attorneys in Miami to get their kids off the hook. Barry's parents chose Melvin Kliner, and he had double-crossed them. According to Barry, Kliner was bought off and pled Barry to a charge that he wasn't involved in. The result was that Barry got 12 years, and the lawsuits and appeals from that bit of Kliner trickery were just beginning.

I had no way of knowing if Barry was telling me the truth, and I didn't really care. Most of his time in the yard was spent with a group of white kids from South Florida, swapping tales of girls, cars, speedboats, and parties—the same stuff that Barry's classmates were talking about with fraternity brothers at the University of Miami or the University of Florida. However, every day after a few hours of talking shit with his buddies, he would drift over to where I was. I was 14 years older than he, and I think he wanted to hang out with me to get an idea of what his mind-set might be when he got out of prison. He was going to be 31 when he got out, he kept telling me.

I wasn't an expert on the parole system when I was at BTU, but I did know enough to know that no one served his whole sentence day for day. But Barry didn't buy my assurances that he was going to be out way before he was 30. When we talked, his cocky attitude about having been born with a silver spoon in his mouth would vanish, and he would sink into a depression about what he had done to screw things up for himself and hurt his family so deeply. Everyone in the joint had a similar tale of woe, but I felt sorry for Barry. I think I saw a little bit of me and kids I grew up with in Barry Abrams, and even though he seemed to be coping with his situation outwardly, inside the panic was beginning to mount. All his parents' money couldn't prevent him from going to prison, and even though everyone he talked to on his five-minute phone calls or received letters from assured him that he was going to get out soon, maybe he wouldn't. Maybe the rest of his teenage years and most of his 20s were going to be spent locked up—no Porsches, no cigarette boats, no spring-break trips to the Cayman Islands, no sex on the beach with hard-bodied Kappa Kappa Gamma sorority girls—just doing time, years and years of time in the joint.

By chance, Barry Abrams and I became eligible for our first approved visit on the same weekend. For me, it was the first time I was able to see Karen since her visit at the Martin County jail and the first time I had been able to touch her since we had embraced during the last seconds I was a free man—more than three months earlier.

I knew Karen was coming, and when I heard my name called on the loudspeaker, I presented myself at the doors that led to the visitor's park. I was strip-searched and then cleared to enter the visiting area.

Karen wasn't there waiting, so I asked a guard what I should do. He said that they were having trouble with the metal detector and were searching everyone's handbags by hand, so I should just sit down and wait for her.

While I waited, I looked around at who was in the visitor's park. There were several inmates visiting with their wives and kids, and there were some pods of free people who had been cleared in, who were waiting for the inmates they had come to visit to get cleared through. Every one of these family units looked like they had had some hard years in their past, maybe a life of sharecropping or truck driving or construction work, except for one group that I guessed had to be Barry's parents and sister.

Barry had told me that his sister, who was two years older than he, did some modeling for underwear ads. The girl sitting with the older couple was tall, skinny, and flat-chested, but she had the beautiful long blonde hair that only movie stars seemed to have and that you knew meant weekly $200 trips to the hair salon. The father was wearing a blue blazer, tie, and gray slacks, while the mother was attired in a beige designer pantsuit and had a large diamond hanging from around her neck. While I waited, I heard an inmate sitting next to me ask his wife what she thought the diamond around the lady's neck was worth. It appeared that there might be a jewelry robbery in the visitor's park of the state prison.

After a few minutes, Barry was cleared through, and he beelined it right over to the people I had guessed were his mother, father, and sister. I watched them engage in a long group hug with everyone crying until a guard came over and told them that they were only allowed one quick embrace. Barry's mother backed a step away to survey her son and pronounced, in Jewish mother fashion, that he had lost weight and looked fabulous. Then the Abrams family sat down at the picnic table to begin catching up on the past two months' events.

Right after the Abrams reunion, Karen entered. We got the same lecture the Abrams got about embracing too long, and then we settled into a corner table across from each other where we looked into each other's eyes, held hands, and played footsie when the guards weren't looking our way.

I didn't have a watch, but I glanced at Karen's, expecting to see that a half hour had passed, and was amazed that we had been talking for three hours straight. When there was only an hour to go on the visiting period, Karen and I got up to get some drinks from the vending machine. As we passed the Abrams' table, Barry stopped us and introduced his parents and sister, after which I presented Karen. We chatted for a few minutes, and Mrs. Abrams said that she had heard about me in Barry's letters and that she was glad I was being such a good friend to her son. Mr. Abrams asked Karen what kind of work she did, and then we separated for the little time that was left in the visiting period.

The first letter I got from Karen reflecting on our Saturday visit arrived for Tuesday's mail call. Karen said that after she was cleared out of the prison she ran into the Abrams in the parking lot and that they had talked for 30 minutes about the various problems everyone was having with Melvin Kliner. In her letter she remarked that she thought I had said that Barry was doing 12 years for cocaine possession, but Mr. Abrams had said that he was doing that 12 years plus a life sentence for murder.

Barry had also gotten a letter that Tuesday evening, but since we were in different dorms we didn't hook up until the next day when the dorm doors were opened and all the inmates except the dorm cleaners had to move outside to the yard.

Barry came up to me, and he had a lot on his mind. "How come you never told me that your wife was such a knockout?" Barry began as he repeated a theme he had been telling me since the visit. "My parents were really impressed. I guess they spent some time talking in the parking lot after the visit."

"You got a letter last night, I assume," I said. "In Karen's letter she said your dad invited her to ride up with them.

With the long drive and the cost of staying in a hotel, your dad might want to think about chartering a plane to come up here. I think he could probably rent a Cessna for the trip with the pilot for $250. Instead of an eight-hour drive each way, they could fly up in under two hours."

"How come you never told me you were a pilot?" Barry wanted to know. "Is all that stuff Karen told my parents true: flying jets, Vietnam missions, flying in big-weight marijuana loads?"

"Yeah, it's true," I answered.

"Well, why didn't you tell me? And you have a Porsche?" Barry looked like my not telling him about the flying was a letdown, but withholding information that I had a Porsche was an outrage.

I told Barry that what I did or didn't tell him about my background wasn't worth worrying about; in fact, I didn't tell anyone about my background. However, if he wanted to hear some stories, I'd tell him as long as he promised to keep the information to himself.

I liked Barry, and I thought I knew him well enough to know that he wasn't going to be someone who would be looking for some angle to threaten Karen or me. I had met his mother and father, and the reality was that he had told me so much about himself that he was probably worried that if I didn't confide a few things about myself to him, that I might be the one trying to pull off a slimy jailhouse scam.

I didn't even care if Barry told his jitterbug homeboys about my background. He often would drop names about fancy hotels he had stayed at or celebrities he had hung out with in Aspen, and I guessed that I'd become a bit of a character that he could pass on to others; I might be flying a 747 loaded with 300,000 tons of marijuana rather than an Aero Commander loaded with 1,200 pounds, but it would be harmless. Barry was a good guy, and I wondered if he was going to tell me about the murder side of his conviction; it wasn't something that I was going to bring up.

Now that Barry knew about my flying and smuggling background, he wanted to know every little detail. He said that he had been trying to talk his grandfather into buying a Learjet, and if he did, then he was going to learn how to fly it. I told Barry that I would teach him to fly when he got out, and I'd even introduce him to my marijuana contact in Colombia. It was harmless shit-talking, but it seemed to perk up Barry's spirits and give him something to look forward too.

The one thing that Barry wanted to know that I wouldn't tell him was how much money I had. He couldn't believe it when I flat out said that I would never tell anyone that piece of information.

He had heard about the Porsche, and I had told him that I had owned an airplane that had been seized by the U.S. Customs, and now he wanted to hear that inner-circle confiding from me about my net worth.

"Barry," I told him, "I don't discuss my money situation with anyone, so there's no point in asking me."

"Come on," Barry replied as we were playing catch in the yard, "you've got to have $100,000 stashed away, right?"

"Look, I don't have anything."

"What about the Porsche, that's got to be worth 20 Gs," Barry said, wanting me to give him some number to assure him that maybe if he had met me on the outside he would have been impressed with the possessions that surrounded me.

"I've got no house, no Rolex watches, no more airplanes, no boats—but you're right, I do have a five-year-old Porsche. So, if you really need to have a net worth figure for me, let's say $6,000," I replied, amused at how persistent he was in wanting to hear a dollar figure. I had a feeling that a lot of Barry's time with his buddies was spent talking about what kind of cars their respective parents drove and what address they called home.

"I don't believe you," Barry concluded. "I know you've got to have at least $50,000 hidden somewhere."

The next Saturday both the Abrams and Karen visited. Karen's and my visit was less frenzied, and it took less time to cover all the legal developments, so we had time to sit with the Abrams at their invitation for an hour.

We talked about where Barry was going to go to college when he won his appeal, and then I told Mr. Abrams how to call around and get quotes as to what it would cost to charter a plane for a day and where would be a good spot to land and get a rental car to drive over to BTU for a visit.

By the time visiting hours were over, Karen and I almost felt like part of the family, with Barry being the younger brother. The parents were upbeat about winning the appeal, Barry was upbeat about getting out and going on to college, and I still hadn't heard anything about a life sentence for murder. If there was a life sentence for murder, these people were doing a great job of being in denial.

We separated with Mr. Abrams saying that he'd call Karen when he got the information on chartering an aircraft, and that if his daughter didn't come, Karen would be more than welcome to fly up with them. However, that never happened because the following Tuesday I was awakened at 5 A.M. and told to pack my shit. I was getting shipped to my permanent prison.

Barry was the one guy I had met at BTU that I would have liked to say good-bye to, but he was in one of the other dorms and the connecting doors were locked. Karen did call the Abrams to tell them that I'd been shipped back to Lake Butler, and they said that they'd keep in touch to let her know where Barry went when he finally got out of BTU.

Karen never heard from the Abrams, and I thought that

I wouldn't be seeing Barry again. He was 19 and probably going to one of the gladiator schools for kids convicted of a violent crime. Thus, three months later, when I looked out the window of the law library and saw Barry Abrams waiting in the call-out line, I was pleasantly surprised.

Barry was wearing the blue pants and shirt of a temporary inmate. I called Barry's name first to come in; we shook hands, and I introduced him to Joe Peel.

Barry began by filling me in on what he'd been doing since I last saw him. A week after I left, he had been shipped to Immokalee Correctional Institution on the west side of Florida. Joe knew this prison well and said that it was probably the most dangerous place in Florida since it was made up of black street criminals from Miami, where everyone was in a gang, and you had to fight almost every day if you wanted to be left alone.

Barry said that Immokalee was horrible. Everything he owned had been stolen, and most of the white inmates were Aryan Nation idiots, who would have nothing to do with him because he was Jewish. That left him alone to face the black gangs. He had gotten out of there because his new lawyer was able to petition the Bureau of Prisons to get him reassigned to a prison where he would have access to Jewish religious services. So he was back at Lake Butler to get reassigned.

"I might be able to help you with that," Joe said. "How much time are you doing?"

Barry looked at me with a shame-faced look: "I've got a life sentence," he said. "It's running concurrently with 12 years for cocaine possession and distribution."

"What did you get life for?" Joe wanted to know.

"Second-degree murder," Barry said. "I still can't believe it, but I've got a life sentence for a murder that I didn't do."

Barry wanted Joe to look at some legal work his new attorneys had drafted, so I arranged a new call-out pass for Barry to come back to the law library after lunch. Once Barry left, I filled Joe in on what I knew about him and how this was the first time he had told me that he was in for a murder.

"How come he's trying to hide it?" I asked Joe.

"He's probably ashamed of what he did and figured he wasn't going to see you once you left BTU and there was no reason you had to know. Or I've seen guys who block their sentence out of their minds because they can't deal with it. I don't know, but if he wants me to help him, he's going to have to level about his situation."

When Barry came back for our after-lunch meeting, he brought a shoebox full of legal papers with him. "I was hoping that you could review all this stuff and tell me what you think," Barry began. "This is just the work done since after my trial with new motions to try and get me back into court."

"Do you have the transcripts from the original trial?" Joe wanted to know.

"My parents have a copy. I could get it if you wanted it."

"It all depends on what you want me to do," Joe explained. "Kenny tells me that you've had a bunch of big-name attorneys on this case. If you're happy with them, that's great; if you want an opinion on the work they've done, I can do that; or if you want me to get more involved, that's an option also."

Barry prided himself on being able to converse and make his own deals with people much older than he was. He wasn't afraid to ask the pointed questions and make sure he knew what he was getting into. "For you to review all the material, how much would it cost me?" Barry wanted to know.

"Nothing," Joe answered with a serious face. "No one

in this office takes money for doing legal work for other inmates."

"How about attorney-client privilege—would that apply?" Barry asked.

"It's never come up as a legal issue, but in the strictest interpretation I doubt attorney-client privilege would apply," Joe said. "First off, I'm disbarred, so in the legal vernacular, I'm not a lawyer anymore. Second, the other people who help me out definitely aren't lawyers. And, third, if we did end up doing some legal work out of this office, we wouldn't be signing it. It would be submitted for your signature as the petitioner. I think I know what you're worried about—is there any chance that I or Kenny, for that matter, could be subpoenaed to give testimony about what you told us in the law library?"

"That's the one point my attorneys kept telling me," Barry confided. "Don't talk to anyone in prison about my situation because it could come back to haunt me."

"That's excellent advice, and advice few convicts follow," Joe replied. "But in the three years I've been running this law library and the 10 years or so that I've legally been able to help convicts with legal work, I've never even heard a rumor that I was going to get a summons to give testimony about what another inmate might or might not have told me. To answer your question: I doubt that it would ever happen. The ACLU would jump right in, and it would be a long fight that I'm sure the Bureau of Corrections or the Florida judiciary doesn't want to start. You know, the more I think about it, the more complex the answer is. No one has ever asked me about attorney-client privilege; that's a great question. I'd say if you're worried about it, then you probably shouldn't talk to me. I can review your paperwork, though; that's already a part of the record. It's up to you."

Barry thought about what Joe had just told him. "No, I'd really appreciate it if you looked at all the transcripts, and I'm sure my parents would be happy to pay what you wanted."

"Barry, I don't take any money, period. Once I take a look at all the transcripts, we're probably going to have to go over this again, but let's start out with what happened to get you in this mess."

Joe got his yellow legal pad, cigarettes, and lighter in the ready position. He cleaned his glasses and got his chair in a comfortable listening position. "Do you mind if Kenny listens?" Joe asked. "He might pick up on something that I miss."

My staying in the room was OK with Barry. Unless he had been bullshitting me, I'd already heard most of the facts regarding the cocaine dealing; all that would be new was the particulars of the murder charge. I went out to the vending machine and got RC Colas for Barry and me and then settled in to hear just what Barry had done to get himself a life sentence for murder.

Barry was an all-American kid with all the advantages. His father owned an insurance company in Miami, and two of his grandparents were major benefactors of charitable causes in the Boston area. Barry was outgoing, athletic, and a popular kid at the private Palm Crest School. He was a teenager any parents would have been proud of.

The Palm Crest School wasn't the type of private prep school found on the upper East Coast. The Palm Crest School didn't worry about what color or religion you were. In the boom years of Miami, as drug money and South American investments poured in, the only thing that the school considered was whether a prospective entrant could afford the tuition, which was comparable to that of the top private high schools in the United States. The kids who went to Palm Crest were mostly from wealthy South American, Jewish, or nouveau riche families—the operative word being "wealthy."

Barry's family was wealthy, but the families of his two best friends at the school were not only wealthy, but also

socially prominent. Chadwick Plant II's father owned an
NFL franchise as well as one of the largest construction
firms in the South, and Frank Bertucci's father was
Roman "The Whale" Bertucci, a 400-pound mobster
identified by the FBI as one of the leading underworld
figures in South Florida.

The troubles started when Chad, a kid with a dazzling
personality; Frank, a moody rebel without a cause; and
Barry turned 16, got their driver's licenses, and became
mobile. They were locals in one of America's most glam-
orous tourist areas, and they knew where to go and had the
money to enjoy themselves when they got there. Making
nightlife activities even easier was the fact that "The
Whale" owned Miami's most exciting nightclub, The Farm,
where the beautiful people of Miami wanted to be seen.

The Farm was patronized by the most beautiful hookers,
the most fashionable gays, and the new millionaires from
the drug business; had ties to organized crime; and always
featured nationally known bands. All of this added up to a
nightclub where even a $100 tip to the bouncers at the door
couldn't get you in on a weekend night if you weren't on the
"friends of The Farm" list.

Barry, Chad, and Frank were on the list. Roman liked
having the boys around because at least then he knew
where Frank was hanging out and what he was doing. Or so
he thought.

Ironically, the boys' trouble started at The Farm, sniff-
ing lines of cocaine in the bathroom. Within a year their
use had progressed to the point where Chad and Frank were
selling almost a pound of cocaine a month to their classmates at Palm Crest. Barry said that he wasn't involved in
the dealing because he didn't particularly like cocaine, plus
he was playing on the football and basketball teams and his
weekends weren't as free as Chad's and Frank's. Barry knew

that Chad and Frank stayed pretty coked up on the weekends, and he knew that their supplier was one of the bartenders at The Farm.

Barry told Joe and me that he used cocaine once in a while, but he wasn't interested in dealing it. However, Chad and Frank not only dealt it, they had visions of being major distributors. Their dealing soon reached the point where they couldn't get enough product from their supplier, and they began arguing over who got what.

The arguments got nasty, and, by the time they graduated, Frank was making threats that his father was going to beat up on Chad. Barry said that no one took this seriously because they all knew that Frank's father strongly disapproved of drugs. If he found out about Frank's dealing and consumption, it was Frank who would get his ass kicked.

Joe stopped Barry's narrative at this point. "You mean that the three of you are spending most of your weekend nights at Frank's father's nightclub; you're 17, 18 years old; you're drinking; you're probably messing around with the hookers; and the old man's big worry is his kid using drugs? The other stuff doesn't bother him?"

Barry said that Roman's big thing was keeping Frank out of trouble. Frank's mother had died when they were sophomores in high school, and because Roman was always out at nights, he wanted Frank and his friends to hang out at The Farm. Roman knew that as long as Frank was at The Farm and even thinking of doing something too crazy, Roman would hear about it.

"The arguments continued," Barry explained as his voice lowered and the speed of his words slowed down. "Chad and Frank quit hanging out together. I'd see Chad quite a bit, but Frank was a pain in the ass. Frank was moody; he'd sleep till noon, never wanted to go out on the boat; all he did was snort coke and run around trying to score some weight so he could deal it.

"Finally, Chad asked me to mediate between him and Frank. I was the only one who knew what they were doing, as far as where their supply was coming from. Their supplier at The Farm had cut them off because he was afraid of Roman finding out, and I think that Chad believed that I could convince Frank to cooperate. Then they could go to their supplier and tell him that they'd solved their problems and wanted their supply restored."

"You've got me confused," Joe cut in. "Tell me if I've got this right. You're not dealing. The bartender at The Farm has quit supplying Frank and Chad. Frank and Chad are constantly arguing about who gets what percent of the supply that they aren't getting anymore, and they're looking to you to solve their problems so they can go back to the bartender and say that everything is all patched up and they'd like him to supply them with cocaine again."

"That's right," Barry confirmed.

This all seemed too cockeyed to me. "Wait a minute," I said. "You guys are in South Florida, the cocaine capital of the world. If Chad and Frank had been dealing a pound a month and, I assume, cutting its purity once they got it, these guys were making at least $20,000 a month. Why didn't they just go their separate ways and find their own supply? Why were they both immobilized because one bartender at The Farm doesn't want to supply them anymore?"

"I know Frank was scared to death that his dad would find out, and Chad, well, if you knew him, it would be like Prince Charles of England going into Harlem to buy drugs. The only reason I think that these guys were so fucked up about getting the bartender to supply them again was because it was so easy. Neither one of them wanted to do the work and take the risks that would be involved in finding a new supplier."

Barry's story continued with him explaining that he agreed to moderate the Chad-and-Frank problem. Frank came by one afternoon driving his Camaro, and he was so coked up that he couldn't even back the car out of the driveway. Barry got behind the wheel, and they motored over to pick up Chad at his house.

When Chad came out, Frank moved to the backseat and Chad got into the front passenger's seat. As soon as they had pulled out of Chad's driveway, Frank started yelling at Chad that he was going to kill him if he didn't go to the bartender and tell him that he was dropping out and that all the supply should go to Frank.

"I'm driving," Barry said, "Chad is telling Frank that he's nuts, Frank's yelling he's going to kill Chad, and then the next time I look at Chad, Frank has him pinned with one arm around his neck and is stabbing him with a hunting knife in the chest. I'm yelling for him to stop, but he just keeps on stabbing. Blood is flying all over the car, and I can't stop or pull off because there are no shoulders on the road, plus Frank is yelling that if I stop he's going to kill me, too. Frank must have stabbed Chad 40 times. When he's done, he's got that crazed Jack Nicholson look from *The Shining* on his face, and he's yelling that Chad had to die and now we have to get rid of the body.

"Frank told me to drive out to the Everglades. We got off the main road, made a couple of turns onto some dirt roads in the sugarcane fields, and then Frank pulled Chad's body out of the front seat and threw it in an irrigation ditch."

"Why didn't he kill you?" I asked.

"I don't know," Barry replied. "I thought for sure he would. But after he had finished with Chad, he seemed to calm down. I thought about slamming on the brakes and bolting from the car, but I thought he could get a couple of stabs into me before I could get the seat belt off and get out of the car, so I did what he said and kept driving."

"Was Chad dead when you threw him in the ditch?" Joe wanted to know.

"No doubt about it," Barry answered. "Once Frank had thrown Chad in the ditch, Frank told me to get in the water and slide the body under a culvert and cover it up with these slimy vines that were in the water. When I moved Chad, he was face down, and there were no bubbles. I'm sure he was dead."

Barry continued by telling us how he had talked Frank into leaving him off on Route 441. He'd gone into a service station and washed the blood off his shorts and shirt and then hitchhiked home.

Two days later, the body was found by some farm workers, and the story took over the front page of the newspapers in South Florida.

"I lasted a day after the body was discovered," Barry said. "Then I told my father what had happened. We went right to the police, and I told them everything.

"Meanwhile, Frank had driven the car back to his dad's condo and hadn't even bothered to clean up the inside. The parking guy saw the mess, and Frank told him to clean it up. When the story hit the papers, the parking attendant knew that Chad hung around with Frank a lot, and he tipped off the police that a couple of days earlier he had cleaned up Frank's car to get rid of what Frank said was spilled spaghetti sauce. The attendant said he had tasted the dried sauce and it definitely didn't taste like anything edible to him. The cops came out, took a sample of the blood that they found that the attendant had missed cleaning up, and did a test. The blood matched Chad's, and as I was at the police station telling the police what had happened, the police were on their way to Frank's to arrest him for killing Chad."

"Did you have a lawyer when you went to the police with your story?" Joe questioned.

"Yes."

"And he approved of your telling the police what happened?" Joe asked.

"For the three days after Frank killed Chad, I was an emotional basket case," Barry said. "I couldn't sleep, I couldn't eat, and I knew that Frank was nuts and would kill someone again. I couldn't take it; I told my dad and the lawyer that I wanted to tell the police."

Joe was writing nonstop on his legal pad. "How about a confession? Did you sign one, and was there any talk of immunity from prosecution before you told the police what happened?"

"I'm not sure on the minute-by-minute details," Barry confessed, "but I think that by the time I started writing my story, Frank was also at the police station and he said that I was the one who killed Chad. I guess the cops didn't know who to believe, and they said that there would be no immunity. I just wanted to tell the truth so Chad's parents would know what had happened."

"So you said Frank did it, and Frank said you did it. There were no other witnesses?" Joe asked.

"None."

We had been listening to Barry for an hour, and Joe called for a bathroom break. When Joe came back and got his cigarette lit, we picked up the story from where both Frank and Barry were arrested for first-degree murder.

"My lawyer thought that I was going to be charged with nothing more serious than an accessory after the fact because I didn't go to the police right away," Barry said. "The killing had happened in Frank's car, the police had found the knife that was the murder weapon in the trunk, the knife was Frank's and had his prints all over it—none of mine—and Frank had the motive to kill Chad. But I got charged with first-degree murder just like Frank. I think bail started out at $500,000 for both of us. Frank made bail first, and then I got out."

"When did Melvin Kliner become your attorney?" I asked. "He wasn't the guy you had when you first went in to confess to the police, was he?"

"No," Barry answered. "After I got charged with first-degree murder, my grandfather in Boston got involved. He talked to a lot of the famous criminal lawyers—F. Lee Bailey, Edward Bennett Williams, and a couple of others—but the guy he selected was a Boston lawyer named Martin Soladar. Soladar had worked with Kliner on some big drug cases, and he hired Kliner to be his local counsel in Miami so he didn't have to fly down there for every motion and every court appearance."

"I know one case they worked on together," I chimed in. "When my smuggling partner, Mike Buff, was busted in Boston for changing $10s into $100s at a bank, the cops searched his rented car and found $330,000 in a suitcase in the trunk. It was an illegal search, but, unfortunately for Mike, he was already out on an appeal bond from our smuggling arrest. Mike hired Soladar to represent him on the Boston arrest, and I know Soladar and Kliner talked quite a bit about how to prevent Mike's appeal bond from getting revoked."

"What happened?" Barry wanted to know. "I think I got fucked by those guys."

"Mike had to appear back in front of the Florida judge with Kliner," I said. "The judge raised Mike's bail from $25,000 to $125,000, but he let him stay out of prison. Then Soladar got the Boston case dismissed because it was an illegal search with no probable cause. But Soladar's big battle was to try to get Mike back the $330,000. The IRS wanted the money, as did the Boston cops and the DEA. It took two years, but eventually Mike got $100,000 back. The lawyer's fees plus withholding by the IRS ate up over two-thirds of the money."

"Let's get back on track here," Joe said. "It sounds like all the evidence pointed to Frank being the killer. I don't see why you weren't offered a deal of some kind to become a state's witness and testify against Frank."

"I was never offered any kind of deal as far as I know," Barry said, "and I'm still not even sure what happened."

"What do you mean?" Joe inquired.

"What I mean is that a few weeks before my trial, Martin Soladar withdraws from the case because he said he had a mild heart attack. Now, Kliner becomes the only attorney who is going to handle my trial. Then Frank does a plea bargain."

"A plea bargain," Joe exclaimed. "A plea bargain to what?"

"I think it was second-degree murder, and part of the deal is that he is going to testify against me at my trial. He got five years plus a lot of probation time."

"So the prosecutors think you're the one who actually committed the killing?" Joe summarized. "They kept your charges at first-degree murder?"

"That's what happened. Kliner is telling me not to worry, that he'll definitely win the trial and I'll be found not guilty. Jesus, my grandfather is paying him something like $200,000 and he's this big-name attorney, so we believed him when he said he'd win the trial.

"Right before the trial, Kliner calls and says that he'd worked out a deal where I'd plead to second-degree murder, just like Frank, and I'd be getting the same five years Frank got. Kliner said that if I didn't take the deal, and I was convicted of first-degree murder, then I might get the death penalty. Now, Kliner isn't so confident that he'll win the trial, and he suggests I take the deal. I do, and months later when I go before the judge to be sentenced, Kliner tells me to answer yes when the judge asks me if I understand how I can be sentenced. I do what Kliner tells me, and I get a life sentence."

"This is unbelievable," Joe said as he cleaned his glasses to show how appalled he was. "This is all in the court transcripts?"

"I think so," Barry answered. "I think Frank's father bribed the judge, bribed the prosecutors, and paid off Kliner. I don't think Soladar had any heart attack; I think the Mafia told him to get out of the case and to make sure that Kliner stayed on to set up the plea bargain. I don't know what else it could be—I didn't kill Chad. All I was, was in the car driving when Frank went nuts."

Barry didn't cry as he finished his story. A year of prison had left him beyond tears. He knew he had just told Joe and me a fantastic, almost unbelievable story. If you believed what Barry had said, it was his innocence and family money pitted against the full force of the South Florida Mafia, and the Mafia had ruled. Barry seemed almost resigned to the fact that he was going to be in prison for a long, long time.

"Where's the case now?" Joe asked. "Kliner isn't still your lawyer, is he?"

"No, he was fired. My family's hired a firm in Fort Lauderdale to try to get me a trial, but I guess that since I pled guilty that I'm not allowed an appeal."

"Right," Joe said, "but there're ways to try to get you back into court."

"I'm sure they're going to try. My dad says that it looks pretty good, but I don't really know what's going on."

"If you're confident that your appeal lawyers are working for you, there's really not much more that I can do," Joe concluded. "I'd be happy to look at what you've got, and I can let you know what I think of the work if you'd like."

"Thanks, I'd really appreciate that," Barry said. "I'd like to think that I can trust these guys who are working on my appeal, but after Kliner, I'm not sure there's any lawyer in the world I'd totally believe now."

Barry Abrams' case was more than just big money versus big power—politicians were also involved. A U.S. senator from Massachusetts who knew Barry's grandparents was inquiring into what had happened, as well as two U.S. congressmen from South Florida. The Florida prison officials were worried that something might happen to Barry while he was at the gladiator school and were more than happy to cooperate in bringing him back to Lake Butler.

Once Barry asked Joe Peel to take a look at the legal work being done on his behalf, Joe went to Colonel Dooly to request that Barry not be shipped off to another prison, at least until the review was completed. Colonel Dooly told Joe that Barry wasn't going anywhere; he was staying at Lake Butler.

Again, Karen and I began socializing with Barry and his parents during weekend visits. If Joe had a visitor, he'd also come over to hear the latest in legal developments in Barry's case. Mr. Abrams was so impressed with Joe's knowledge that he commented that he wished there was a way Joe could handle Barry's appeal.

Joe went through all the court transcripts the Abrams provided. Since there never was a trial, there was no record about evidence, but the record was very clear that Barry had accepted the plea bargain knowing that he could be sentenced to life in prison.

Joe and I both believed Barry's conspiracy theory. Joe believed it because he had been a crooked judge and knew how much power a judge had in manipulating a desired outcome. I believed Barry because I had been through the same type of situation with Melvin Kliner. I knew that I would have done whatever Kliner had told me to do. I had paid him a lot of money and he was a well-known attorney, so if he had told me that I had to stand up in front of a judge as part of his plan to get me a good plea bargain—I would have done it.

If he was paid enough money or scared that he or his family would be killed by agents of "The Whale," I had no doubt that Kliner would cave in. What he did to me by almost getting me a failure-to-appear charge was nothing compared to what he had done to Barry Abrams, and he had sold out Barry in a way that showed what a brilliant lawyer could get away with.

Law firms came and went with regard to Barry's appeals, but he never was able to get back into court. Politicians wrote letters, the media wrote stories, and everyone who heard about the case thought Barry had been screwed. The only result was that Barry never had to go back to a gladiator school. He was assigned to the permanent state prison in Dade County, and he was released on parole after serving the minimum of seven years that was required according to his parole guidelines. He was 26 years old when he got out.

After Barry was released, he went to work for his father's insurance company. Then a strange thing happened—he had been out of the joint for three months when he was shot in the head while in his car waiting for a red light to change. He died instantly. No one was ever arrested. Miami police explained the murder as a mob hit, probably because of all the waves Barry and his family had made to try to prove that Barry was innocent. Barry was a reminder to Roman that his son was a drug-dealing murderer—something Roman didn't like being reminded of.

Long after Barry Abrams was gone from this planet, a friend of mine sent me a cover story from a Sunday *Miami*

Herald. The picture on the cover of the Sunday supplement magazine was Melvin Kliner, and the captions underneath stated that the famed South Florida drug lawyer was going to prison for 20 years on money-laundering and drug conspiracy convictions. Kliner had played all the angles—he did the Mafia's bidding, he accepted huge fees from clients and then didn't do the work he had contracted for, and he crossed the line to get involved in the huge profits of drug smuggling.

If anyone ever got what he deserved in the Barry Abrams case, it was Melvin Kliner. It will give him a chance at redemption—maybe Kliner will become the next Joe Peel, doing legal work for inmates at no charge . . . but I doubt it.

CHECKING OUT

I HAD 12 HOURS' ADVANCE NOTICE that I was going to be shipped from Lake Butler to a work-release facility in Fort Lauderdale. The inmate assistant chaplain was able to sneak a look at the transfer list, and he told Joe, who passed the good news on to me.

When I left Vietnam, I had flown a combat mission just 48 hours before getting on the California-bound commercial jet leaving Saigon. Good-byes in Vietnam were easy; the guys I had become friendly with would be just months behind me in going back to the States to pick up their lives with their kids and wives. Most of these fellow air force pilots I would see again. We'd shared the bonding experience of high-adrenaline air combat, but we knew that five years after leaving Vietnam, we'd be talking about kids, airline careers, and maybe a ski trip, rather than what we had gone through in Southeast Asia.

I spent my last evening in prison in the hobby shop. Except for Joe Peel, I wouldn't say that any of the inmates were close friends, but there were people in that room I genuinely liked and with whom I'd shared some interesting times. However, I was 261 leaving, and I knew that some of these guys were facing 15 or 20 more years before they would be turned loose. I looked at Jack Green, who'd be in his 70s by the time he checked out, but he was still talking about brushing up on his flying skills and getting right into cocaine smuggling. Jack wanted to make sure I stayed in touch with him so he could look me up when he got out and I could teach him the flying knowledge he would need to go for a $2 million payday in the cocaine business.

Joe Peel was the one convict I would miss. When I knew that I was getting close to being transferred to a work-release facility, I had talked to Joe about whether I should refuse work release and stay at Lake Butler to get another four months in at the law library. Joe had said that staying at Lake Butler when I could be down in Fort Lauderdale was a bad idea.

"Your life isn't in prison," he said. "Get on down there where your pretty wife can visit without having to ride a bus 10 hours each way and start thinking about what you're going to do when you get out."

Joe was right, of course. But, still, it was hard to realize that Joe had done 20 years and there was no end in sight. He might be in prison for another 20 years, and that would mean dying in prison for him.

Joe Peel had made my prison years more interesting than my Vietnam years or even my drug-smuggling period. By becoming a part of his world, I had seen all the aspects of life behind bars from the protected position as the favorite son of the most beloved inmate in the history of the Florida prison system.

I was hoping that I really believed what I was saying when I told Joe that I would see him on the outside, but I didn't know. I wasn't even sure if being on the outside meant anything to him anymore.

My last morning at Lake Butler, I was shaken awake by a guard at 4:30 and told to pack my shit—I was being shipped. As I was putting my letters and legal papers into my shoebox, Joe walked over from his bunk with his first cigarette of the day already fired up. He didn't say anything.

A minute later I was packed and ready to go. Joe walked with me to the TV room to wait for the guard to appear to open the doors and escort me to out-processing.

The moment every convict dreams of was just minutes away for me, but I was in no particular hurry for it to happen. I had entered prison worried about getting gang-raped or stabbed. I was leaving prison thinking of the man standing next to me, quietly smoking a cigarette, and how he embodied the triumph of the human spirit.

The guard opened the door to the outside corridor and motioned for me to step out. "Sorry, Joe," the guard said, "I'd love to let you go, too."

Joe and I embraced, then I stepped into the corridor as the guard slammed the steel door shut right behind me. I never saw Joe Peel again.

If there is a God and he came to Earth, what form would he take? When I left Lake Butler, at least for a few minutes, I was pretty sure that I knew the answer.

When I entered the Florida prison system, I was going into the biggest unknown of my life. When I'd left for college or gone to Vietnam, at least I felt that I was prepared for what awaited me. Of what would happen to me once I entered prison, I knew nothing. If the sentencing judge had really wanted to ensure that I would never break another law in my life, he had had the chance when I stood before him to get my punishment demanded by the state of Florida. A long probation with strict reporting to a parole officer would have been the end of my criminal career. But the judge went for the next day's newspaper headlines—"Maximum Sentence for War Hero, First-Time Drug Smuggler."

This is the time when a judge should give a person a second chance—successfully complete probation and you can avoid prison. This is the one chance the justice system has to keep the career criminal classification off a large number of first-timers entering prison. A sentence of probation keeps the fear of prison alive, and it just might be enough to cause a person to change his ways and avoid what would be a sure trip to the joint if convicted of a second crime. Because, once a person goes behind bars, he quickly realizes that he can adapt to the circumstances, and the fear factor of doing time in a penitentiary is eliminated.

I left prison at the age of 34, and the fear factor was long gone. Prison was something that I certainly didn't want to experience again, but it had added more data to the equation of whether I would re-enter the drug-smuggling business. The equation was simple: potential monetary gain versus potential time I might have to spend in prison.

I had been lucky with my prison experiences. I had met a bizarre group of people and witnessed some unusual situations. But that is all quickly forgotten. Anyone who has ever completed a prison term walks out of the joint intending never to go back. I was no different, and so far I haven't.

TO KAREN

GETTING ARRESTED, BEING CONVICTED, and serving time in prison does one good thing for you: it shows you who you will go out of their way to visit and stay in contact with you during a time when you can't give much in return. Throughout my two years of legal wrangling to stay out of prison, 15 months inside, four months in the halfway house, and two years on probation, my wife, Karen, always made me think that the best part of her day was thinking about our next visit or the letter she knew would be waiting for her when she got home from work.

Karen never missed a visit, though it always meant a 10-hour overnight ride on a broken-down church bus and a lot of pent-up frustration for both of us because we were constantly watched and never had any privacy to talk quietly, touch, or just be alone together. When you check into the joint, in many ways, your family checks in with you, and there aren't too many relationships that can survive that type of strain.

And that brings up my last tale from the joint.

Karen is beautiful, with long blonde hair and a 265

great figure. She tans in the summer, stays in marine-boot-camp shape year-round, and has a toothpaste-ad smile. Often, when we were visiting at the Martin County jail, I could see guys staring at her through the Plexiglas visiting window on the other side of the corridor. These guys were in cell block B, and if there were no visits going on in cell block B, there was nothing to prevent the inmates from staring at Karen's back while she was visiting me.

By the third time Karen visited, the faces in the block B visiting windows began changing every few minutes as both black and white prisoners wanted to eyeball her.

I didn't know what was going on until Leroy the Jitterbug, who had been put in cell block B for two weeks after the Jason incident, clued me in when he returned to C block. He reported that several of the guys regularly paid off a black guy to end his visit early so they could use the visiting window to ogle Karen.

"They'd jack off right there," Leroy said. "The fuckers wouldn't even go into the shower or get in their bunks. Geez, cum would be all over the wall after your wife left!"

Leroy said that he was appalled by their behavior and tried to stop it, but that was just Leroy talking shit. I always wondered why Leroy's face would be staring through the Plexiglas when I knew he wasn't waiting for a visitor. I didn't get too upset, though, because at least these jack-offs were lucky enough to have a beautiful girl to stare at and fantasize that when they got out someone like Karen would be waiting for them.

Despite behavior like this, Karen was there every week. She fought my legal battles, brought me news of friends and family, handled my outside business affairs, kept my prison account filled, and sought help for me from the most unlikely sources—but, most of all, she made sure that I knew she'd be waiting for me when I got out.

So for this and more, I thank you for helping to make my prison experience such that writing this book was possible.